Dacia Maraini
Writing Like Breathing I

Beloved Writing
Fifty Years of Engagement

Edited and Compiled by
Michelangelo La Luna

SOPHIA

III

Series of Art History Literature and Science

Literature
2

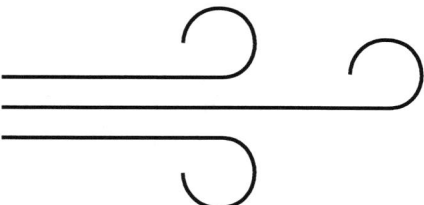

SOPHIA
Series of Art History Literature and Science

LITERATURE:
Dacia Maraini. Writing Like Breathing I

SERIES GENERAL EDITOR:
Michelangelo La Luna
University of Rhode Island

SCIENTIFIC COMMITTEE:
Elvira Di Fabio, Harvard University
Roberto Gaudio, University of Calabria
Giovanni Morello, Apostolic Vatican Library
Giulio Ferroni, Sapienza University of Rome
Giuseppe Roma, University of Calabria
Lisa Sarti, Borough of Manhattan Community College
G. Pino Scaglione, University of Trento
Maurizio Seracini, Monash University
Jane Tylus, New York University

LIST LAB DIRECTOR:
G. Pino Scaglione

OTHER BOOKS OF THE SERIES SOPHIA:
Literature
1. Michelangelo La Luna. *La corrispondenza tra Girolamo De Rada Angelo De Gubernatis (1870-1900) et alii*. Rossano: conSenso publishing, 2016.

History
1. Mario Massoni. *Le Istorie della Città di Rossano di Carlo Blasco*. Rossano: conSenso publishing, 2016.

    SOPHIA gives life to a series that seeks to unite the disciplines of art, literature and science, by reproducing the figure of the Renaissance man that modern times have tried to forget.

    SOPHIA also intends to act as a bridge between Europe and North America, facilitating the circulation of works that deserve to have a home in both worlds.

    Its Scientific Committee is therefore comprised of experts from various disciplines who will contribute to the various branches of this new publishing venture.

Michelangelo La Luna
Professor of Italian
Director of the Italian Engineering Program
University of Rhode Island

A Dacia
per tutto ciò che ci ha dato,
con grande affetto

Index

Foreword
    Michelangelo La Luna   6

I. Autobiography
    (Extracts from):
    The Ship for Kobe. The Japanese Journals of My Mother   15
    The Great Celebration   23

II. Novels
    (Extracts from):
    The Age of Malaise   63
    Woman at War   76
    Colomba   96
    Clare of Assisi: In Praise of Disobedience   102

III. Short Stories
    A Christmas in the Snow Globe   120
    Little Aylan   126
    Viollca the Albanian Girl   130
    A Number on Her Arm   141
    Might as Well Live   149
    Serena the Bride   155
    A Sicilian Nun   157
    Splendor   167
    The Little Girl and the Earthquake   173
    Marina Fell Down the Stairs   181
    The Secret Bride   191
    The Poet-Director and the Wonderful Soprano   206
    A Woman, a Man, a Donkey   223

IV. Poems
    Original Poems:
    At Night; Rome; Like Sea Bass Underwater   230
    (Extracts from):
    Traveling in the Gait of a Fox: Poetry 1983-1991   233
    New Year's Eve in Hospital   242

V. Bibliography   248

VI. Index of Names   264

VII. Index of Places   268

VIII. Index of Topics   270

Foreword

Writing Like Breathing is an homage to Dacia Maraini, celebrating a writing career that has spanned over half a century, covering all forms of literature (prose, poetry and drama). It is a unique collection comprising some of her most important works, the majority of which have never been translated into English. The series is divided into four major volumes that are meant to give a full picture of Maraini's production from 1962 to the present:

I. Autobiography, novels, short stories and poems

I. Plays

II. Articles

IV. Essays, talks, conversations and interviews.

Writing like Breathing truly embraces academic collaboration, as it is the product of scholars from numerous countries, including Canada, Italy, the United Kingdom and the United States. The volumes will be a welcome and enjoyable addition for students and researchers of Dacia Maraini, her work, Italian culture, and the standing of women in the world.

Beloved Writing shows how today's most prominent Italian writer has embraced and fought for a vast number of issues: women's rights, abuse of women and children, emigration, discrimination, politics, the Holocaust, among many others. Moreover, this collection of Maraini's autobiographies, novels, short stories, and poems, emphasizes the author's long relationship with Japan and the United States, countries to which she has devoted several books and articles, both autobiographical and fictional.

Dacia Maraini and Michelangelo La Luna
at Harvard University (2012).
Photo by Elvira Di Fabio.

Some unpublished manuscripts enrich this unique first volume: two short stories ("A Christmas in the Snow Globe" and "Aylan") and three poems ("At Night", "Rome", "Like Sea Bass Underwater"). The other volumes contain unpublished plays ("Diotima and Socrates," "To Protect You Better, My Child," "Geco," "Bakunin," "My Name is Antonino Calderone," "Celia Carli, Ornithologist," and "Lia, Who Thought Herself Antigone"), talks, conversations, and interviews given by the author at American universities.

I would like to thank everybody for the precious contributions they made to this challenging work: a full list would be too extensive and ultimately incomplete. Special thanks go to G. Pino Scaglione, List Lab Director, who believes in *SOPHIA's* audacious project of building a bridge between Italy and English-speaking countries, such as the United States of America, Canada and the United Kingdom. In fact, our editorial plan is to complete an homage to Italy's most prominent writer with a volume of essays—a Festschrift—and to publish in translation works of other major contemporary authors.

I would also like to thank the publishers Rizzoli RCS, Einaudi, Feminist Press, Giulio Perrone, and Giuseppe Laterza Editori for granting us the rights to publish Maraini's work. A thank you goes also to Eugenio Murrali, Walter Scancarello and to those institutes who have provided some of the oldest and most inaccessible material: L'Archivio Storico del Banco di Napoli, Biblioteca Area Umanistica "E. Fagiani" and Biblioteca Tarantelli at the University of Calabria, Biblioteca di Storia Moderna e Contemporanea (Rome), Biblioteca Comunale "C. Natale" of Crispiano (Taranto), Biblioteca Città di Arezzo and Biblioteca Estense Universitaria (Modena).

Last but not least, I would really like to thank Dacia for her support and assistance and I wish her more "Writing and Breathing" in the years to come.

Michelangelo La Luna
University of Rhode Island
June 2, 2016

A Note to the reader: Some translations are introduced by a preface and enriched by footnotes written by the editor and the translators. To help the reader Translator's Notes (TN) are also enclosed in the translation itself in brackets.

Tabula Gratulatoria*

Scholars
Agresta, Angelene, Montclair State University, *United States of America*
Albertini, Stefano, New York University, *United States of America*
Alfano, Barbara, Bennington College, *United States of America*
Anatrone, Sole, University of California, Berkeley, *United States of America*
Benedikt, Eva, Filmmaker, *United States of America* (special thanks for text revisions)
Benetti, Mara, University College London, *United Kingdom*
Bogusz, Sylvia, University of Rhode Island, *United States of America*
Braico, Giovanni, New York University, *United States of America*
Bush, Amanda Rose, University of Texas at Austin, *United States of America*
Butts, Kayla, University of Rhode Island, *United States of America*
Calabretta-Sajder, Ryan, University of Arkansas, *United States of America*
Capotorto, Vittorio, Italytime New York, *United States of America*
Cellinese, Anna, Stanford University, *United States of America*
Contreras, Julio, University of Rhode Island, *United States of America*
Costello, Todd, University of Rhode Island, *United States of America*
D'Agnillo, Renzo, "Gabriele D'Annunzio" University of Chieti, *Italy*
Di Fabio, Elvira, Harvard University, *United States of America*
Di Paolo, Paolo, Writer, *Italy*
Feltrin-Morris, Marella, Ithaca College, *United States of America*
Frizzi, Adria, University of Texas at Austin, *United States of America*
Giufre, Stacy, University of Massachusetts Amherst, *United States of America*
Gonzalez, Maureen, Italytime New York, *United States of America*
Gorjup, Branko, University of Toronto, *Canada*
Gunn, Genni, Novelist, poet, and translator, *Canada*
Haberek, Kristin, University of Rhode Island, *United States of America* (special thanks for text revisions)
Hicks-Bartlett, Alani, University of California, Berkeley, *United States of America*
Iacovella, Anna, Yale University, *United States of America*
Iturralde, Paul, University of Rhode Island, *United States of America*
Jackson, Emily, Theater Artist, *United States of America*
Johnston, Taylor B., University of California, Berkeley, *United States of America*

---

* The table includes all scholars and institutes that worked for the entire series *Writing Like Breathing*.

Karnes, Samuel, University of Rhode Island, *United States of America*
Kay Nicolette, New Shoes Theatre, *United Kingdom*
Kemp, Matthew, University of Rhode Island, *United States of America* (special thanks for text revisions)
La Luna, Michelangelo, University of Rhode Island, *United States of America*
Lancellotta, Rosa, University of Rhode Island, *United States of America*
LaPenta, Kathleen, Fordham University, *United States of America*
Levers, Stanley, University of California, Berkeley, *United States of America*
Magistro, Elise, Scripps College, *United States of America*
Mariotti, Elisabetta, International Association of Conference Interpreters, *Italy*
Matozzo, Caterina, New York University, *United States of America*
Mattavelli, Sara, University of Wisconsin-Madison, *United States of America*
Mojico, Xavier, University of Texas at Austin, *United States of America*
Montecalvo, Brianna, University of Rhode Island, *United States of America*
Morelli, Maria, University of Leicester, *United Kingdom*
Murrali, Eugenio, Libera Università Internazionale degli Studi Sociali Guido Carli (LUISS), *Italy*
Nietupski, Jessica, University of Rhode Island, *United States of America*
Noson, Kate, University of California, Berkeley, *United States of America*
Olson, Antonella Del-Fattore, University of Texas at Austin, *United States of America*
Olson, Bobby, Free Lance Translator, *United States of America*
Oresman, Kelsi-Mariah, University of Rhode Island, *United States of America*
Ortler, Kelley, University of Rhode Island, *United States of America*
Ortner, Samantha, University of Rhode Island, *United States of America*
Owens, Katie, University of Rhode Island, *United States of America*
Picchietti, Virginia A., University of Scranton, *United States of America*
Pinderman, Luke, University of Rhode Island, *United States of America*
Porretto, Elizabeth, University of Chicago, *United States of America*
Roma, Daniela, Pianist, *Italy*
Roma, Giuseppe, University of Calabria, *Italy* (special thanks for advice)
Russoniello, Marta, Montclair State University, *United States of America*
Scaglione, Pino G., University of Trento, *Italy*
Scancarello, Walter, University of Florence, *Italy*
Schwarten, James, John Cabot University, *Italy*
Searle, Wendy, University of Connecticut, *United States of America*
Seger, Monica, The College of William & Mary, *United States of America*
Shea, Leslie, University of Rhode Island, *United States of America*
Shields, Daniel, University of Rhode Island, *United States of America*
Spottiswood, Elspeth, Translator, *United Kingdom*

Standen, Alex, University College London, *United Kingdom*
Streifer, Monica, University of California Los Angeles, *United States of America*
Tortolani, Lisa, University of Connecticut, *United States of America* (special thanks for text revisions)
Trubiano, Marisa, Montclair State University, *United States of America*
Tylus, Jane, New York University, *United States of America*
Varkey, ReenMary, University of Connecticut, *United States of America* (special thanks for assistance)
Vegna, Veronica, University of Chicago, *United States of America*
Wood, Sharon, University of Leicester, *United Kingdom*

Institutes
Archivio Storico del Banco di Napoli, *Italy*
Bennington College, *United States of America*
Biblioteca Area Umanistica "E. Fagiani" at the University of Calabria, *Italy*
Biblioteca Città di Arezzo, *Italy*
Biblioteca Comunale "C. Natale" of Crispiano (Taranto), *Italy*
Biblioteca di Storia Moderna e Contemporanea, *Italy*
Biblioteca Estense Universitaria, *Italy*
Biblioteca Tarantelli at the University of Calabria, *Italy*
College of William & Mary, *United States of America*
Einaudi Publishing Company, *Italy*
Feminist Press, *United States of America*
Fordham University, *United States of America*
"Gabriele D'Annunzio" University of Chieti, *Italy*
Giulio Perrone Publishing Company, *Italy*
Giuseppe Laterza Publishing Company, *Italy*
Harvard University, *United States of America*
International Association of Conference Interpreters, *Italy*
Italytime New York, *United States of America*
Ithaca College, *United States of America*
John Cabot University, *Italy*
Libera Università Internazionale degli Studi Sociali Guido Carli (LUISS), *Italy*
Middlebury College, *United States of America*
Montclair State University, *United States of America*
New Shoes Theatre, *United Kingdom*
New York University, *United States of America*
Rizzoli RCS Publishing Company, *Italy*
Scripps College, *United States of America*
Stanford University, *United States of America*

University College London, *United Kingdom*
University of Arkansas, *United States of America*
University of Calabria, *Italy*
University of California, Los Angeles, *United States of America*
University of California, Berkeley, *United States of America*
University of Chicago, *United States of America*
University of Connecticut, *United States of America*
University of Leicester, *United Kingdom*
University of Massachusetts Amherst, *United States of America*
University of Rhode Island, *United States of America*
University of Scranton, *United States of America*
University of Texas at Austin, *United States of America*
University of Toronto, *Canada*
University of Trento, *Italy*
University of Wisconsin-Madison, *United States of America*
Wheaton College, *United States of America*
Yale University, *United States of America*

Dacia Maraini in New York.

Topazia Alliata and Dacia Maraini in Japan (1939). Photo by Fosco Maraini.

I

Autobiography

The Ship for Kobe.
The Japanese Journals of My Mother

Translation by Genni Gunn
Novelist, poet, and translator*

1942. My mother's diary is now silent. She can't recall if she kept any trace of the daily news of 1942 and 1943, before entering the camp, where there certainly would have been no way to write or read.

"Perhaps I stopped keeping the diary about my daughters because the climate had changed. We lived in apprehension. The newspapers repeated words ordered by the government. And the people said, "Hitar, psuy-oi-né," Hitler is powerful, right? with a mixture of admiration and fear.

"Those who were not in agreement with the German and Japanese invasions (in March Japan invaded the Dutch West Indies, the USA bombed Tokyo and in August the Solomon Islands were occupied by the Japanese; in September began the Siege of Leningrad), those who were not in agreement remained silent, fearful of violent retribution. I was convinced that Hitler would not win. I don't know what gave me this conviction, but I was certain. Our situation was very delicate: we were part of an exchange program: so many Japanese scholarships and so many Italian ones. The diplomatic circles kept an eye on us. There were some at the embassy who thought like we did, the young Sforza attaché, for example. But even he couldn't speak."

My mother tries to remember the atmosphere of these traumatic years and her voice tightens. "The climate among Italians in Japan was changing: everyone looked at each other suspiciously. Some were skeptical towards fascism, like Sforza. Instead, Jannelli, the ambassador believed in it. He would stand there, rigid, and salute with his outstretched hand. Others, however, were beginning to doubt, like Cavalchini of San Severino, for example, the naval attaché who spoke without speaking, but made us understand that he hated Hitler and the senseless politics of the Italian Republic of Salò,[1] subservient to the Germans and now without dignity and pride."

"But the news, the genuine news, how did you get it?"

"Through the radio we secretly listened to. I also recall two French nationals who knew something about the killing of Jews in the extermina-

---

* Original title of the book: Maraini, Dacia. *La nave per Kobe. Diari giapponesi di mia madre*. Milan: Rizzoli, 2012. The pages translated are 165–176.

tion camps. One day, the woman whispered: you know that they burn people in ovens after having gassed them, women and children included? I said: That's not possible. Who told you this? It really seemed to be an invention. I thought it must be one of those numerous extreme rumours that circulate during war. Who could possibly organize something as monstrous as the systematic extermination of an entire people, guilty only of belonging to a different religion? However this is exactly what occurred. I have no idea how our friend Baron Fain heard of it."

The news circulated, evidently, but there was no official confirmation. Neither the Church nor the American government wanted to say how things stood until after the war, when photographers and filmmakers crossed to the other side of the barbed wire and discovered several survivors, who had escaped the genocide—all skin and bones—keeping warm under a blanket, their mouths in toothless smiles.

It's the final months of '42. My sister Toni is born after hours and hours of pain, the umbilical cord wrapped three times around her neck. That twisting within her refuge of flesh and blood seems, if I think of it today, a premonition of the terrible events that would soon change our lives.

"It seemed my last child would die and I with her. She was suffocating and didn't want to come out. They gave me an injection to induce labour, and I began once more. . . a pain so acute, I was unable to hold back my cries . . . I recall the Canadian nurse looking after me said, "Pleasure is paid with pain," an incredible punitive attitude towards women in labour. However, the hospital was well-kept, clean and efficient. After hours of suffering, Toni was born, purplish and half-asphyxiated by the cord cinched around her neck. When it came to the stitches, I asked for anaesthetic, and they replied it had all been sent to the front for the soldiers. Thus, I had to endure this, biting my lip.

"When Fosco arrived, I thought he might have objected to the third female child; instead he was pleased: better three girls than two girls and a boy, he said. And I was delighted. Paradoxically, Toni, who was born from such pain, was a happy, calm newborn. She never cried and as soon as she was able, she began to climb on everything."

I ask her if it's true, that they had in mind a different name for the last child. "Yes, we wanted to call her Kiku-chrysanthemum, but fascism did not permit foreign names, and in the end, we called her Antonella, which became Toni. We didn't want to have to repeat the vicissitudes of Yuki's christening: after giving the embassy the newborn's name, all the papers were sent to Italy, but were returned with the comment that Yuki was not a valid name for the birth certificate. Fosco refused to budge, saying he was free to name his daughter whatever he wanted. They would not accept this, and for months, Yuki remained without a name. In the end, we had to resort to Luisa, "They'll have their way on paper, but we'll call her Yuki." And in fact, Luisa has remained only the official name on her birth certificate. For us, she has always been Yuki.

"When it came to Toni, perhaps the question of her name didn't seem as important: the war was making itself felt with increasing arrogance, and Fosco didn't want to insist. We named her after her grandfather Antonio. However, I liked Kiku."

Who knows whether Toni's destiny might have been different had she been named Kiku–chrysanthemum. In Italy, the chrysanthemum is the flower of the dead; I didn't know if my little sister would have experienced symbolic hardships with that name. She certainly fit into the anthropological strategy of my father: if she is born in Japan, she will be partly Japanese and her name will establish a geographic reality, which though not aligned with her birth certificate, will be revelatory of a cultural belonging.

In Japan, the chrysanthemum is a sacred flower, a flower symbolizing the sun's longevity and heat. Its petals, they say, are arranged in the shape of solar rays and thus imitate the star of life. "Oh! At Nara / The scent of chrysanthemums / And old Buddhas!" writes the poet Basho in 1673. "Furthermore," explain Chevalier and Gheerbrant, "The chrysanthemum, *kiku*, evokes, through a homonym, the word *kiku-ri*, which means listening to the truth, from which is derived *Kukuri*, the name of one of the primordial *kami*."

For the Chinese, by contrast, the chrysanthemum is the autumn flower and represents the time of rest after harvest. Among flowers, the philosopher Chou Tun-i says, the chrysanthemum is "the one that conceals itself and escapes the world." Nothing could be more true as it pertains to my sister Toni, who hides under leaves like a solitary snail that has lost its shell and doesn't want to get wet.

She writes with grace and vigour, but hides the pages, like Jane Austen did in her time, almost as if writing were a sin of vanity. She has passionately divided herself between writing and motherhood. She has two grown daughters, Mujah and Nour, of which one is a theatre actor in New York, and the other studies anthropology at the university in Rome.

Toni has instinctively followed the paternal project of anthropological adherence to places of suffering and joy chosen by study or passion. She set up house in Morocco, marrying an elegant Arab painter; has lived many years in Casablanca, writing and organizing festivals of the arts. Her daughters are as fluent in Arabic and French as they are in Italian. At the beginning of 2001, her elder daughter gave birth to a boy, Gabriele Fosco, son of the charming and accomplished New York actor of Irish origin, Daniel McDonald.

"November of '42. The Japanese newspapers spoke of the naval battle of Guadalcanal (an island in the Solomon archipelago) where so many young soldiers had died. I could not feed Toni, because my breasts had no milk. I think it may have been because of that terrible labour in childbirth," my mother says, appropriately continuing the diary she didn't write back then, digging into her crystalline, tempestuous memory.

The word 'Guadalcanal' transports me to distant lost days. *Guadalcanal*, but what does it remind me of? I read it was a naval battle between the Japanese and Americans in the stretch of sea between the islands of Florida and Tulagi; a battle that lasted from the 11th to the 15th of November, during the week of my birthday. The small war planes had to destroy the airport the Americans had seized from the Japanese in August.

If I close my eyes, I can see them: they fly low, and are slow and clumsy and dark like large pregnant ducks. That's how I would have come to know them in the sky of the Nagoya concentration camp. In those bellies are the eggs, and now they'll come out and spit red yolks on the heads of the crowd, I told myself. I really saw those eggs—pale against a pale sky—emerge from the belly, one by one, and slide towards earth. However the shells did not open to spill soft yellow tasty yolks, but to spit out small iron monsters and fire that caused wounds and death to whoever found himself within range. How many times I heard the hissing of splinters over my head while we ran to hide in the trench doubling as an air-raid shelter. The deafening sound of motors in tandem at night is still there, inside my ear. It was the sound of fear.

But the night of November 13 of '42 in Guadalcanal something went wrong for the ducks whose bellies were full of metal eggs. A dim light lit up the edges of the sky. A missile approached like an arrow and hit, dead-center, the airplane, which spun then fell in a column of smoke. The cocky ducks of death were caught mid-act and struck. It would have been the first in a series of setbacks that brought the definitive defeat of Japan.

"I didn't have a drop of milk for baby Toni Kiku," my mother explains. "I didn't know what to do. Dr. Wittemberg told me to give her cow's milk, but where was I to find cow's milk? And so, I began to search the entire city and its environs and in the end, I found a farmer who had a pregnant cow. I told him about the baby without milk, and he was kind enough to let me milk the cow. In general, Japanese civilians were generous and hospitable. Only the military was cruel, sadistic and stupidly nationalistic. Our nanny, Moriokasan, for example, was the only one among our friends who had the courage to come and visit us in the concentration camp, risking arrest. And in fact, she was beaten. And the second time, they wouldn't even let her approach."

"Moriokasan had a soldier husband who was in Hiroshima when the atomic bomb exploded. Miraculously, he survived. I remember his stories retold: he was in the barracks, eating rice and *zukemono* when he saw an immense light, then everything began to shake around him, followed by an absolute darkness into which he passed out. When he regained consciousness some minutes later, he found himself inside a small artificial lake, about a kilometer from the barracks. The immersion in water had saved him from the firestorm. Of the thousands of his fellow soldiers, all that remained were shadows seared on stones. He survived a few more years, until the residual radiation of the blast took effect, and he died of a form of cancer common to the survivors of the bombing of Hiroshima.

"They called it 'black rain,' that which fell after the bomb, and against which the citizens who rushed to help the wounded spread throughout the city didn't think to defend themselves. That black water was radioactive and continued to kill for years and years. Like a long, unjust death, it gathered people in the midst of the euphoria of reconstruction, unrelentingly attacking their limbs until they became gnawed as if by a greedy, obscene mouth. All because the Americans withheld warnings about the dangers of the bomb's aftermath. No one in Japan knew the consequences of radiation contained in the drops of rain that washed the sky after the atomic mushroom."

"I would add two thirds water to the milk, because it was too fatty, and I could give it to her without boiling it, so as not to lose the vitamins, as I had been told by Wittemberg. And Toni, drinking the milk of the Japanese cow, became very strong. She grew in front of our eyes, laughed and played; she was an extraordinary girl. Only a year later, in the Nagoya concentration camp, did she turn into an angry, defiant child, constantly yelling: I'm hungry! I'm hungry! So much so, that everyone begged me to silence her, but how? I worried, because she had no new teeth. During our entire stay in the camp, she didn't grow even an inch. My menstrual periods stopped. And we were all full of parasites. Do you remember how we deloused each other like monkeys...? The only difference is that we didn't eat those disgusting bugs once squished...even if almost, because of our great hunger, we could have..." laughs my delightful mother, making black humour out of that atrocity.

The filth, the parasites are things that humiliate the body and render it greedy and wild. I still recall the poisoning from worms that swelled the belly and emerged from our bums instead of feces, because there was nothing to expel. Damned worms took advantage of our weakness to lodge in our intestines, and eat every kernel of rice they found. And I recall the shame of seeing those lice dance on the bed in the morning, fat with our blood. I had become excellent at catching them. But as many as I squished came out of the folds in our clothes, from the seams of our underwear. No matter how much my mother washed everything over and over, we remained infested.

Yuki can now stand with help for quite a few seconds and does not want to talk. She holds out her hand when she wants to be picked up, and kicks furiously. She can sit unaided, but she falls to one side, and needs cushions arranged around her.

And a few days later, a huge title on the diary page:
YUKI'S FIRST WORDS
July 5th. Almost a year. For the first time, Yuki is standing on her own.
Words: Tatta! Odì. Dacia-ciàn.
July 14 onnicià (connichiwa)
àdà (ya-da)
babài (banzai) celebration, best wishes for a thousand years of good health and immortality
o-bàba (obasan) the nanny.

One day, in the convent where we lived after we were transferred to Tempaku from Nagoya, a monk died. I still see him, seated, leaning against the wall, his chin against his chest. The worn clothes, the hollow face, the small feet wrapped in the soiled 'tabi,' he had died and no one had noticed. Not even us children, who thought he had fallen asleep. Until the monk's grandchild, the small and kind Keiko cried, "Look!" From the body of the man, from his threadbare clothes descended thousands of bugs, which quickly formed into disciplined columns and headed for the door. Proof that the blood was cooling. Proof that there was nothing more to eat.

"Remember to explain that I didn't go to a concentration camp simply to follow a beloved husband," my mother says, petting her white cat to whom she speaks as if he were a baby. "The Japanese military authority called both of us, papà and me, separately, and asked us to sign up for the Republica di Salò. Fosco answered, "I am an official of the Alpini and can't sign anything against them." On my own, I said Nazism didn't concur with my ideas, that I did not like racism. We stared at each other from afar, Fosco and I, and understood we'd made the same choice. From then on, they locked us in a house under police watch. We could not go out, nor telephone, nor write to anyone. You came to me with a branch of citronella, do you remember? 'Smell, Mama, it will cheer you up,' you said.

At the start, they wanted to separate us. But then the wife of the mayor of Nagoya, who was Christian, came to our rescue. Who knows what would have happened if they had put you in a school for children of "traitors": this is what they called us with outright contempt. The wife of the mayor of Nagoya said, "No, leave them together, you can't separate a mother from her children." And so, after those initial days of house arrest, they came to get us, and took us towards the south."

But this is another story and falls outside the love diaries written by my mother and resurrected by chance from my father's Florentine dresser. I promised my sister that I'd let her tell that story. Therefore, I ask my readers to be patient, to listen to what follows the events thus far: the years in the concentration camp, so intense and painful, the war, the daily life of the camp. For many years, I tried to tell this story, but I have always paused, breathless, at the edge of the woods, in both shame and dismay. Suddenly in front of me appears a faceless man, who walks quickly. And I run, run, until I reach a truck and I tell the driver about the terrible encounter. And he turns his empty face towards me, and says, "Like me?"

---

1. Republic of Salò was a satellite state of Nazi Germany during the latter part of World War II (from 1943 until 1945). It was the second and last incarnation of the Fascist Italian state and it was led by Duce Benito Mussolini and his reformed Republican Fascist Party.

Maraini's family home in Japan (1939).
Photo by Fosco Maraini.

Dacia and Fosco Maraini in Japan (1940?).
Photo by Topazia Alliata.

The Great Celebration

Translation by Elvira Di Fabio
Harvard University[*]

I[2]

In the Japanese concentration camp my father and I would often sit under a tree: a cherry tree whose sun-dried leaves would be crushed and rolled inside a larger leaf to form a cigarette. I can still smell that cigarette of cherry fragments, a bit like fine honey, delicious to smell even if it scraped the throat of the person who was smoking it and, in the long run, brought on a headache.

Under that cherry tree which did not, however, bear fruit because it had grown wild, my father would teach me the multiplication tables.
"How much is five times five?"
"Twenty-five, dad."
"And six times seven?"
"I don't remember."
"Try to sing the numbers, sing along with me, like this: two times two is four, three times three is nine, four times four is sixteen…Ok, now you do it!"
And I'd try, singing along with him. And in that way, I learned very quickly. I've never forgotten my multiplication tables precisely because of those chants under the cherry tree. Even now if I want to remember how much eight times eight is I have to sing it in my mind, remembering my father's voice.

For my birthday in the concentration camp, papà Fosco gave me the best present I could ever wish for—a wooden Pinocchio doll carved from a branch of that very cherry tree. It was a crude and rather imperfect puppet. My very young father didn't have the proper instruments for carving and especially for securing the limbs, but given that I was completely deprived of toys, I found it to be an unexpected and fitting gift. I brought it wherever I went.
"Will you tell me the story of Pinocchio, dad?"

---

[*] Original title of the book: Dacia Maraini, La grande festa (Milan: Rizzoli, 2012).

But he didn't remember children's stories and fairy tales. He knew everything about the stars, he knew everything about the origin of the universe, he knew everything about geography and history, but he didn't remember children's stories. Or he scorned them, I don't know. They were a woman's business.

So, I went to my mother, "Will you tell me the story of Pinocchio, mom?"

And she, patiently, while sewing the guards' shirts in exchange for an egg or a potato for her two starving little girls, would tell me the story of Pinocchio and of Geppetto, of the talking cricket and of the little fairy with blue hair. It was the first truly Italian story that I learned about. I knew many fairy tales but they were all Japanese. I had heard them from our nanny Moriokasan, also called Oka-chan, which means little mother, seeing that she watched and took care of us as a mother would have. Oka-chan would tell us terrifying tales of ghosts that went around the camp at night in search of disobedient children, of unfaithful wives who would be strangled or turned into foxes. Foxes, who, on the nights of the full moon, would then sit on the edge of a well waiting for a kind man to come along and free them, and with an enchanted kiss would give them back their human form.

Only years later, while reading David Garnett's *Lady into Fox*, was I reminded of that Japanese tale which I had heard as a child. But Garnett gives the metamorphosis a positive spin. For him the woman is transformed into a fox because she is closer to nature, and is capable, through love, to transform herself, even at the cost of losing her human privileges. Garnett's lady, in fact, falls in love with a male fox and gives birth to little foxes. But she is killed, because men kill foxes, even if she harbors within herself a young and beautiful woman, the wife of a man who no longer recognized her. While in the Japanese tale the woman transformed into a fox suffers a punishment and expresses her pain curled up on the well's edge on the nights of the full moon.

It must be true that foxes have this ability to disguise themselves as human beings, even if they cannot be tamed. One day in September, in my home in Pescasseroli I surprised a fox that was seated on a chair at the table that had just been cleared. It seemed to be peacefully waiting to partake of some scrumptious dish. As soon as I drew near, it ran off. But that doesn't take away from the fact that it had stayed there, calmly, while we were resting, pretending to be a person seated at the dinner table. We had surreptitiously observed it from behind a window.

The ancient fabulists were right: nothing sticks to memory like a fairy tale told to a child. Admonition, instruction, sensual experience, advice, encouragement, revelation of the senses and of the intellect. As Bruno Bettelheim asserts. Perrault's dreadful, instructive fables had a profound meaning: to raise the awareness of evil in those who live in childish indifference, to have them recognize the forms and the flavors of that monster that hides in each of us, whether child or adult.

"Today we address children in a minimalist and affected language, made up entirely of diminutives and sing-song, which falsifies realty," sternly writes my friend Josepha. "We think of the child as an innocent little thing to look after and spoil. The ancients treated the child as a man, even if he was still small. It was necessary to have him learn, with seriousness and even a certain brutality, what they considered constituted the essence of society, so that he would not then find himself unprepared. Children had to grow up quickly and learn in a timely way. Life didn't last very long. The little boy once grown had to soon go off to war and the little girl had to have children at thirteen, fourteen years old."

Pinocchio, too, is a didactic fable, used to teach children to study, not to waste time at play, to save money, to respect their father. But Collodi never dreamed that his novel would have delved into the depths of the collective subconscious, that it would have touched very harsh, symbolic places, unexplored by the human spirit. The story of the disobedient puppet was transformed, despite its author's simplistic intentions, into a dense and mysterious book that can be interpreted in many different ways.

I read it today as the moving and delightful tale of the eternal and ever repressed longing of paternal tenderness by a man without wife or children. But it can also be read as the voyage of a child Ulysses who braves the world and nature to tackle the arcane passage of time. A breathless, impatient restlessness.

Or even yet as the totally masculine dream of a world without women—the only woman who appears is dead and has the marvelous inconsistency of a doll with woolen hair—a world in which men give birth to sons, they look after them and create a relationship of absolute love with their own son, as they saw their mothers do and of whom they are in some way envious.

Or even yet as the surreal and fantastic tale of an impossible metamorphosis: a piece of wood that turns into a man. The dream of omnipotence by a humble artisan. God created man by kneading a bit of mud, so couldn't a poor cobbler, in love with life, do the same thing by drawing out from a mute log a talking puppet who would then become, through the magic of love, a real child?

Pinocchio is also a story of hunger. I, who lived on edible dreams while my stomach contorted from the deprivation of food, was fascinated to hear that even in faraway Italy there were children who went hungry and fed on the skins of pears.

"Pinocchio, who had no feet because they had been burned off by the brazier's fire, asked his father for something to eat. But there's nothing in the house except for a pear. Geppetto hands it to the puppet, and you know what he says, 'Dear father, do me the favor of peeling this pear, please.' His father is shocked and calls him Boccuccia. 'A poor little boy like you can't afford to be so picky.' And do you know what Pinocchio says in reply? 'It may be as you say, papà, but I would never eat a fruit that's not been peeled. I can't stand fruit skins.' See how picky Pinocchio was? Almost like you, who refused to eat the boiled ferns the other day."

I knew it was sacrilege to refuse to eat my vegetables, but those ferns were so bitter that I simply couldn't swallow them. I still recall the smell of that bitterness and can see myself petrified in front of that dish while tears rolled down my cheeks.

"And what did Geppetto say, mom?"

"Geppetto didn't say anything but he took the skins and the core and placed them on a dish at the corner of the table.

"And what about Pinocchio?"

"Pinocchio didn't even glance at those skins, until a few hours later when he was suddenly hungry again. Then he ate skins and core and all."

That's what I ended up doing with the ferns. We, too, would have eaten skins and core and all. Except that we didn't have a single pear to peel. We had tried to eat anything, even acorns. We figured that if pigs could fill up on them, then so could we! So we tried to dry them, grind them into a powder, mix that into a dough and cook it. But what turned out was a gruel that pasted your tongue to your palate, as bitter as gall and utterly indigestible. Everything that came within reach was immediately nabbed and devoured. A mouse, a lizard, a snake. Killed, skinned and boiled. Crappy meat, tough and woody. But anything was better than that horrible hunger that was slowly eating away at us.

II[3]

"Eighty percent of American deaths now occur in the hospital," Nuland[4] reveals. "The figure has gradually risen since 1949, when it was 50 percent; in 1958, it reached 61 percent, and in 1977, it was 70 percent. The increase is not only because so many of the dying have needed the high level of acute care that can be provided only within the hospital's walls. [...] We have somehow been so taken up with the wonders of modern science that our society puts the emphasis in the wrong place. It is the dying that is the important thing—the central player in the drama is the dying man […]."

"In ages past, the hour of death was, insofar as circumstances permitted, seen as a time of spiritual sanctity, and of a last communion with those being left behind. *A great celebration.*[5] The dying expected this to be so, and it was not easily denied them. It was their consolation and the consolation of their loved ones for the parting and especially for the miseries that had very likely preceded it. For many, this last communion was the focus not only of the sense that a good death was being granted them but of the hope they saw in the existence of God and an afterlife."

The entire system of creative imagination—cinema, theater, literature, comic strips—revolves around the fear of death and therefore of the dead. Is this why we drive nails into coffins with such determination? I've always asked myself the reason why so many nails and so many screws are needed to secure the lids of caskets. Do we perhaps fear the surreptitious appearance of a hand, which slowly becomes an arm and then an entire body thirsty for blood that will wander by night when the moon is full in search of a neck to suck on?

Vampires and ghosts, this is what the dead represent for us westerners. We're afraid of them and we bury them as deeply as possible, nowadays even enclosing them in those horrible cement caissons, weighing them down with stone slabs or mounds of fresh lime. Let them be put away and locked up! Lest they even think of coming out of some hole, some crack, to pollute the robust and powerful life of the living!

Easterners have a much more loving and kind relationship with their dead. Perhaps because of their belief in reincarnation, of their conviction that, immediately upon exhaling his last breath, the deceased begins a process of transformation. Metamorphosis awaits him and he has no desire to go off and disturb the earthbound, nor does he want to suck the blood of the living, he does not fear garlic and the crucifix.

Every evening, the Japanese prepare dinner for their dead, expecting them to come and eat the freshly made rice balls, the saucers with tsukemono that every mother has learned to make for the living and for the dead, accompanied by a fresh egg and fragrant saké.

"Ours is the law of Karma. It is a law that weighs on a scale the things that are just and the things that are unjust. If you led a good life, then you are reincarnated as a prince, as a king, or as a wise man. If you behaved poorly, you are transformed into a frog, or a cockroach, or a snake." This is the hoarse voice of Oka-chan, the little mamma with bobbed hair, black as a raven's. "It depends on the animal that was born in that moment and is willing to receive you. Do you understand, Daciuzza?"

Daciuzza is what my father called me. My mother preferred Dacina. In Rome they've always called me Da'. Ninetto Davoli, who's always been my bosom friend, begins his merry stories with an "Ah Da'"!

"After many incarnations, you can reach Nirvana," my little Japanese mother Oka-chan would explain, "and there is no more pain, you know, time no longer passes, there's no fear of suffering, no wars, no wickedness, even death doesn't exist there. You are seated and in front of you is a beautiful landscape all made of flowers and trees full of fruit. If you're hungry, just reach out your hand and take an apple, or a bunch of cherries. You don't even have to get up."

"But that's Heaven like the Bible tells us," I would retort thinking back to a Dürer painting of Adam and Eve, naked, a young and winsome couple, with a fig leaf gently and modestly placed over their genitals, their limbs white, soft. But in the branches of a magnificent tree (a baobab? a mango? or maybe an oak? Does Heaven have a tropical climate or a temperate Mediterranean one?) lies hidden an asp from whose vicious mouth emerges a pointed, slandering tongue…

"Eve yielded to temptation and ate the forbidden apple, the apple of knowledge, and for this they were banished from Paradise." This is the voice of the priest from Bagheria, the very one who once, when we were alone in the sacristy, grabbed me voraciously and gave me a kiss on the mouth. I was so dumbfounded that I didn't dare react. Luckily, he limited himself to the one kiss. The man who was supposed to teach me how to live and how to pray, the pious man that everyone considered almost a saint, treated me as if I were his little girlfriend! Was that the temptation of the diabolical serpent? I gave all the blame to myself, foolish little girl. The serpent turns to the woman because it's well known that women are weak, they have no sense of morality, they are wild and nasty, and on account of stupid vanity, they prefer to listen to the word of the serpent rather than that of God. These were the sermons that were heard in church.

Like Eve, I probably had committed the sin of ingenuousness, I had seduced that holy man without even knowing it, through female irresponsibility and weakness, despite my most ingenuous thirteen years of age. Inevitably it had to be my fault. The pious man, so devout and so convincing in his church sermons on morality could not possibility claim any responsibility. That act was a sin, though, I had no doubts. He himself had led me to understand this by hiding himself and by taking all the precautions not to have been seen and then forewarning me not to say anything to anyone. And, in fact, for thirty years I never said a word

III[6]

When I was at Harvard for a month as visiting professor, having been invited by the amiable and most cultured Franco Fido who collects rare books, as soon as I had a free hour I used to go for a walk in the city cemetery. It was a welcoming and serene place, crossed by a playful stream, rich in great vigorous trees, meticulously landscaped with flowers and bushes. In the midst of these, slates of stones stood up with a simple name engraved upon it. No sign of cupolas or little miniature churches. No gilding, frills and unnecessary whimsicalities.

That's what a cemetery should be like. Even in Japan the cemeteries are places of meditation and peace. Not to mention those of the Scandinavian countries, where among the tombs one can even find spaces and structures where children can play. And no one is appalled if a little one runs after a ball trampling the grass that surrounds the simple and humble graves of the dearly departed. Only a cross or a stone signals that there below lies the deceased.

Who had the monstrous idea to put the dead in cement chests of drawers? What perverse imagination could have suggested honoring our beloved ones by pressing them like linen in those drawers of inert gray matter?

The answer is always the same: there's no more space, the dead are multiplying and where can we put them? That's why I think cremation is better. But if you really want to bury them, at least take care to put them underground, not suspended in air, squashed one on top of the other. As to be expected, the very wealthy have little temples, usually hideous, in which to encase the family corpses. A space that costs as much as an apartment in the center of the city. The poor, on the other hand, are placed in drawers, and the absolute destitute end up in mass graves.

"And yet," Josepha writes, "It's really a matter of an attitude of the mind. The deceased and the living can meet each other in a garden, in a field, in a sunny refined courtyard with potted plants, but to stack them up like that, one on top of the other in a cold and inhospitable building material like cement, reveals an incapacity for imagination that makes one shudder."

The noble dead never come out of their tombs, they don't climb out of their stinking vaults with bruised eyes and sharp canines ready to suck your blood. What sense of guilt drives you to be so afraid of those bodies that are decomposing in their wooden casings lined with zinc?

What do we have to atone on their account that we fear them almost more than the living? It's as if we had killed them ourselves and as murderers we dread their gazes, their reproaches and perhaps even their revenge.

IV

Giuseppe, who was only forty-seven years old, did not think of dying. He was an actor, a director, a musician. He looked to the future with confidence and he looked at me with love. We met at an after-theatre dinner, in Trastevere. I couldn't take my eyes off of his, which were brilliantly blue, timid and inquisitive. At the end of the dinner we knew we would be seeing one another again. And we had not exchanged a single word.

Little by little I learned to know him: he came from the Umbrian countryside. An irascible father who died at an early age, a gentle, sweet mother despite her rigid appearance: Caterina, a woman used to working hard, one who does all she can for others, for relatives, for her children, for her grandchildren. Accustomed to settling for a cubbyhole so as to leave room for others. For years she made her bed on the couch because she did not have her own bedroom. An uneducated woman, but with a strong and precise sense of her responsibilities and of the world's hierarchy. A small woman, with short hair, a shy smile, with calloused hands and a great desire to dance.

I never met Giuseppe's father. I quickly became friends with his mother. And even with his sister Daniela with the blond curls. She looked so much like her brother, almost like twins. Small nose, thin lips, bright eyes, lovely long-fingered hands, quick to smile and to accept others. Daniela is married to Carlo, who is surly by nature, though generous, attentive and decisive. They are both from Trevi, a little town clambered among the Umbrian hills. They've known each other since they were children. Yet they married late, only when she became pregnant. They got married at my place in the mountains of Pescasseroli d'Abruzzo: she in white, her hair done up by a most talented local hairdresser, he in black, in the town's small eighteenth-century church.

Giuseppe was happy. He looked at his sister with pride and love. And she delighted in it. She was in fact beautiful, fully pregnant, her breasts swollen, her face radiant, her lovely blond curls rolled and falling over her ears like grapes ready for picking.

At the great wedding lunch prepared by old Picchio there were first courses, second first courses, and even third first courses, then second second courses, and third second courses, etc., all the way to the desserts, fruit, coffee, liquors, just like a traditional wedding. Even the relatives were happy, despite the midday heat. It was August 1, 1998.

Their daughter, Francesca, is now a little lady with long honey-colored hair, a very talented skater. In the meanwhile, Daniela and Carlo had a second child and they called her Aurora.

Every now and then Giuseppe was seized by a sudden anger that would thoroughly upset his balance. What made him angry was another's disregard, distraction or carelessness towards him. "It's like, I cut myself down to size, humble myself, I'm ready to help you in any way possible, and you treat me as if I were incompetent?" Many, in fact, because of his humility and kindness, ended up turning it against him with disdain. And he would fill with indignation to the point of screaming.

I never treated him with disdain. I never treat anyone that way. But I have witnessed his furious flare-ups when someone didn't take him seriously. He would shake and became aggressive. But his rage would soon fizzle out and he would gloomily brood over imaginary retaliations.

The first time we took a walk together along the streets of Rome, I noticed he was limping.
"Does your leg hurt?"
"No, I was born this way, a defect in my hip."
I would often see him take a homeopathic remedy by which he swore blindly: Bryonia granules. He always kept a small tube on his nightstand. It didn't seem to me that it had any effect. He walked badly and he tired quickly.

He finally decided to go to an orthopedic specialist who told him he needed to have surgery as soon as possible otherwise his hip would have continued to twist to the point that he would no longer be able to walk.

A relative of his had been operated on by doctors at the school in Lyon and he was quite happy with the experience. The famous Professor Legret (a great surgeon who died prematurely in an accident while canoeing down a South American river with rocky shores) and Dr. Gassen (a man with a generous smile and sharp eye) came down to Florence every month from Lyon to operate on Italian patients in the Santa Chiara Hospital.

Giuseppe made an appointment, filled two bags of blood so as not to resort to transfusions, and underwent surgery at the hands of the great French surgeon who had the bearing of a working-class priest rather than a medical doctor.

It's difficult to imagine Giuseppe struggling with transfusions back then because whenever he'd see a needle or even a bit of blood, he would faint. But in any case, the deed was done. And so one day I accompanied him, together with this mother and sister, to the Florentine hospital. The next day I had to leave because I was expected in Berlin. I called him twice a day.

"I don't know what they gave me, but while they were operating on me I was singing. I was all happy and I've never felt so good in my life. It was a local anesthetic, so I saw everything, but I didn't feel a thing, a miracle. I do have some pain now, but nothing like before. In a few days I'll be walking again."

And that's just what happened. First with two crutches, then with only one, and finally none at all. A quick and complete recovery.

He was transferred to the rehabilitation clinic Frate Sole in Figline Valdarno a few miles outside Florence. That's where I, too, went a few years later, when I was run over by a car while I was bicycling, and I fell and broke my hip. Thanks to a diligent and unyielding physiotherapist named Vienna, I quickly recovered. She was as strict as a sergeant, but precise and attentive. Battle between the two of us arose only when I presumed to read while I did my exercises and she prohibited me from doing so. It goes without saying that she always won.

When I met him, Giuseppe didn't know how to ski or how to swim. I dragged him along in the snow, and after a few lessons he was able to descend the snowy slopes. He liked swimming more. "You know, today I swam eighty lengths," he would triumphantly announce to me over the phone. He was proud of that body, which, humiliated and lame for so many years, had now become strong and agile.

We would go cycling along the bicycle path. We'd stop for an ice cream. Giuseppe was ready to laugh at everything. He was a joyous person and determined to see a friend in his neighbor. Defenseless, perhaps, but never cowardly, never bored. He liked parties. He'd prepare frittatas for his friends, finger sandwiches with tuna and mayonnaise, almonds covered with caramelized sugar, Russian potato salad, ice-cold drinks. His friends were a motley crew: Francesco, an intelligent young man with a law degree who, unable to find a job that matched his qualifications, had to settle for mailman, married a pretty young woman, but began to suffer from depression. On account of the treatments, he gained weight and lost all his hair. Massimo is an accountant but he loves the theater and can recite Baudelaire from memory. He had been engaged to a Slav, Alessandra, but he found her to be too severe and demanding, so they split up. Chantal, a French actress who from time to time would arrive from Paris, with short skirts and a sarcastic and seductive air. Antonello and Gianluca, loving longtime friends, passionate about theater, they had opened a restaurant and with the money that they earned, they set up a theatrical company that even Giuseppe was part of. But the money soon ran out, and they went back to the restaurant business. Alberto the handsome, elegant costume designer, whom he lost track of after a move. Candida and Donatella, two friends from Trevi, one redhead and the other blonde, loving, intrepid, he didn't see them very often, but he was very fond of them. Marisa, passionate costume designer, she married an office worker, they had two children and then he died of a tumor at thirty-six.

In the rehabilitation clinic after the hip surgery, Giuseppe had become friends with a young dentist from Modena, Pietro the gentle, who was living a conflicting love for an older woman. He often betrayed her and she kept quiet, but one day she threw him out of the house and he suffered greatly because of it. He put on weight without even noticing and as a result, when he fell, he broke his just operated hip yet a second time. The two friends phoned each other often, one from Modena, the other from Rome. Sometimes we went together to visit him. He was always cheerful, playing his part. He liked to eat well, gossip a bit. At a certain point he stopped calling. "Call him!" I would said, "and ask him why he hasn't been in touch. Maybe he's sick again." But he didn't dare.

"I'm afraid he might be dead."

"What? Why?"

"I don't know, but a friend who disappears like that means that he's no more."

"I say he's alive. Try to call him."

"I don't feel like it." It was strange, that desire not to know. As if his own destiny depended on that of his friend.

We were in New York. In a hotel where a lot of Italians went, on 42nd street. In a room that was longer than it was wide. On the 12th floor with windows that faced other windows. You had to keep the curtains always drawn if you didn't want to be seen. Even if no one seemed to idle in front of an open window. On the other side of the tightly closed windows you could see bodies ever in motion. Offices with the lights eternally on, men in shirt and tie, some poor wretched cactus plants that languished on the edge of the tables, and hands that stretched out toward the ringing telephones.

Of course it must have seemed strange, that look of a man who, from the inside of a courtyard with a thousand open windows, stopped and gazed at the tripping of a ballerina, at the comings and goings of an old married couple, at the disorderly dinners of a humble family with many children, at the solitude of an old woman. I'm thinking of Hitchcock and his wonderful film, *Rear Window*. For American sensibility it was the gaze of a curious man breaking the rules, a crank, an oddball. He was justified only in the fact that he had his leg in a cast.

Here in Italy we assume that people pry into other people's windows and spy in on what's going on. That's why there are shutters, curtains, opaque windows. No one except an exhibitionist, however, would dream of undressing in front of the window of a well-lit room. In America it's assumed—because of decency, discretion, disinterest—that no one wants to steal a glance into the private space of others. It's a fact that most windows are unprotected by curtains and people move about their homes as if the neighbors across the way didn't exist.

One morning in this hotel room on the 12th floor Giuseppe discovered that his gums were swollen, that they hurt and he couldn't brush his teeth because of the pain. Shall we go to a dentist? But who and where? We didn't know any dentists in New York. We called a friend and he gave us the name of a doctor saying that he was "very good." We called him and made an appointment. In the meantime Giuseppe developed a fever of 101. We attributed the fever to the swollen gums. It was urgent that he see a doctor.

It was three days before our departure and we had to quickly find a remedy. The doctor received us in a very small and cluttered office. There were no other patients. It was after hours. Straight away he let us know that he was doing us a favor in seeing us at that hour. For that reason, he wanted two hundred dollars up front and in cash. We complained. But Giuseppe had a high fever and he didn't feel like arguing. The dentist was adamant and demanded his 200 dollars in cash before he would even look in his mouth.

We should have left right then and there. Instead, we stupidly stayed. The dentist examined the patient and decreed: he has to be operated on immediately! All the gums had to be resected. The cost of the surgery: one thousand two hundred dollars. He was so sure of himself. And he said that if it wasn't done immediately, there was the risk of a highly dangerous septicemia.

What to do? We had to make a decision right away. We did the math. We didn't have enough cash, but by making ATM withdrawals, each from our own accounts, we could manage. It goes without saying that we had to pay right then and there and in cash. I ran to the ATM while the harsh and greedy dentist operated on poor Giuseppe.

I will never forget the look he gave me just before submitting to the knife. For a moment I instinctively wanted to take him by the arm and carry him away. But I didn't, and I don't know why. A doctor's authority is always binding. He had said with such certainty that it would have been dangerous to delay the surgery even by a day. There was a doubt in my mind about his good faith, but what if he was right? What if blood poisoning would have threatened his life? What if delaying the surgery by even an hour would have been fatal? Could we have risked it? We acquiesced. Without considering—it's hard to believe that a doctor could be so perverse as to approach needless surgery just for the sake of money—that the demand for cold hard cash should have set off an alarm.

When I returned with the money the operation was almost over. Giuseppe had not suffered any pain and the gums looked almost normal. There was nothing left to do but to thank the doctor for having taken us after-hours, to hand over the money, and leave. And that's what we did.

Back at the hotel, though, the fever wasn't going down. Giuseppe got into bed. Every eight hours I gave him a shot of antibiotics. In the evening I would go out to get him some warm soup at the corner store that, in addition to newspapers, cigarettes and apples, also sold fried rice, chicken broth, potato salad, bottled water and onion rings. I would bring him some cut-up fruit in a plastic bowl, some mint tea. He wasn't in any pain, but he was so tired and the fever gave no sign of letting up. I called another doctor, who couldn't come by, though. He advised us to go to the hospital. But Giuseppe didn't want to. "It will soon pass, it's only a toothache. Let's wait until we're back in Italy."

The next morning I had a meeting with students at Columbia University. I went, but I tried to finish up quickly; I didn't want to leave him alone for too long. When I got back to the hotel, I found him exhausted and sweaty in the untidy room. I hurried off to get two bottles of water. The concierge reproached me for bringing food into the room. When I told him that my partner was sick, he retorted that if I wanted he would call a doctor. The cost: five hundred dollars. I told him that we were leaving the next day.

It was the date indicated on the ticket. The plane was to take off in the late afternoon, but we had to leave the room in the morning. I asked the manager if he would allow us to stay in the room at least until three o'clock, but he was inflexible. I had to pay for another night in order to stay in the room for a few hours past checkout. Giuseppe's fever was still high. His thirst great. The pain throughout his whole body never left him. I was beginning to think that this was something more than just a toothache.

The return flight was agony. Giuseppe didn't manage to sleep for a moment. He complained of a terrible headache. He couldn't manage to swallow his food. And his high fever persisted. At first he was so cold I had to put two blankets over him, his and mine. Then, at mid-flight, he was hot and sweating, and couldn't even stand having his shirt on.

We finally arrived in Rome, without having slept, with our nerves on edge, we grabbed a taxi and I accompanied him to his place. I helped him with the suitcase. His mother had come by to see him so I left him, worn out and feverish, in her care. I went home exhausted and went straight to sleep.

The next day Giuseppe was better. Two days later, his fever was gone, and he was able to take up his normal routine: theater workshop with schoolchildren in the morning, planning other performances with this sister in the afternoon, the evening with me. We would go to the theater, the movies, dinner with friends. His gums no longer swollen, the fever gone. It really seemed like everything was back to normal. To be on the safe side, and on his doctor's advice, he went to have a blood test. The results were expected in by Monday. This was on Friday.

We went to the countryside as we usually did to spend Saturday and Sunday out in the open with our dog Ginni and cat Carbone. We cooked for our friends who had come over for dinner: Beppe and Monica (he works at the State Mint and she is a dynamic actress from Rignano), Vincenzo (a talented actor who understands *pietas*), Renata (an actress and director of a thousand creative ideas), Deanna and Laura (one a painter with a pleasing hand, the other a meticulous and talented translator, who came from their home in Sant'Oreste). We cheerfully dined on pasta with garlic and oil, fish fry, mixed green salad, and an apple dessert that I had made. We chatted joyfully, without knowing that that would be the last happy dinner we would have shared in our common life together.

The next morning at seven o'clock there was a call from the lab. Extremely urgent: Mr. Giuseppe Moretti, you must go to medical services for information that cannot be delayed. On a Saturday? How come? Well, we'll just wait and see on Monday, Giuseppe says. But the person on the other end insists: no, you must come in right away. So we returned to Rome, taking the cat and dog with us, giving up on a Saturday and Sunday of nature walks.

At the lab, without much ado, they told him that his blood tests were shocking: more than four hundred thousand white blood cells, an invasion, which meant a serious blood disease, acute myeloid leukemia. He had to immediately have other tests done at the hematological institute.

It had all happened so quickly that none of us thought of something beyond remedy. Our friends tried to reassure us by saying that leukemia is now curable. All that's needed, therefore, is the proper treatment.

The tests that followed confirmed the verdict. He had to be admitted right then and immediately begin treatments. His mother, his sister and I accompanied him to the hospital. There were no rooms available. But they were obliged to keep him because he had to begin chemotherapy that very night.

We three women went home at midnight, leaving him on a stretcher in the hallway, next to two other sick people who had just arrived. One died during the night. The other would later become his roommate.

The next day they found him a room with four beds, on the third floor. I would soon learn my way around the hospital and its timetable. I went back and forth the whole day long, bringing Giuseppe fruit, flowers and books. I learned to wipe my shoes on a disinfectant matt, slip into a full-length, leaf-green smock, to secure the elastic of the white mask at the nape of my neck, to stuff my hair into an apple-green cap, to wash my hands with antiseptic.

I also came to know his roommates. The very elegant man in a silk robe, a bracelet on his wrist, computer on his bed, several phones about. He put on display photographs of himself in uniform, next to great American movie stars. He used to work at the Ciampino airport where the famous actors landed in private planes and he was there to assist them every time. In exchange, he would have his picture taken next to those illustrious guests, stiffly erect and with a sparkling smile. His wife was kind, more demure, she wore her hair in a ponytail. She dressed like a teenager with short skirts and leopard bodices. She would read a book while he talked on the phone.

After two cycles of chemotherapy, he went home. In his place, a boy who never peeled himself away from his PlayStation. He began at eight in the morning and continued straight through to midnight. He never looked anyone in the eye. Shaved head, long arms, a t-shirt with a burly blue duckling on a white background, his pajama pants rolled up on his ankles.

The most amiable was a chef with big, dark beautiful eyes. Dark-haired, stocky, restless, he had a quick wit. He cooked at a restaurant at Castelli Romani. He had lymphoma, but he never lost heart. Bald head, naked arms, a tattoo on his shoulder, he would face the various cycles of chemo with courageous cheerfulness. His wife, a matronly woman, pretty, would bring him clean linens every day. They would call, even after the chef was discharged, to see how Giuseppe was doing.

Luckily, the hospital is next to my mother's house. So, whenever I had to leave the room, I went to her place, and she is always happy to see me.

The chemotherapy had its impact. The fever went away. Giuseppe's veins began to fill up with red blood cells. Despite his hair loss—that brown curly hair that he was so proud of, at an age when almost all of his friends were becoming bald, he prided himself on having thick, curly and abundant hair—despite his swollen face, his life resumed its pace: getting up early to go to the schools, eating a sandwich while he set up and broke down scenes with Barbara and Luisa, the two actresses who performed with him, coming home tired at around 3 o'clock. Resting for an hour. Taking up the work for the schools again (organization, offers, negotiations: the schools didn't pay because they didn't have any money. Each child who wanted to see the play would buy a ticket for five euros).

The teachers loved Giuseppe for his kind disposition, for his availability, for the plays that entertained the children. Plays where the good and the bad were easily recognized. One day when he was playing the part of the bad guy, a little girl stormed onto the stage and kicked him in the shins, calling him a "monster"!

Barbara, petite, pretty, with big expressive eyes, was expecting a baby, but she acted until the very last, ever enthusiastic and disciplined. Luisa the chubby one often played the part of the wicked fairy, and she was so convincing that the children would always insult her and throw little paper balls at her.

Then there was a part in Salvatore Maira's movie. Giuseppe left for Padua where they were filming from morning to night. "I'm so happy to be feeling well," he would tell me over the phone, "I struggle a bit more than usual, but I can manage."

"Don't tire yourself out too much."

"I have to get up early in the morning. It's wonderful getting out of bed with the sun that seems to melt in a lake of clouds. There are always delays on the set, but I just pick up a book and read. Or else I practice my guitar. I lock myself in a storeroom and forget everything."

It really did seem like the disease had been vanquished. A bad dream from which he had come out victorious. After all, hadn't the same happened to many of his hospital mates? After two or three cycles of chemotherapy, they'd lose their hair, they'd learn to go around with a cap drawn low on their forehead, but then ever so slowly, they would regain their colors, their hair would grow back and they would return to a normal life.

Others died but almost out of sight. As soon as they got worse, they would be sent home so as not to dishearten those who shared the same room. When they couldn't be sent home, the hospital personnel would surround the bed with two screens and a priest would come by to anoint the patient with extreme unction. The room would be emptied. The nurses would run here and there. Silence would fall all about. If the lot fell to him, it won't fall to me—that's what the sick would think as they strolled nervously up and down the hallway. Almost as if death was a voracious dragon with an extreme and insatiable appetite. All you had to do was throw him a body to eat and he would be still and quiet for a day or so while he digested.

At mealtime the tinkling trays would arrive. The pasta with tomato sauce or the four-cheese rice would be offered in small bowls sealed with a pearly plastic wrap. The seal on the bowl was torn open. Inside the pasta was still warm but overcooked every time. Giuseppe's mother, the petite and daring Caterina, would often bring him homemade dishes that she herself prepared: grilled eggplant, fresh green beans with lemon or vinegar, a juicy steak. Those stricken with this disease were not on a restricted diet. Even if it seemed strange to me to offer someone with a high fever and confined to his bed fried breaded cutlets or noodles dressed in a rich, heavy gravy smelling of browned onions. The meat inside those Styrofoam bowls was shriveled and withered, completely devoid of taste.

I still have a segment of that lovely film by Maira in which Giuseppe, smiling, exits the scene and waves. And he truly seems to be coming out alive, with a sweet and shy grin that stretches his tired lips. His head completely bald, his dreamy eyes, he put up a tenacious and merry fight against the disease.

The fever actually had once again begun to appear. The doctors advised another round of chemotherapy. And so, as soon as the film shoot was done, he was readmitted to the hospital. But he didn't stay for very long. His body responded well to the harsh chemo treatments. He also seemed to be responding to the medications—he'd take dozens a day and they caused nausea and a debilitating torpor—but he was happy that the disease was in remission, as the doctors kept telling him.

The doctor who was responsible for his ward, Maria Paola Iorio, would come into his room with a smile, always helpful, always kind. She gave him hope. Despite the death of his other two roommates. "Leukemia can be cured. Sixty percent of patients survive, whereas before everyone died from it, it was an unforgiving disease. You just have to oppose its destructive forces with all your might, you must want to live, and you will make it."

And he would muster up all his willpower. As soon as he would feel better, he'd take up his work with the schools. Barbara in the meantime had had a son whose father wanted to name Gianmaria, and she carried him around with her in a basket. The child was very good and never cried.

Giuseppe even received an offer for another film. But he was unsure about accepting it. He now felt much less secure and was afraid of another relapse. Yet he never gave up on the schools; it was his only source of income, besides. Despite the growing exhaustion and shortness of breath. He no longer suggested going out for a bike ride or even to the movies in the evening. We'd stay home and watch TV, lying down on the couch.

His mother had come to live with him and give him a hand. I'd go to their place every night. I would sadly look at that bald head, those swollen hands, those dark circles under his eyes. And yet, it seemed that nothing could shake his optimism. Even though I suspected it was a way of confronting the disease, in order to resist the temptation to give in to despair.

Before dinner I would join him for a walk. But after ten minutes we would have to turn back because he was tired. My little dog, Bionda, would trot along ahead of us. Luckily right by his house there was a path that followed the bend of the river Aniene, accompanied by the smell of acacia flowers and cane, but at certain points even that of garbage rotting along the banks.

Every hundred meters or so, we had to sit on one of the park benches because he was short of breath. "I've turned into a old retiree," he would say smiling, "Come on, let's go!" and he would get up with some effort from the bench to prove to me that he could make it, he still had so much energy in his body. But it was only willpower, a stubborn willpower to resist that devastating disease.

By now his only hope was a transplant. We had to find someone who was compatible and willing to donate some bone marrow. I was not compatible, neither was his mother. "Let's try with your sister, Daniela," the doctor suggested. But she too was incompatible. We had to track down a donor as soon as possible. Giuseppe's name was entered on the international lists of those in need of bone marrow transplants.

Months went by without the slightest sign of a donor. The bone marrow donation is much simpler and painless compared to a kidney. It's almost like drawing blood. Afterward, as long as you eat well, you can quickly regenerate what you donated. And yet there are still few donors compared to the number in need.

Months of fear and anticipation passed. Then one morning, the good news: there's a transplant offer. It comes from America. A willing young woman has offered to donate her marrow to a patient she doesn't even know. An Italian on the other side of the ocean. He was next on the list, and the precious substance arrived from America by plane, locked in a refrigerator.

The next morning we were all in the hospital awaiting the outcome of the transplant. It took hours but the graft had been completed "with positive results," as the doctor said triumphantly.

We shed tears of joy. Caterina regained her coloring. Daniela brought her two little girls to visit their "ailing uncle." He very much loved his little nieces, Francesca and Aurora. One slender, tall, elegant, the other more petite, very smart, but more delicate.

How to thank the kind American girl who had given of her marrow to a young Italian actor and musician who lived on the other side of the ocean? Unfortunately there was no way to learn her address or her name: the donor must remain secret.

For months I thought about the letter I would have written to her: "Dear anonymous young woman, I know only that you are American and that you are young. But I also know that you are generous. I don't know, however, what reasoning prompted you to act with such generosity; the desire to help your neighbor by sacrificing something as precious as the most secret lymph that runs through our bones? The duty of a good citizen who knows that she must help her fellow man? A religious need? Civil engagement? A self-imposed challenge? An urge to win over the esteem of others? Or to get into Heaven as soon as possible? Or simply the instinct of a person who understands the suffering of another human being and seeks to alleviate it in some way? It's curious of course that you, on the other side of the world, gave life back to a 47-year-old man in a county that you may not even know. Is this the generosity of globalization? I so wish to meet you so I could thank you in person. If thanks to you Giuseppe should be cured, I will try in every way possible to get a hold of your address and come with him to talk to you." I would write and rewrite the letter, every time adding something different, in the hours when I would toss and turn in bed unable to sleep.

    I once wrote a short story about a man who, having received the heart of a young man who died in an accident, sees his life transformed: an obsession pursued him. He wants to know at all costs who that boy to whom he owes his life was, and he wants to know how he died, every detail of the accident and who was responsible. Feeling guilty for having unconsciously wished for, not the death of that particular young man, but of any person whatsoever who could leave a heart of which he would then take possession. "If your life depends on the death of another person don't you feel caught in an obscene trap, something perverse from which you cannot escape despite your innocence?"

    "The Aztecs and the Mayans did it without any fuss," wrote Josepha from the far-off Americas. "They'd take a prisoner, they would bring him to the top of the stairs of one of those very tall and dreadful altars made of stones and skulls, they would make him lie down naked on a rock and with a quick and precise cut they would pierce his chest and take out his still-beating heart, which they would then offer up to their god as a peace offering. The elated spectators would scream their delight.

    "Isn't it more honest to do it in that manner rather than secretly in some sleazy illegal hospital somewhere, with the purpose of making illicit money?" My friend Josepha has a dramatic imagination and I make fun of her without offending her. Fortunately, in Giuseppe's case it didn't take someone's death but a rather smaller sacrifice.

    Another year went by in the company of the disease, with its ups and downs. The transplant was a success; it truly seemed to be the definitive solution. His body became whole again, it was producing lots of red blood cells and his heart was quietly pumping, his hair had begun to grow back, the fever was nowhere to be seen.

We couldn't plan on trips together, however. On the weekends we would to the countryside to relax. No horseback riding, no bicycles. Only a bit of swimming every once in a while. School tired him, theater wore him out. But he held on, with steadfast willpower. He continued to get up early in the morning to bring his shows to the schools, with Barbara and Luisa and the car loaded up. He crammed everything into the poor car: the set, made of huge backdrops which he had painted and that each time were unrolled and then rolled back up again once the performance was over, to then be relegated to the car's rooftop, not to mention the costumes, the tape recorder with all the music, the two speakers and the four spotlights.

We would eat at home in the evening, he no longer felt like going out to friends' houses or to a restaurant. Parties that used to cheer him up so much in the past, were now a distant memory. The medication he was taking wore him down and unnerved him. He had become fearful and he would be irritated if the fruit hadn't been immersed in an antiseptic for hours, if a package of cookies had expired, if the milk hadn't been boiled properly. He felt that he was on the path to recovery, but he was still fragile and vulnerable. He didn't drink a drop a wine, stayed clear of coffee, and everything made him suspicious. And yet, despite his suspicions and his irritations, he held on to that gentle candor that simmered in the depths of his blue eyes. A candor that made him dear to his friends and to those who loved him. A timid smile, a gesture of comical surrender, a slight movement of his long neck would wipe out all sad rigidity that the disease had placed on him. "Darling, where are you? I miss you," he would whisper over the phone, reaching me in my now solitary travels.

But the disease had not at all been quelled. It was smoldering sly and cruel in the depths of that body that was only apparently gaining strength.

"The word leukemia comes from the Greek *leukós*," explained Josepha who likes to teach and inform with the grace of a wise cricket. "*Leukós* meaning white, and *aíma* meaning blood, that is, white blood. You know that in many cultures white is the sign of mourning, so who knows if there is an underlying consonance between the white of the diseased cells and the feeling of loss."

Josepha's pedantry is joyous and is born of a sincere love for the other, from an instinctive and cheerful urge to help, to succor, to inform, to prevent. Our friendship was born from my admiration for her didactic courage and her surprise at my absurd and childishly crippling shyness. She asserts things that I am thinking but often don't have the nerve to state clearly.

Despite the successful transplant, despite the apparent recovery, the white blood cells—that persistent *leukós* in his blood—were not taking it upon themselves to clear out. Hence the tiredness, the breathlessness. And hence the continuous transfusions.

Friends from all over Italy offered their blood. Which was not always compatible. But always generously donated. The actors especially, the many actors who had been his travel mates in the world of theater and of cinema, a few musicians, and even writer-friends, my friends who loved him so, offered to help him.

"For the Chaldeans, divine blood mixed with the earth gave origin to life. Blood gives birth to plants and metals," Josepha would say, "The arrows flung toward the sky-blue cupola by Shou-hsin made blood rain down. The blood of the Holy Grail is the drink of immortality. The wine drunk at the altar represents the blood of Christ. The blood of the sacrificed animal was donated to the gods as a plea for their protection and goodwill. Menstrual blood, on the other hand, is thought to be the sign of impurity by many cultures."

"Why is it that blood which is considered so precious turns impure when it comes from a woman's body?"

"Because all religions consider woman to be impure. Her blood links the soul to something obscure and unknown, which is seen as a danger. Hence, the impurity."

"But why, instead of producing so many white blood cells and so many red blood cells, does blood suddenly begin to produce mostly white blood cells, which then eat the red blood cells to the point of not leaving any alive? The red is killed by the white. The white wins as if in a ferocious war between the will to live and the will to die. Why does the will to die prevail in certain cases and in others not?" I would ask Josepha, as if she were an oracle. But it actually was a way to dialogue with myself. I've always asked myself why certain parasitic diseases lean toward the death of the body that nourishes them when they should wish it to live so they might continue the nourishment. By killing off the matter which feeds them, don't the parasites kill themselves first and foremost? Isn't that paradoxical?

"Do you remember the story of the scorpion who manages to get a ride across the river by a dog who knows how to swim? Halfway across the scorpion stings the dog, who, as it flounders while drowning, asks the scorpion: Why did you do that? I was taking you to the other side of the river, and if I die, you, too, will die by drowning. And the scorpion replies: I can't help it. It's my nature. Indeed, dog and scorpion both die. Do you remember?"

"Strange parable. What does it mean? That the fate of nature is like an unmovable kernel deep within our hearts and it is that which determines our actions, despite our education, our choices, our freewill?"

"Do you remember Fromm, his 'anatomy of human destructiveness'? Apparently, only man has a taste for destroying a life without any motive or objective. Animals kill to eat, to defend themselves, to take out an enemy. Man kills for the pleasure of doing so..."

"And you believe in this determinism, Josepha? You astound me."

"Fromm actually uses the words 'sensual pleasure' in reference to those who kill and torture. A totally human and mysterious sensual pleasure."

A sudden high fever brought Giuseppe back to the hospital. The other patients knew him by now. Some had died, others still alive and they comforted one another. The physician Maria Paola reassured him by telling him about those who had been discharged and were happily living in some Italian city. Dr. Mandelli's hematologic clinic in Rome's Policlinico, today directed by professor Robin Foà, has a widespread reputation and people stricken with leukemia come from all over the world to its annexed ward on Via Benevento.

Giuseppe started having transfusions again—how many times have I tried to sensitize public opinion about the lack of blood for the sick in hospitals!—and cycles of chemotherapy. Blood was in poor supply. In spite of the many generous people who would show up at the ward to donate blood, many others walk straight by without even giving it much thought. There are never enough donors for those who are in need of blood.

In order to administer blood to the veins, a small hole is made in the patient's chest, where the principal vein is located. This vein in turn distributes the precious vital liquid to all the others. The hole is tapped by a small plastic valve. The problem is that the opening, being exposed to the air, often becomes infected and it is then necessary to take it out, disinfect everything and change the valve. This is not a trifling matter, it involves a small but painful operation.

Giuseppe had learned on his own how to open and close the valve, disinfecting it every time. But this didn't prevent it from becoming obstructed and infected every so often. And when that happened, he had to undergo that painful surgery in the operating room, with a minimum of local anesthesia, in order to put the valve back in its place.

His life became more complicated with each passing day. The disease seemed to want to complete its destiny, to run its course to the very end despite the endless medications, chemotherapy, radiation, successful transplant, exactly as the scorpion in the fable, because its destructive nature was more powerful than any possible treatment.

His medications increased. His diet became more and more strict. Weakness prevented Giuseppe from tackling any type of work. Every now and then he'd still go to perform at the schools but he'd come back more tired and despondent than ever. By now he himself would ask to go to the hospital because he felt more protected there.

They had transferred him to the upper floor, in a tiny private room, where the personnel would enter completely covered in antiseptic gowns, gloves, slippers instead of shoes, caps, masks that covered almost their entire face with only their eyes exposed.

When I would go to visit him, both in the morning and again in the afternoon, I would leave the car parked along the street and before entering, I'd raise my eyes to his small window that in fact faced Via Benevento and which was always lit up by a neon light.

Sometimes I'd catch sight of his bald head, limpid behind the pane. I knew he was waiting for me. But I also knew he wanted to see our little dog before I'd lock her in the car. And to indulge him, I'd let her get out of the car, I'd take her in my arms, raising her toward the window. He'd raise his arm with a fond greeting, and in turn I would raise one of Bionda's paws so that she would wave back to him.

The little dog looked up, as if she could see the window and knew that her beloved Giuseppe stood behind it, as if she wanted to tell him to get well soon so that he could resume his routine of going to the schools in the morning and for a walk in the countryside on the weekends.

Every time I go by Via Benevento on my way to my mother's place, I raise my head to look at the little window where Giuseppe would wave to us, to me and Bionda. I can see him there behind those closed windowpanes, his head bald, his face swollen from cortisone, his feverish eyes, so sweet and resigned. We are alone now, I say to Bionda who places a paw on my shoulder as if to encourage me to move on.

It was December. It was cold outside. The hospital was excessively heated. In the hallway that led to Giuseppe's tiny room the nurses had put up a small Christmas tree with red baubles and sparkling silver and white garlands.

In previous years, for Christmas, Giuseppe and I would run around, going here and there to different stores to find gifts for his nieces and my niece and nephew. Francesca and Aurora, his sister's children; Fosco and

Ondina, the children of my sister Toni's daughter, Mujah.

Normally we celebrated Christmas Eve at Giuseppe's with all the relatives, followed by another celebration on Christmas day at my mother's place. Presents, adorned trees, nuts, tombola. These things may be a bit tedious for the adults, but for the children they are a source of joy and surprise.

Little Fosco, who is as nimble as his great-grandfather was in climbing trees and rocks and who hides his shyness under sudden and very sad smiles, lets loose in his games speaking a mixture of English and Italian. I believe he is the one who suffered the most from the death of his father, a very handsome New York actor struck down by a brain tumor at the age of forty-six. Although Mujah now has a new and very loving partner, her beautiful chestnut-colored eyes affectionately light up whenever she speaks of her husband Daniel. Ondina, Fosco's sister, is a strong-willed and very intelligent child, driven by an enormous phosphorescent energy. One day her mother showed me a small mound of ashes that she has stored in a plastic bag inside a precious vessel of Vietnamese stone. "He's all here," she said with a rational tenderness that struck me. "But we will not forget him."

That Christmas, though, there were no presents, no trees, no surprises. I spent my day in the hospital, relieved by Daniela and by mamma Caterina. The little girls were not allowed to visit. Giuseppe seemed less and less interested in eating. His legs were swollen and every day his face became more ashen. But he didn't want to give in to the worsening of the disease. He kept on planning projects. Especially with this mother, probably as a way of comforting her. He perhaps knew deep down that he wasn't going to make it. His body seemed to be draining day by day, his breath grew more labored, and the desire to stay lying in bed ever more imposing.

One morning he developed an intestinal blockage. He was in pain and immediately threw up anything he'd try to eat. He couldn't even swallow a bread crumb. He had to be fed intravenously. They talked about an operation, but the doctors were uncertain: would he make it through the surgery? Gradually his stomach even refused water, which was vomited along with fresh blood.

His thirst, though, had not vanished; on the contrary, it became more nagging with every minute. "Don't give him anything to drink!" the doctor insisted. But he would ask for water. And we, who would hide any evidence of water, were like cruel prison guards. He would look at us with pleading eyes. Sly eyes, at that. One day I held a plastic cup full of water: he tore it from my hands with a quick, recalcitrant gesture and brought it to his lips. In the rush, he crushed the cup, spilling the water on the bed sheet.

That thin hand that gripped the cup tore my heart. It was the thirst of man lost in the desert and we moved bottles and cups out of his reach. Was it not a futile act of cruelty?

Christmas. The bells of the nearby church rang out in celebration. The echo of a children's choir in the distance infiltrated the hermetically sealed windowpanes. The air was balmy. Birds flew low and their chirping was so loud that it reached us through the windows which could not be opened for fear of bacteria. Oxygen entered through a hole in the ceiling over which an aseptic filter was applied.

The lights were always on, the smell of medications filled the room. Every now and then the noise of carts loaded with bowls of warm food covered in plastic could be heard, but it came from the floor below. All that was heard on our floor were the hissing and gurgling of the oxygen coming from a tube in the wall, the groans of the sick and the muffled steps of the nurses who went from one room to the next.

Sometimes Giuseppe would ask me about Bionda. "Can I say hi to her from the window?" "Do you feel like getting up?" "Yes," he'd reply but then as soon as he was on his feet he would falter, and his attentive mother would help him back to bed. "I think if you both hold on to me, I can do it."

He was very attached to Bionda. He would take her while I was traveling, and he would bring her with him to the schools making her sit in the car's rear window. It was funny seeing them pull out, the car loaded up with equipment, a very pregnant Barbara with her black curls hanging down to her shoulders, the stout Luisa with her radiant smile, and the dog, perched on the shelf bobbing her head just like those foam dogs that some drivers have to keep them company.

When I returned from my business trips, Giuseppe would come to get me at the airport. I'd come out of the arrival gate pushing a cart and I'd wait for him at the curbside. I would see a green car in the distance, with Giuseppe at the wheel and Bionda sitting erect next to him, looking intently ahead as if she were showing him the way. When she spotted me, she began to wag her tail, she looked out the window and began to snort cheerfully.

At home, while I'd be cooking for the two of us, Giuseppe would prepare the little dog's meal, carefully checking that the meat was not too fatty, the rice was well cooked, there was no salt, the water was neither too warm nor too cold.

After he died, Bionda kept looking for him and she still does. When she catches sight of a parked green car, she stops, places her paws on the window and tries to see if he's inside.

A sad Christmas. A family dinner with the shadow of a sick person who is dying. The hospital next door made Giuseppe's absence at the Christmas Eve family gathering all the more sad and depressing. I imagined him beyond that sealed window, his head bare, his eyes wide, his expression sweet despite the fear. The solitary prisoner of a merciless disease.

Still, his sister and his mother believed that he would make it. In every little smile, every time he would get out of bed even for a few seconds, they would see a sign of recovery. While the doctor had said that at that point there was nothing else that could be done. But Christmas passed without major changes, on the contrary, it seemed that the patient revived a little. Now he was talking and sat up leaning against the pillows. He had stopped eating, but it seemed like the nourishment he was getting intravenously satiated. The bags of blood increased. His color leaned toward rosy.

We thought recovery was on its way. The nurses encouraged that thought: with the typical dispatch of someone who deals with adults turned children: come now, open your mouth, and don't dribble. Turn to your side so I can give you a shot, there, I'll straighten out your sheet, and don't dirty it anymore now, etc. For the nurses, the terminally ill are little bunglers who are not very obedient and are to be treated with a brisk and impatient tenderness. Little children who will soon leave the world but are unaware of their unhappy fate. They are to be pampered but at the same time tortured with impositions that even the nurses consider futile.

It was clear from the relaxed rigor that the nurses placed on enforcing hygienic precautions, from our being allowed to visit at any time day or night, that no one expected any improvements. They showed a certain regard for the relatives who would soon suffer terrible grief, but at the same time they couldn't hide the rush to free the room for another terminally ill patient who would take over that bed.

New Year's was approaching. The air was growing colder, but made electric by the city bustle. You could hear the sounds of firecrackers that the Romans were testing and which they would shoot off on New Year's Eve to say goodbye to the old year. In the air there were festive songs, rock music slipped out of closed windows, television sets clamored with their rituals "for the people," people crowded the shops for their last-minute shopping, everywhere there was the sweet smell of candied *panettone*, the fragrance of fresh flowers and of roasted chestnuts.

We spent the night of the 30th at Giuseppe's bedside. He seemed to be a bit better. He was trying to tell us about a dream he had that night. But often he would get lost in his narrative, his eyes staring at the wall as if he were listening to a cry that came from afar. His pupils would glass over and his breath became short. His legs hurt so that he kicked his sheets and groaned aloud.

Thirst tormented him. Caterina would moisten his lips with some wet cotton. But he never seemed to be satisfied by those beads of water. His weak hands would turn to the bottle that was usually on his nightstand, and they would grab at the air in a desperate attempt to drink. But then he'd doze off and his ashen face would lose any sign of expression.

The doctor had openly told us that there was nothing left to be done. She asked if we wanted to "alleviate him," at least he would not have suffered and he would have died in peace. This gave way to an argument. Daniela and Caterina wanted in no way to artificially soothe his pain because it would have been like accepting his death in advance. I, on the other hand, thought of accepting the doctor's recommendation. She had been working there for twenty years, she knew the disease's course, she knew when the end was near and she only wanted to alleviate the final agony.

Both Caterina and Daniela, however, distrusted her, didn't believe her, they wanted to resist at all costs, counting on a revival of that young male body that was undoubtedly battling against a disease from which it would surely come out victorious.

Giuseppe's body held on for yet another day, through all the pain and contractions. He insistently asked to drink, but every once in a while he would smile, he would squeeze his sister's hand. And she was more convinced than ever that he would make it. That's why she stubbornly kept on refusing sedation.

On the night of the 31st we stayed by his bedside well into the night. Outside there were celebrations. You could hear the bangs of the firecrackers, the cheerfulness of the fireworks, the laughter, the singing by groups of young people who wandered through the city, the shouts celebrating the new year.

Then, seeing that our patient had dozed off and seemed to be breathing well, we each returned to our own homes: Daniela to her husband and two daughters, Caterina with her, to make her bed in the living room as she normally did, and I to my home near the Tiber where the night gulls noisily bickered.

At three in the morning, a telephone call: come, Giuseppe is sick again. I dressed in a hurry, took the car and rushed off to the hospital. Daniela and Caterina were already there. Giuseppe was delirious. His eyes were closed and he was shaken by painful contractions. The doctor once again suggested sedating him, once again mother and sister answered no. I was in favor of sedation, but not being officially part of the family, my opinion weighed far less than theirs.

Four five six o'clock. I was sitting on one side of the bed squeezing Giuseppe's left hand in both of mine. Caterina and Daniela were sitting on the other side of the bed and they would alternate holding his right hand that rushed to tear away the oxygen tube. Giuseppe no longer opened his eyes. His breathing became more and more labored, his chest swelled, he seemed to be suffering. His twisted mouth now sought air, no longer water.

At a certain point, and it was now ten in the morning, he suddenly stopped gasping. "He has finally fallen asleep," Caterina said relieved. Instead, he had stopped living.

The first day of the year 2009, while the city was falling asleep, exhausted from the celebrations, many men Giuseppe's age where closing the shutters after having drunk and danced for the better part of the night.

A radiant morning, warmed by the sun, the streets deserted, a lonely street-cleaner was picking up the remnants of the party: Romans have the terrible habit of throwing old objects out their windows. That's why it's considered dangerous to walk about during the hours just before and just after midnight. Together with the old year, household items that are no longer useful are thrown out the window, without giving a thought to who might be walking by below. In fact, emergency rooms are invaded, on the morning of the first of the year, by people who were hit on the head by a worn-out mattress or a scorched pot, or by people who were wounded from throwing a lit firecracker, taking part in a brawl, falling down the stairs drunk.

Our Giuseppe was there, now mute, still contracted, his face stretched into a strange and mysterious smile, his eyes closed, his mouth open like that of little birds when they ask their mother to feed them because they are not yet able to provide for themselves. The last request for water that we in turn denied him is a guilt that sticks in my memory, a torture for which I will not be able to forgive myself. Why didn't I insist that he be "alleviated" as the doctor said, instead of letting him die twisted in pain, with labored and frantic breathing? I don't know, I'll never know. A sense of humility toward the will of his mother who adored him after all, but who didn't want to believe in her son's death even with all the evidence?

Exactly like Pasolini's mother who up until the end denied the violent death of her son. I'd go visit her at her house in the Eur district of Rome and as soon as she'd see me, she would say, "Come, I'm make you some coffee. Pier Paolo is in the garden, I'll go call him. Sit down, tell me what you're up to." Pier Paolo had died months before.

One of the many dearly departed in the garden of distant thoughts. I imagine him there, always in motion, as when he would travel with us. A white t-shirt and a pair of blue shorts. His hair cut short, square-rimmed eyeglasses. He's running today, too, nimble and having fun, in the midst of a group of youths, kicking with a swift foot a dirty and half-deflated soccer ball. Pier Paolo, are you there where I see you? I feel like asking him. And I watch him while, surprised, he lifts his head stealing a few seconds away from his attention as soccer player in the middle of the field. He brings his hand to his eyes blinded by the African sun and he looks at me. This time he doesn't speak, as he has many other times in my dreams where he would appear ready to pick up where he left off, scolding his technicians because they weren't taking him seriously. "Dacia, tell him that he's dead, he can't make a movie." And he, shrugging his shoulders, "Fools, I'm here ready to pick up where we left off, even if this death made me lose ten kilos. But that's enough small talk, let's get back to work!"

I see him from a distance. He is so intent on playing that it bothers him to stop even for a few seconds. He slightly raises a slender hand as if to say, "Yes, I know you're there, watching me. Don't lose sight of me." And he quickly starts running again, his sinewy legs, the lightweight track shoes with spikes, his red knee-high socks, blue shorts and white t-shirt. He moves like a chased roebuck, skipping and running in a zig zag pattern. He is agile and light, bouncy and delicate, his muscles that you can tell are like steel, tense in the effort, his beautiful carved face, his eyes intent, sweet, dreamy. Are you looking at me again, Pier Paolo? I like when you put your hand to your forehead, against the sun, and you nod as if to say, hi!

Even after more than thirty years, we still don't know how Pasolini died. The young man who ran over him with the stolen car pleaded guilty and this sufficed for the judges to condemn him to seven years in prison because he was a minor. The time served was in fact only three years. And now more than thirty years after the crime, Pelosi has confessed that he was not the one who killed Pasolini that day.

We knew that right away. It was impossible that in a hand to hand in which Pier Paolo was reduced to a fountain of blood, the person who had presumably killed him did not have a single red stain on him. And there were many shoe prints on the ground and a sweater in the car that did not belong to Pier Paolo, as well as the trace of a bloody hand on the car's hatchback that matched neither Pier Paolo nor Pelosi, his would-be assassin.

Mind you, he wasn't murdered with a gun, but beaten with a plank, kicked and punched. He had defended himself, he had struggled and whoever fought with him would have to have had traces of that fight on his clothes. Instead nothing, Pelosi's clothing was clean and not a single tear. It's likely that Pier Paolo was already dead when he ran over him with the car, but who had thrashed him in that manner? Who had so raged at his body to render it unrecognizable?

Pelosi confessed that there were others with him on that cursed night in Ostia. But he didn't name names. Who were the accomplices? Why won't he say? Is he still afraid? Who wanted Pasolini dead? A group of angry thugs? Hired criminals sent by someone who hated him? Or did others, more powerful, want to shut him up because he knew things that mustn't be revealed?

Pasolini was writing a book on the mystery surrounding the death of Mattei, and on the arms and oil trafficking in Africa. Might that be the reason he was silenced? Perhaps. Who knows if we will ever know? Maybe they'll find out in fifty years when all the witnesses and the people who loved him will be dead, including me.

"The terrible, obscene mystery remains," wisely pontificates Josepha. "How obscene all the mysteries of our recent past, not because they deal with sexual issues—in a Catholic society the obscene is only about sex—but because they are made up of secret, non-confessable plots, in which not only the criminal society is implicated, but the State itself with its institutions, like the Secret Service out of control, and a segment of the police that is corrupt and in murky collusion with the mafia."

The morning of January 2nd, I returned to the hematology hospital but Giuseppe had already been taken away. A terribly sad meeting with friends and family at the morgue. What is a body that no longer hosts a person? Caterina kept on touching his swollen, livid legs, she kissed his cheeks, his mouth.

I, on the other hand, began to experience a detachment from the body that I had loved and embraced. Memory's conquest was beginning. That's the reason why I hate funerals, the cult of tombs. I don't believe in gravesides as a place of meetings and regrets. The body buried is destined to rot underground and I don't find it healthy for my thoughts to linger on that mound.

After the death of a loved one, the task is to learn how to live together with his memory. Memory grows, as do the living, while the dead body remains inert and mute and tends only to deteriorate. Memory produces visions and fanciful ideas, while the grave is a seal on the past that nails you to a piece of earth, a slab of stone with a name engraved upon it. That's why I immediately began to retrieve his pictures, the recordings of his voice, his performances. That's why I established a prize in his honor.

Giuseppe had had a brilliant idea: to mix modern pop music with high poetry, both past and present-day. He had set to music verses by Leopardi, Pascoli, Montale, Alda Merini, Pasolini and Elsa Morante. His gamble of matching the high with the low gave birth to the proposal for a contest aimed at young songwriters. The idea was a success. That first year young composers arrived from all over Italy to Gioia dei Marsi, where the township fondly named a cultural center in his name. They brought songs that joined together the words of Foscolo, D'Annunzio, Cecco Angiolieri, Natalia Ginzburg, Valerio Magrelli and Patrizia Cavalli, with melodies that flowed out restless and complex from guitars, pianos, harmonicas, flutes and many other instruments. For me, this is the euphoria of the remembrance that gives voice and thought to the projects of a young man who died too soon.

"You mustn't mourn the dead because they will rise again in us like the Phoenix," Josepha writes to console me. And I think of the beautiful bird with soft and delicate colors that I had seen is so many reproductions. "The ancient Egyptians called it Bennu," expounds professorial the enchanting Josepha. "A wagtail transformed into a heron, Bennu lived on the rock Benben, in the temple of Heliopolis. It represented the sun that dies in the evening and is reborn every morning at dawn, symbol of eternal life. It had a yellow neck, red body feathers and a blue tail, its beak was golden, and it had long silver legs."

"In other words, a monster."

"No, a marvel of colors. But even the Phoenix dies and do you want to know how? Every five hundred years its feathers wear thin and then the Phoenix gets ready to disappear. It looks for a quiet, secluded place, in the hollow of an oak, for example, and there it accumulates small branches of sandalwood, of myrtle, frankincense and myrrh. There, it settles down and lets itself die burned by the rays of the sun. But after the smoke has been dispersed by the wind, under the fragrant ashes lies an egg. From the egg, the new Phoenix is born."

"But how did the name Bennu become Phoenix?"

"Bennu was also called Heron and the Greeks called it Phoenix. Herodotus speaks about it as a sacred eagle that spits fire and flies on high... Some consider it the metaphor of the soul. Jesus rose again, exactly like the Egyptian Phoenix."

"But no egg and no myrrh."

"Myrrh is offered at his birth, remember the three Wise Men? They bear gifts of gold, frankincense and myrrh, the materials with which the Phoenix bedecks itself."

The phantasmagoria of the Phoenix keeps me company when I can't sleep.

More than anything, however, I like the stories of those who entered Hades in order to take a dead person back to earth. They are more human.

"Like Orpheus and Eurydice?"

"But Orpheus doesn't succeed in bringing Eurydice back to life."

"In fact, the dead cannot live again. Yet, the sound of his lyre was so wonderful that everyone listened to it spellbound. Even the river's waters began to dance, the trees bowed to lend an ear to its notes, the birds stopped flying to listen to its music and the wild animals came out of their dens enraptured."

"Orpheus loved Eurydice but did Eurydice love Orpheus?"

"Legend states as much. But of course there was another youth, a certain Aristaeus who sought her and chased after her in the forest."

"And did she love this Aristaeus?"

"Virgil says no, that she was running away from Aristaeus, and in her flight she ran into a viper that killed her. Seneca also tells the story."

"And what if Eurydice went into the forest to meet Aristaeus?"

"You're crafty. The ancient tales tell of an Orpheus and a Eurydice who loved each other dearly. She died because of a snakebite and he decided to descend into the realm of the dead in order to bring her back to life."

"And what did he do to reach Eurydice?" I knew, but I wanted her to tell it, because the tale, every tale fills me with joyful expectations.

"He asked Charon for a passage across the river Styx and Charon could not refuse him. While he rowed, he listened to the lyre and he wept with emotion. Not even Cerberus, the three-headed dog that tore apart any living being who tried to enter the kingdom of the dead, barked upon his arrival, but it soon crouched peacefully, perking up its ears. And the Furies, instead of attacking him, stood spellbound following the harmony of that lyre.

"Thus, Orpheus reached Eurydice and took her by the hand. But Hades stopped him and told him that he would have granted him this enormous favor, in the name of his music and of his love, on the condition that he not turn around to look at his beloved until they were completely out of the realm of the dead. Orpheus agreed. And he began to climb up the narrow, dark path that led to life. Behind him came Eurydice wrapped in a white tunic, and behind her followed Hermes, who had been sent by Hades to make sure that Orpheus would remain true to the deal. But when they arrived just at the border of the realm of the deceased, seeing a light that illuminated the path and thinking that they were already at the exit, Orpheus turned around, radiant, toward his bride and right at that moment she, reaching out her arms in a vain and desperate attempt to grab on to the outstretched hands of her man, was snatched again by the forces of darkness and brought back."

Josepha knows how to tell a story. I am fascinated by her words that take root in an amazing memory that accompanies her like a beloved sister. I, who am so deprived of memory that like an ant I collect every morsel of remembrance and drag it laboriously to a den that is ever threatened by ruin, I envy her luminous ability to unite words to facts, to stories that palpitate on her tongue like living substances.

Stories that were stratified and germinated long ago, and have acquired the splendor of myth. Stories that are revamped with each telling such as the Egyptian Phoenix, the Bennu with the golden beak. A wild and resplendent eagle that flies toward the sun so as to burst into flames and then die and hence come back to life. Is this the wonder of the passage of time, from generation to generation?

"And where are the troubles, the sorrows, the wounds, the mortifications, the fears that accompany our hapless, daily life?" I ask. "Saint Catherine of Siena would gulp down the water that had been used to wash a person dead from the plague, covered with sores and boils. Was that an act of defiance toward death for love of life?"

"Our religion prefers sacrifice to happiness. If anything, it menacingly states: do not trust that you will reach some earthy bliss, life is sorrow and tears, only in the afterlife, if you were good and obedient, will you find reward and joy. That's why sweat and pus have preference over the great flight of the bird with the golden beak and wings the colors of the peace banner."

That evening I decide to re-read the words of Virgil that trickle on the ear like a bitter, aromatic liqueur. "The transparent shadows and phantoms of those deprived of light, driven by his song, came from the lowest depths of Erebus, like many thousands of birds that hide among the leaves, when evening or wintry rain drives them from the hills. The corpses of men and women were walking there...among them noble heroes, boys and unmarried girls, women burned at the stake before the eyes of their relatives: they came down surrounded by the black mud and the pale reeds of the vile marsh of stagnant waters called Cocytus, holding them captive while the Styx flows through nine circles. The House of Death and the deep abyss of Tartarus were stupefied, and so the Furies with black snacks twined in their hair, and so too Cerberus its three mouths agape in astonishment, and the whirling of Ixion's fiery wheel stopped with the wind."

Virgil compares Eurydice, who is sucked into the night, to a "soft smoke." Are the dead made of smoke? In my mind's eye appears the recollection of those disturbing male bodies, stout and elderly, clothed and masked as women in the theater of Noh. Covered in wondrous silk and satin garb, with bright flashy colors, with extraordinary elegance, they move according to rules established hundreds of years ago, representing dead characters who converse with the living. The grandiose theatrical smoke of an abstract and symbolic ritual.

I once saw an actor die in a Noh performance in Tokyo. Everyone thought that his tremor of gestures, his tentative and unsteady, yet ever controlled and harmonious steps were part of the theatrical performance. The splendor of Noh, they thought. Instead, the actor who was waving his fan with a somewhat shaky gracefulness before his enigmatic and serene woman's face, was in fact dying. He didn't dare ask for help. Besides, no one stopped him in his dying gestures. He continued to act the part of the soft-spoken girl until his last breath. And in the end he fell outstretched on the stage.

Two attendants came to carry him off by the arms and legs. In the hauling, the female mask slid to one side and the wrinkled, waxy face of an elderly man appeared, a contorted mouth with a trickle of blood. An image that is difficult to forget. The fiction of the fiction was unraveling before our astonished eyes.

The performance was not interrupted, however. There wasn't a moment of pause or of silence in honor of that poor actor who died in the midst of his work. The Hayashi vigorously resumed the ancient music with their flutes and drums, accentuating the guttural cries which in that dramatic moment sounded to our ears like the desperate howls of a wolf.

"But what happened to Orpheus, now alone and despairing?" I ask, giving voice to my insatiable hunger for narration.

"It's brazen and childish to always want to know how stories will end," Josepha reprimands me, "Tales are sometimes left hanging and it's only right to leave them incomplete."

But I insist, "I may be brazen and childish, but I like to know how stories end, which is something I have in common with all the readers in the world."

Josepha twists her mouth, as only she knows how to do, with a mixture of snobbish boredom and fond irony. This time we're together in Boston in front of a cup of green tea.

"If you really want to know, I'll tell you how the story of Orpheus ends, even if it's brutal. There are several versions of his death, but the most well known narrates that Orpheus, no longer able to look upon the face of a woman other than Eurydice, retired to a hilltop and opens a music school for youngsters. This preference for the male sex, however, seems to bother the female followers of Dionysus, the Maenads, who interpreted it as an insult to the female sex and that's why one day the school was invaded, Orpheus taken prisoner, killed and cut to pieces. His head was thrown into the river Ebro."

"It would appear to be an accusation of homosexuality on the part of Dionysus' female followers."

"It may very well have been."

"But by the same token weren't the Maenads a community made up entirely of women? Weren't they likewise homosexual?"

"Others state that the Maenads were irritated by the fact that Orpheus, instead of evoking Dionysus, adored the Sun god. The Maenads were in any case dreadful women, who in moments of collective fury became extremely strong, they would quarter whole oxen with their bare hands and feed on the raw meat. You know, don't you, what they did to Pentheus who dared to call into question Dionysus's divinity?"

"Yes, I know, but go on. I like to hear you tell it."

"King Pentheus did not believe in the divinity of Dionysus and when the Maenads began their procession with their beloved lord at the head, he had him arrested and put into prison. Dionysus, without saying a word, made use of an earthquake to escape to freedom. In the meantime, from Mount Cithaeron, where the Maenads had gathered, came the terrifying news: the women infuriated by Dionysus' imprisonment, had thrown themselves on a herd of cows and quartered them live, had invaded a village, destroyed the homes and burned the granaries. At that point, Pentheus, against the advice of his grandfather Cadmus and of the blind seer Tiresias, decided to disguise himself as a woman and go to spy on the Maenads, among whom was his mother Agave. But he was discovered as he was spying from a tree, dressed as a woman. They captured him and quartered him as they had done with Orpheus. They tore him to pieces. Agave herself, his very mother, stuck his head on a spike and carried it triumphantly, screaming that they had quartered a lion."

"So they weren't aware of having torn apart a man?" I ask, having always felt a bit perplexed by the Maenads' fury.

"You've touched upon a rather delicate and mysterious point: to what extent were the Maenads conscious of what they were doing? By Agave's reaction, one would say they were not at all aware. Dionysus made them drunk and delirious."

"So they were insane? Pure bodies manipulated by an angry and vindictive god..."

"Insane, yes, but only for a brief period. To the point that when Agave realizes she had murdered her son and was carrying his head impaled on a spike, she almost dies from shame and horror."

"So it was not a matter of a religious choice, however savage, but of a perdition, a surrender to the mocking forces of evil. What was the message Euripides meant to give with his Maenads?"

"He probably wanted to show that the beautiful civilization that was constructed on an Apollonian ideal based on harmony was crumbling in the face of the clash with formidable new forces coming from unknown countries that the Greeks called barbarians."

"But why did these unknown and barbaric forces inhabit only female bodies?"

"The Greeks viewed women as being more animalistic than men. A body to be dominated and controlled, that, if left on its own, could bring havoc and destruction."

"It takes a lot of creative imagination to transform the female body into a destructive force, a body that instead constructs and gives life."

"If a sex wants to dominate another, it has to inevitably attribute to it something terrible and dangerous. It has to transform it into the enemy if it truly wants to subjugate it. And they succeeded quite well, don't you think?"

"But why does one sex want to dominate the other?"

"Power, my child, is a primordial instinct," Josepha calls me child when she wants to be the wise mother and even her voice changes in those moments, it becomes lower, noble and convincing.

"Any animal whatsoever, any man, weak or strong as they may be, wants to have the liberty to decide for himself and for others, to govern and dominate. Naturally, even women would have liked to govern, but not having the tools to do so, they revolted like the poor farmers of old, with ferocious jacquerie. Instead of arms they would use their hands, and when they didn't have manual strength because those hands were accustomed to embroidery, they would use cunning and poison. The women of the lower class, however, had robust hands that had grown strong from washing clothes at the fountain, pulling up bucketfuls of water from the wells, strangling chickens, chopping wood, lighting the fire, mixing polenta, kneading bread, milking cows, blending ashes and lard to make soap, beating milk into butter."

"Do you think that Euripides truly believed that the Athenian women of his time were capable of tearing a man to pieces with their bare hands?"

"Virgil writes in the *Georgics* that the severed head of Orpheus, white as marble, tossed by the waves, repeated over and over, 'Ah, Eurydice! Wretched Eurydice!' while his tongue already turned blue from death was becoming more and more stiff and black."

"A gruesome sight."

"That's what Virgil relates."

"Does the story end there? With the severed head in the middle of the waves that murmurs: Ah, Eurydice?"

"No, it doesn't end there. Everyone mourned the death of Orpheus whose music moved them to tears: the nymphs dressed in black, the wild animals unnerved turned to run in search of weaker prey, the Muses began to bellow like cows whose calves had been taken away from them. The gods, who in the meantime had grown very angry over the senseless crime committed by the Maenads, sent the plague to Thrace as punishment.

"The population, after months of suffering and death, decided to ask the oracle for an opinion, and the oracle declared that everything was happening because the severed head of Orpheus was asking for revenge. The head was found and placed in the cave of Antissa. And there he began to prophesy, and was so successful that the people, rather than go to the priests of Apollo, ran to him. At that point, Apollo himself came down to visit the head of Orpheus, and he ordered him to stop foretelling the future.

"From that day the head fell silent. But the nightingales sang for him. And Zeus, to compensate poor Orpheus, brought back to the heavens the instrument with which he used to accompany his song. Thus was born the constellation of the Lyre, in loving memory of a great musician who used to enchant with his notes and his incomparable voice."

"And who knows, perhaps that constellation also signifies a memory on behalf of a poet's homosexuality and freedom to teach."

"Are you thinking of Pasolini?"

"Not a constellation, but a star in his honor, what do you say?"

---

2. Ibid., 95–102.
3. Ibid., 115–120.
4. Translator's Note: The Italian text is a quote from an Italian translation of Sherwin B. Nuland, *How We Die: Reflections on Life's Final Chapter* (New York: Alfred A. Knopf, 1994), 255-256. The text reported in this translation is quoted from the original English text.
5. In the original Italian version Maraini adds *Una grande festa*, which is also the title of her book. The expression does not appear in the original text by Nuland.
6. Maraini, *La grande festa*, 128–130.
7. Ibid., 148–209.

Alberto Moravia in Japan (1967).
Photo by Dacia Maraini.

Alberto Moravia and Dacia Maraini with a Japanese monk (Japan, 1967).

II

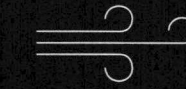

Novels

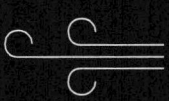

The Age of Malaise

Note to the 1996 Edition
written by Dacia Maraini

Translation by Marta Russoniello
Montclair State University*

I never re-read my books. I prefer to let them sleep, far behind. Actually, they don't sleep at all because they travel the world, and I happen to come across them, filled with unfamiliar writing, bound by a jacket in which I don't recognize myself. A month ago in Germany I found myself face-to-face with a copy of a new edition of *L'età del malessere* (*The Age of Malaise*) by Rowohlt Verlag, fitted with a really strange cover: a young man leans over with his motor scooter to approach a buxom brunette who is walking swinging her hips. I looked inside to check that it was actually *L'età del malessere* like they had told me. It was definitely my novel from '63. How far away it seemed! And not only because of that stereotypical image. Many years have passed and my thoughts have taken different routes, followed different rhythms.

About my past books I sometimes remember the emotions that accompanied their writing: searching for words, working on metaphors, the closeness to a character, the physical sense of a landscape, of a house, created for that occasion. I remember how I would switch between the tendency to write paratactic phrases, short and concise, almost syncopated, and the urge to ease into long descriptions that followed the lazy flow of my wandering thoughts.

I have never been able to choose between the fast and contracted rhythms of a concrete, measured prose, and the slow, expanded rhythms of a baroque and sensual narration. At times, I definitely lean towards a desperate sobriety; at other times, I indulge in the rich opulence of imagery.

Recently in a school where they had read *L'età del malessere* some students asked me: is Enrica you? Of course, Enrica resembles me, but at the same time she is separate from me, far away and unknown.

---

* Dacia Maraini, *L'età del malessere* (Turin: Einaudi, 1996), 5-6.

Characters are born from us, they are flesh of our flesh, but at the same time they are different from us, developing their own personality, their own particular destiny. It is a bit like what happens to children born from a female body: they bear the signs of their parents' personalities, but then they develop on their own, often even in unpredictable and unexpected ways.

Just like Pirandello tells us, characters tend to take over the narrative and impose their own motives. I have often found myself to be in disagreement with my characters who wanted to act differently than what I expected. Only to find out, with the progression of the story, that they were right. The characters are always right, because their only interest is to be true to themselves, while the author, with an eye to the general story, tends to sacrifice the individual, imposing his or her own vision for the narrative which doesn't always correspond with the deepest needs of the single character.

Today, I can say that Enrica is foreign to me, she has moved too far away from me. Yet I cherish the memory of the pleasure I felt when writing about her, following her slowly along roads that were both familiar and foreign, to me.

I never know when I write if, on the stylistic level, I will be able to give body to the journeys of the imagination. Style, as Roland Barthes says, "[is] the product of a thrust, not an intention...a vertical and lonely dimension of thought...it is the writer's 'thing', his [or her] glory and his [or her] prison...; it is the private portion of the ritual, it rises up from the writer's myth-laden depths and unfolds beyond his [or her] area of control."[8]

How better to describe the carnality of style, that is the result of the linguistic organization of the complex and unique relationship that a writer establishes with him-or herself and the world?

---

8. The English translation of the quote was adapted from Roland Barthes, "What Is Writing?" *Writing Degree Zero*, trans. Annette Lavers and Colin Smith (New York: Hill and Wang, 1968), 10-11 and 32-33.

The Age of Malaise

Translation by Kathleen LaPenta
Fordham University*

Cesare's father came to open the door for me. He was wearing a gray housecoat with red flannel lining. He nodded hello with his large graying head of hair and smiled at me as usual, with a malicious air.

"Do you want to see Cesare?"

"Yes."

"I'll call him for you."

Cesare had already heard me arrive and he called to his father to send me back to his room.

"He's studying," his father said wryly "Exams are in a month."

He accompanied me to his son's room and there he stopped, hand on the doorknob.

"He's so diligent! He studies a lot," he said, still not opening the door.

"I'll go and read the newspaper," he added with a timid smile. "I have nothing else to do: read the newspaper, listen to the radio and every now and then I drink a coffee."

"Finally he opened the door and let me in. Then he shut it gently and I heard him walking down the hall, dragging his feet along in his slippers."

"I've been waiting for you for half an hour," said Cesare.

" I had things to do."

" What?"

I shrugged my shoulders. Cesare looked at me with a furrowed brow. He looked down at his long, smooth hands and flat fingertips.

"Just a moment, I need to finish this chapter. Have a seat."

His room was filled with furniture. The curtains were closed and there was a lingering odor of smoke and dust. Cesare was studying in his robe with his elbows propped on the desk. The table was covered with books.

"I can't do it," he said after a few moments pushing away the book. His robe fell open to reveal his smooth hairless chest.

"Want to?" he added, his tone of voice changing.

"Yes."

"Why didn't you come before? I can't study when I know you're coming."

"My father. For the insurance," I said.

---

* Dacia Maraini, *L'età del malessere*, 9-24.

"It's always the same story."

I took off my coat and scarf.

"When you come over you should put something better on. I don't like always seeing you in the same dirty sweater."

"You mean the blue dress?"

"That or another one. You look like a slob. Look at yourself!" he said, getting up from his chair and pointing to the mirror in the closet. I looked at the stretched-out neck of my sweater and the sweat stains in the underarms. I lowered my head.

"You see?"

I nodded yes.

"Don't tell me that your father does not have money to buy you a new sweater, one that costs a thousand lire at Upim."

"What does my father have to do with it?" I said laughing. "My father works at the insurance company and only thinks about himself. His family never even sees him. Underneath though I'm clean. I wash my own undergarments."

"Take your clothes off," said Cesare and he shut the closet door. He brought his large blonde head closer to mine. He had blue, grey and yellow eyes—like the eyes of a cat—and large short teeth.

We both undressed and got in bed.

"I forgot to lock the door—he said, sitting up."

"Want me to do it? It doesn't matter, your father won't come in," I added.

"You never know. Sometimes I think that he looks through the key hole. Dad's like a little boy."

"Why does he watch?"

"Out of curiosity. He has fun doing it."

I felt Cesare's cold feet rub up against my ankles. He held me tightly. He finished immediately and then collapsed on the other side of the bed to fall asleep. I stared up at the ornate ceiling; it had pink, purple and black designs, flowers with shiny leaves that were straight like swords. I counted the petals on one flower. I already knew that there were twelve. But each time I did it again, as if I wasn't sure. I felt Cesare's soft and warm chest heaving up and down as he breathed under my arm.

On the walls there were photographs of Holland; a mill, a canal, expansive and verdant fields, a looming gray sea with sailboats and barges full of flowers.

The phone next to the bed rang. Cesare reached out a hand and brought the receiver to his ear.

"Who is it?"

His voice instantly became sweet and he began to speak as if he were alone. It was his fiancée.

"Yes, I'm studying. No, this evening I have to study. Tomorrow at 5, okay? You know that I adore you. Kisses, yes. Give me kisses too."

He turned towards me with a shameful grin as he put down the receiver.

"Does that bother you?"

"No."

"What a stupid thing, marriage," he said, pulling me in closer.

"Why are you marrying her?"

"Just because. I don't really know myself."

"When are you getting married?"

"In April. You and I will need to split up, you know?"

"You already told me."

"And what if I still want to see you?"

"I'm not sure what to do about that."

"I won't have time. I have to graduate in one year. I would like to earn a living so people don't say that I married a rich girl in order to not have to work."

He got out of bed and put on his robe, rolling up his sleeves on his strong blonde arms. He brought his hands to his throat and said that it was sore.

"I've been smoking to much recently, but how am I supposed to study without smoking?" He lit another cigarette, and offered it to me.

"Want some?"

I nodded my head yes, took a puff and blew the smoke out of my nostrils and lips, slowly.

"Get dressed. Now I can start studying again. I need to concentrate."

He opened the door and peeked his head out.

"My father's nowhere in sight, maybe he went out. I'm going to the kitchen to have a coffee. Come on, I'll make some for you" and he headed toward the end of the hallway.

His father was in the kitchen seated next to the window, eyes fixed on the newspaper, though it seemed like he was sleeping. He smiled at us and began reading his newspaper again.

"Some catches of fish have been contaminated by radiation. Crazy stuff," he said suddenly raising his head.

"Do you want some coffee, Dad?"

"Yes, a little. 'The fish, that was unloaded yesterday morning at the docks in Genoa...'" he read "a big deal" he said pounding his hand on the paper. "This stuff is going to poison us all," he added as he began to sip his coffee.

"Another bit of sugar. Good, Cesare!" he continued raising his face out of the newspaper "you know how to make coffee better than me."

As soon as he had finished drinking his coffee, Cesare pushed me to the door without paying attention to his father who continued commenting out loud on the day's news.

"Bye bye honey!" his father shouted.

"Doesn't your father understand what we do?" I asked.

"He pretends nothing happens. He just doesn't want to be bothered."

"He's discreet," I said.

"Whatever!"

He closed the door behind me. I went down the stairs slowly, remembering the alternating gestures of anger and embarrassment with which his warm and nervous body had made love to me.

My father wasn't home when I got there. After a while my mother arrived. Tired and in a bad mood, she went directly to her room and threw herself on the bed.

"Did he say anything to you?" she shouted to me suddenly, anxiously, through the open door.

"No."

"You need to watch out for yourself. Make yourself desirable. Whatever you do, don't give him anything. Understand?"

"Yes."

My mother began undressing in her plain and dank bedroom that was weakly lit with a lamp with no shade. Every now and then she would shout out something to me about Cesare.

"What?"

"I said that they must be well off, the Rapettos. You have never talked to me about their house. How many rooms are there?"

"I don't know" I tried not to look at her as she took off her bra and looked for her nightgown in the closet. One day I would be like her, I thought, fat with flaccid and wrinkled skin.

"You never know. You should have more respect for your mother. I am forty years older than you, have you forgotten? I will always know more about life and so you should listen to me if you don't want to end up in a mess. Understand?"

It didn't matter to her if I responded or not. While she spoke she was closely examining her skin in the mirror and, lowering her head she grabbed a handful of hair to see if it still had color. Then she went to sit on the bed and began massaging her feet as she mumbled to herself.

"Have you studied today?" she asked in the end after a long silence.

"No."

"I'd like to know how you are going to graduate if you never study."

I didn't respond. She went to fetch my books and opened them for me on the table.

"Study," she insisted, pushing me towards the chair.

I left the house nestling into my coat to keep warm. There was a hole in my shoe through which water was seeping. I felt a shiver go down my back. I wrapped my scarf around my neck. The street was empty. The rain had made everyone disappear. It was no longer raining but I could hear water running through the streets. I walked with my head bowed, careful not to step in any puddles. I went to the card shop and bought a notebook. The owner, a thin small man who looked like my father, smiled at me benevolently while he counted my change. "Work hard" he said happily.

I left the store and I continued to walk along the tram tracks towards Avenue April 21st. I stopped, and after having hesitated a moment I crossed the street to make a call at the bar Mocambo.

"Cesare's not here," his father told me. "But I will tell him you called when he gets back" he added affectionately.

"That's okay. When will he be back?" I asked.

"Um, I don't know. He went out at about 3 o' clock. Maybe he went to a friend's house to study," he said.

"Or maybe he went to see his fiancée," I thought to myself as I hung up the phone. When I went outside it was raining again. I covered my head with the handkerchief and I walked along the edge of the wall. I heard the tram and then saw it stop a few feet away. I had barely placed my foot on the platform when it suddenly departed.

As I continued walking, I felt someone grab my arm.

"Hi, Enrica."

"Hi," I said. It was one of my classmates.

"What are you up to?"

"I don't know, nothing really."

He began laughing. "I'm going dancing. Why don't you come with me?"

"Where?"

"To my friend's house, Giordani. Remember him?" I shook my head.

"The tall one with the glasses. He's in the class next to ours."

"Oh, yeah. And where does he live?"

"On Marsala Street."

"Near school?"

"Two houses down."

There was a strong smell of wet raincoats and our rain from our umbrellas was dripping on our feet. I looked at my friend: I didn't remember his name. He had an angular face with high cheekbones and thin lips.

"How old are you?" I asked him.
"I'm twenty, you?"
"Seventeen."
"So are you coming?"
"Ok."

As we walked down the hill he took my hand and began to run in the rain. Mud was splashing up on my legs and coat. I felt my wet hair sticking to my forehead.

"So much rain!" he said.

We passed by the shoe store where I always stopped after school. The shoes seemed even more beautiful in the window display. I stopped again this time, fascinated. He gave me a push and we continued to run down the street together.

We stopped only when we found shelter from the rain, in a blue lobby that smelled of cat pee.

"Are you tired?"
"A little."

He held my hand. I pulled it away and I played with my wet hair. The handkerchief was soaking wet and I felt the rain in my freezing, soaked-through shoes.

"What a mess!" he said looking at the hem of his pants that had changed color.

The stairwell was dark and steep. We arrived at the top out of breath.

"What's your name?" I asked him while we were waiting outside.
"Carlo."

Giordani opened the door. He was dressed in black and had wide, blue eyes that looked at us from behind thick lensed glasses.

"Hi."
"Hello."
"It's pouring!"

The entryway was dank and narrow and had walls lined with framed photographs. "To Colonel Giordani, General Giossi," I read aloud. Carlo looked more closely at the yellowed photograph in the gold frame "To Colonel Giordani, but the signature is illegible," he said pedantically.

We followed Giordani into the living room, which was asymmetrical room and had large glass and wrought iron chandelier hanging in the middle of the ceiling.

I saw lots of girls piled one on top of the other on the couch; in from of them some boys, standing, who were smoking clumsily.

"Want some lemonade? A little anisette?" Giordani was holding the glass and the bottle up close to his eyes as he poured some of the white sticky liquor into the glass.

There was a pile of records next to the gramophone which was set up on an old studded piece of furniture. Carlo began looking at them. They were small 45's, recordings of American and French songs. The music played out of the speaker, at times raucous and aggressive and at others sweet and mawkish. Carlo was tapping his foot to the beat.

"What is Giordani's first name?"

"I don't remember. His father is a colonel," he said smugly. "He's retired now. He fought in several wars and has tons of medals," he added, making another face.

Giordani was walking around, bottle in hand and offering drinks to his guests. As he approached, he would ask people to dance.

"Aren't you having fun?" he asked bashfully.

"Dance, please!" he insisted.

But nobody was dancing. Until he himself grabbed a girl and twirled her around the room.

"It's a rock song and I don't know how to dance to this," he said finally, drying the sweat from his brow. The girl was laughing. Someone else said that it wasn't a rock. Carlo took a disk out of its cover and put it on the gramophone.

"That's better" said Giordani, bringing himself closer to me.

"It's important to have a beat" said Carlo and he winked at Giordani.

Giordani walked up to a girl named Gabriella. She was my classmate. She had red shoulder-length hair and a small, fair complexion specked with freckles up to her hairline. Everyone was watching her because she had on a tight dress, wrapped around her petite and shapely figure.

"Hi Enrica," Giordani said and he began to speak to me about school. He said that a teacher's aide had discovered two kids in the bathroom making out and had made a big scene of it.

"What idiots!" he commented "couldn't they have done it outside? Now everyone knows about it and makes fun of them, calling them the 'toilet couple' and saying that Elisa is so ugly. Who knows what she sees in that ugly dude!"

Giordani took Gabriella by the waist and they danced together holding each other tightly. I emptied my glass and moved towards the window. It was still raining outside. The street was dark and drops of water fell through the reflection of the street light as it swayed in the wind. I could see shadows of passersby running with an umbrella. Every now and then a car's headlights would shine directly on people and, as the car skidded by it would splashing water onto them. In the house across the street, children were chasing each other in a brightly lit room as a woman stood cooking in front of a gas stove.

"Do you want to dance?"

Carlo put his arms around my waist and pulled me in. He was dancing slowly, without paying any attention to the music. He was flushed and kept his eyes half-closed as he rubbed his body up against mine.

We danced two or three turns holding each other close. Then someone turned out the light. A girl let out a scream and others started laughing. Carlo held me closer and began breathing heavily in my ear. I could feel the pressure of his stomach against mine through the wool of his sweater.

Now everyone was dancing in silence. The only sounds in the room were those of feet running down the street outside and of the breath of some of the guys who were all worked up.

"Now it's okay, it's really okay," Giordani repeated from the dark. Carlo laughed.

"Okay," he said and he lightly brushed his lips up against mine.

"We're alone," Giordani was saying "my parents are gone and we should take advantage."

It seemed like no one was listening to him. Someone shouted that the wine was all gone and so Giordani went to get some more after turning the light back on. A girl followed him and came back by herself, red in the face, with her blouse disheveled.

"I found a bottle of Tenerelli," she shouted showing the cognac. A guy tried to take it from her. Others ran up to her, took the bottle and passed it from person to person. They were drinking directly from the bottle, laughing, leaning over and slapping each other on the back.

"Not that!" shouted Giordani, trying to grab the already half empty bottle.

"What's it matter to you?"

"My father will kill me if we drink his bottle. He had it hidden in the bedroom."

"Liar!" the girl confronted him, "it was in the kitchen."

"You're the liar! We laid down on the bed together and found it under the pillow."

Everyone burst out laughing. The girl saw her opportunity, grabbed the bottle again and Giordani gave up grumbling to himself.

Carlo left me to go and dance with Gabriella. He rubbed up against her body as he had done with me. Gabriella placed her cheek on his shoulder. Carlo put his nose in her hair and whispered softly in her ear.

I asked Giordani where the telephone was and he took me to the hallway.

"Do you need the directory?" he asked.

"No."

He stuck around. Shyly, he came closer and tried pulling me in by my waist.

"Leave me alone," I shouted in his ear.

He immediately pulled back his hands and walked off slouching his shoulders. I dialed the number and waited.

"Cesare?"

"What is it?" It was him, but his voice sounded strange.

"What do you want?" He continued, trying to sound patient.

"I'd like to see you."

"I can't, today or tomorrow. I have to study. You know that I have my exam in a few days. I'll call you when I can."

"Ok" I said. "I hung up the phone."

I thought about his voice and I understood why it sounded so strange: he was in bed with another woman. He had responded to me in the same way as when I was with him and we were in the middle of making love. Ninì, his fiancée, was not the kind of girl who would go to bed before marriage, so who was he with?

I could see them lying together in that room that I knew so well. Perhaps Cesare had just fallen asleep. And maybe she, with his leg resting on her thigh, was also sleeping or looking at the ceiling, just as I often also did. He hangs up the phone, then looks at her to see if she knows who I am. He brushes his lips against her shoulder. She smiles. He looks at his watch. He decides that it's time to start studying again. Maybe he will go make coffee in the kitchen and his father will be there reading the newspaper, kind as always and indifferent to everything.

"What are you doing, Enrica?"

Carlo had been standing there without me knowing. He took me by the shoulders, turned me around and kissed me. His lips were soft and his breath smelled of anisette.

"Are you coming?"

I followed him into the dark room where some couples had stopped dancing and were making out. The only light from the streetlamp filtered in through the glass windows and dimly lit the room. The gramophone had been turned down. I could see Gabriella's hair on the sweater of a big guy laying on the couch. She had taken off her shoes and was laughing hysterically.

"What's wrong with her?"

"She drank too much."

Carlo wasn't dancing anymore. He was pushing me against the wall as if he wanted to flatten me, kissing my ears and hair.

"I'm tired of being here. Want to come outside with me?" he asked pulling himself away suddenly.

"See if it's still raining."

He went to the window and opened it. I went over to him and looked through the open window. It seemed to have stopped raining. The wet smell of rain emanated from the street.

After having searched for our coats in the pile on the bed we left Giordani's party without saying goodbye.

In the street it was cold. The humid air surrounded us and stuck to us like a wet piece of gauze.

"I know a place where we can be alone," said Carlo.

"Where?"

"Start walking" he replied.

My shoes were filled with water after a few moments but I still wasn't cold. On the street corner the wind softly blew and the wet asphalt reflected the colors of the cars and windows.

We walked for a long time alongside one another. Cars passed quickly and we could hear the sound of their tires turning through the puddles. Carlo looked ahead somberly. His hands were deep in his coat pockets. I was trying to keep up with him. Sometimes I would fall a few steps behind and had to run to catch up. I was panting and my feet were killing me.

"Where are we going?"

"Quiet! I know."

He looked at me a moment as if he didn't even see me and then he picked up the pace. We passed by a newsstand that was wallpapered with colorful magazines. I got distracted for a moment to look at the magazines but Carlo continued on his way.

"Here we are" he said, finally.

I looked around. We were on a cobblestoned street that was full of holes. On one side there were frames of two houses that were being newly built. Behind a white picket fence there was a garden full of plants and flowers.

"Now what?"

"Follow me."

He looked around, then he lifted a plank of the fence and ducked down low to pass through to the other side.

"But isn't someone there?"

"No. They are putting in plants for an apartment building. The guard is over there at the construction site, so try not to make any noise.

I followed him through the fence. I slipped in the mud and, to prevent myself from falling, I grabbed onto another part of the fence. Carlo nodded at me to be quiet and to follow him. Leaves were stuck to my face, and I could taste water and pollen. Carlo walked confidently, without looking where he was putting his feet. Every now and then he turned to make sure I was still following him.

"Come on," he said several times "hurry up!"

I saw a small shed behind a bush next to the house being built. Maybe it was a place for storing firewood.

We crawled into the shed on all fours. There was barely space for the two of us. There was a large straw mat that was soaking wet on the floor.

Carlo sat down and slumped his shoulders, as if he had suddenly lost interest. His hands trembled and he was having trouble lighting his cigarette.

"It's too wet," I said.

He lowered his head. He threw away a few matches and finally managed to light it. He blew smoke in my face.

The body heat that I had built up during the run had begun to dwindle and I was also feeling cold and tired. I had no desire even to touch him. I looked at the garden beyond the opening of the shed. Water was dripping down from the openings in the fence and I nestled in my coat. I was soaked to the bone.

Carlo threw away the half-finished cigarette and began massaging my feet.

"Are you cold? Are you cold?" he asked.

"No." And it was true. I could feel the warmth of my legs.

Suddenly he was on top of me and was fumbling about in my coat.

"Too many clothes!" he said as he laughed. He snapped off one of my buttons.

We made love furiously while still wearing our clothes. Afterward Carlo fell to my side with a sigh of satisfaction.

He lit another cigarette and offered it to me. We each took a puff. I began to feel the moisture through our coats.

"Shall we go?"

"Yes."

We got mud all over our knees crawling back out of the shed. Carlo pulled me in to him and kissed me. We could hear crunching of the leaves under our feet and some car horns in the distance.

Carlo put his arm around me.

"What time is it?" I asked.

"8:30."

"It's late. My mother's going to yell at me."

"Let her yell."

Carlo walked towards the exit and I followed him. He picked up the piece of fence and put it back in its place once we had gone back out onto the street. We stopped under a street light to look at our clothes.

"Oh my gosh, look at this mud!" Carlo exclaimed. I looked at his back, he was covered in mud to his shoes.

"Your wet, messy hair makes you look like an angry cat!" he told me.

"And I'm not sure what you look like: but something really strange."

We hugged for the last time and then took off to make the tram that was turning down the street.

The tram was full of workers coming home for dinner. They all had tired and hungry faces. I tied my handkerchief around my head, trying to hide my messy hair.

"Where do you live?"

"On Moroni Street."

"I'll walk you home," he said. "I also live over there."

Woman at War

Preface and revised translation by Mara Benetti
University College London

When I first read *Donna in guerra*, I had recently moved to the United Kingdom and was studying at a British university. It was the seventies, and like most young people of my generation, I found myself part of the social and political wave of unrest that swept across many Western countries.

Traditional values and beliefs were being challenged, not least the gender hierarchies within the left itself and the old male ways of doing politics. 'The personal is political' was arguably the most radical slogan of the era, an unequivocal feminist call to arms.

In this context of, often, confused rebellion and great hope, Vannina, the protagonist of *Woman at War*, seemed to be talking directly to me. Her story struck me as being so exemplary that I immediately wished it could reach the largest possible audience. The best way of making sure it would was, of course, to translate it myself.

On an impulse, I wrote to Dacia and asked her to let me have a go.

In spite of the fact that I had never tackled the translation of a literary work, Dacia generously agreed. She only asked me why I wanted to translate into a language that was not my own. "Usually," she said, "people write best in the language of their dreams." I couldn't answer. I only knew I loved the book.

A long period of intense work followed. Dacia was right. It wasn't easy to find the right nuances of expression in a language that I had only recently learnt.

The sensual, almost tactile quality of Vannina's narrative seemed to have no equivalent in the pragmatism of the Anglo-Saxon world. To recreate the larger than life characters was a big challenge.

Faced with these difficulties, I translated the first few chapters and sent them to two literary friends, both English native speakers, Dick Kitto, and Elspeth Spottiswood. They immediately fell in love with the story and offered to help.

Our collaboration was good and fruitful, although complicated by the distance that separated us. Ours were pre-digital times, with no access to computers, online dictionaries, or emails. We proceeded as follows: I typed out the first draught on an old typewriter, put it into an envelope, stamped it and posted it to Dick and Elspeth. They made the necessary corrections in handwriting and sent the manuscript back to me, also by post. From time to time, wanting to thrash out the difficult points, we would ring each other; or catch a train and meet half way.

The project took a long time, even longer when, having just set himself up as a publisher, Dick came upon the first teething problems of the profession.

Throughout our efforts, Dacia stood firmly by our side, offering encouragement and support.

The book was well received by the British public and the critics. The author was highly praised and, to my pleasant surprise, so were the translators.

Thanks to Dick and Elspeth's continued partnership, more translations of Dacia's work followed.

I went travelling and life took me in other directions, although, over thirty years later, here I am in London, teaching Translation Studies at UCL.

Somebody, whose name escapes my memory, said that reading helps one make new friends. I couldn't agree more. Reading and translating *Woman at War* did exactly that. Not only did I learn to appreciate Dacia as a writer, but also, and more importantly, as a human being. Her commitment to giving a voice to those who do not have one was, and still is, outstanding. It is a voice that is as much needed, if not more so, today, as women the world over struggle to gain their full human rights.

We should be hugely grateful to Dacia for making sure that, throughout her writing, this voice is heard.

Woman at War[*]

Naples[9]

1st September
I'm in Naples, in Suna's house on a dark narrow street, I don't even know its name. The house is old, the walls crumbling, the staircase dirty and stinking of cat piss.

The Maldriks' flat consists of four rooms on the third floor. Its windows look out onto the street, but the view is blocked right off by a new freshly painted building.

As soon as Suna switched on the lights there was a scramble of reddish cockroaches.

"This house is from the last century, it's as full of holes as a cheese. You can use as much insecticide as you like, it's no use, the cockroaches are here in their millions."

She took out some clean sheets, some white and pink striped towels, and

---

[*] Original title of the book: Dacia Maraini, *Donna in guerra* (Turin: Einaudi, 1975). The revised translation is based on the first edition of *Woman at War*, translated by Mara Benetti and Elspeth Spottiswood, and published by Lighthouse Books, in association with Writers and Readers Publishing Cooperative Society Ltd (London, 1984).

a lemon-shaped bar of soap. She showed me the room where I would be sleeping.

"This is Oliver's room, do you like it?"

It is lined with dark wood. In the middle there's a brass bed and by the window a table covered with books and exercise books. The smell of rubber shoes, chocolate and dust stagnates in the airless room. The walls are covered with photographs and posters of tennis tournaments. On a shelf there are four trophies of shiny metal. As I opened the wardrobe I thought I saw something dark move.

"What's that?"

"It's a mouse. Are you scared?"

"Mice disgust me."

"The place is alive with them, there was a time when Oliver and I spent whole days driving them out, we used to enjoy ourselves a hell of a lot, but now I don't think about them. Once my father gave me some terrible Dutch poison that strikes them dead in one second. Now and then I'd open a drawer and find a big fat mouse lying there as hard as cement."

"Why did you get such an old run-down flat?"

"Because it's near my father's. His flat is beautiful, larger, and much brighter than this."

She showed me an inlaid wooden chest of drawers, the most precious object in the house. Inside it there was a whole collection of white tennis shorts, rackets, dirty tennis balls, white and blue shoes.

Along the corridor leading to the kitchen hung some small pale-coloured paintings, crowded with human figures.

"My father painted those. Horrendous stuff, but he's very fond of them, if he comes and doesn't find them he's quite capable of making a scene."

I looked at them closely. They'd been painted with great care. They illustrate domestic scenes—a peasant family gathered round the table in a smoky kitchen, their faces lit by the fire; a husband and wife busy decorating a room with bunches of gladioli, the room picked out in sugary light blue; a mother breast—feeding her baby, her arms enclosing him lovingly, her head bent, the whole scene frozen in a syrupy pink.

"He's sentimental in his paintings because everything in his life is going wrong. Even his present wife isn't too good, she insults him, drinks too much and fills up his house with relatives who steal from him non-stop."

"Whose photograph is this?"

"Elizabeth."

"Who's she?"

"My mother."

The photograph is large and clear. There is a background of trees, and on the bench sits a minute fragile woman in a pair of trousers too large for her. Her calm beautiful eyes stare at the camera with a look of determination. There is something uneasy and proud in the way she sits there staring straight in front of her, which immediately endeared here to her. Perhaps she's less beautiful than Suna, yet she's more glowing and more delicate.

"She looks like you. Is she English?"

"Irish, actually. She comes from a family of shepherds in Galway, her surname is O'Connor, her mother died in childbirth when she was born, she has an elder brother whom I've only seen once, he's a big, tall man who always stoops, whereas my grandfather is short and robust. That's it, now I've given you the lowdown on my family."

"Have you ever been to Ireland?"

"Yes, I have once, when I was ten. I went to stay with my Uncle Robert who works for the Post Office in Dublin."

"Did you go by yourself?"

"No, I went with my father, but as soon as we arrived in Dublin he left me in the lurch and went back to London on business, or so he said, though he'd promised to stay with me and I'd even thought it'd be a sort of honeymoon for the two of us, all alone, without that little terror, Oliver. Instead, he abandoned me in a very squalid guesthouse covered with Virginia creeper and told me to wait for Uncle Robert who'd come and pick me up before the end of the day. I can still remember that cold, damp room. I filled the bath tub with steaming hot water, slipped into it, and there I stayed for a couple of hours swallowing my own tears, masturbating desperately. It was one of those old cast-iron tubs with lion's paws for legs. I remember it all perfectly, the window with white curtains, and beyond it the creeper with its red leaves. I'd been dreaming about that journey for months and there I was, as soon as we arrive he ditches me with my bad legs into that foreign bath tub, immersed in steaming hot water, all by myself like a waif, with my hands between my legs tormenting my cunt. What an idiot I was."

"But didn't he love you?"

"He arrived back on the last day, breathless, loaded with suitcases, he hugged Uncle Robert and my grandfather and then we were off."

"Where was your mother then?"

"Elizabeth hadn't been on speaking terms with her father for the past eighteen years, since she got married to the Turk against his will. The funny thing is that the Turk has made it up with him and the rest of the family, and she hasn't."

"Have you ever been to visit your Turkish relatives?"

"We did decide to go once, I'd packed and got everything ready, then there was a terrible row between my father and mother so we didn't go after all. A year later she ran off with Salvatore, and my father never left Naples again. He says that Turkey gives him the creeps, that his relatives are all shits, grown rich from dishonest rackets—as if he'd become rich himself from honest ones. Anyway he doesn't want to go by himself."

"What about his new wife?"

"Emma? She has deep roots in this neighbourhood, an earthquake wouldn't budge her, if she takes one step out of town she feels sick. She needs to live in the street where she was born, chatting with the neighbours, eating fried aubergines and drinking iced coffee topped with cream, to go to the same shops, to sleep every night in the same bed with the same linings, and if you take a single one of these things away from her she gets depressed and falls ill. When they went to Switzerland on their honeymoon, she wouldn't eat, she turned green and she spent every night tossing and turning as if she'd been bitten by a tarantula. The Turk keeps telling us about it, in the end they had to come back straight away and since then they've never gone away anywhere."

"What does your father do?"

"I don't know exactly, he trades, he deals with money, with foreign currencies, he's never told me a thing about his job. I know that after the war he made a lot of money with the Americans, now he doesn't make as much, he even went to prison once but he'd cut off his tongue rather than talk about his business. I know he has two other flats in this neighbourhood, he's a mean, greedy landlord, a menace, his tenants are poor mediocrities with no money, the whole neighbourhood is poverty-stricken, but he doesn't care a damn about anyone, when they don't pay he throws them out and if they refuse to go he 'persuades' them in his own way, by sending round the 'sappers'."

"What are the sappers?"

"He sends over these big bouncers and for a few thousand liras, they break everything up, smash everything, turn everything upside down and steal whatever they find. If it doesn't work the first time he just goes on repeating it, once, twice, three times, until the tenants get fed up and move out."

"This father of yours is a bit of a criminal."

"Not just a bit, a lot, but he's quite a special criminal of great beauty and charm, everyone who sees him falls in love with him."

Midnight

The shops were already closed. We ate biscuits and tinned sardines. The house is hot, one doesn't feel like eating at all. Fortunately the fridge works well, and we filled it with bottles of milk and coke.

Suna went to sleep early. I heard the phone ringing: it was Giacinto. He says he's back at work, that it's very hot in Rome, that our house has been taken over by lice. "When are you coming back?" he asked me anxiously. I said I'd be back in a couple of days.

Oliver's bed is too soft, it sinks right down in the middle as if it were a hole. The oppressive heat prevents me sleeping. I open the window. Outside there's an old woman singing. She's sitting on the ground right in the middle of the street.

2nd *September*
We slept until about ten. As soon as we got up, we gorged ourselves on biscuits and milk. At eleven we went out in search of Santino. Our first destination was the Movement headquarters. We took two trams and eventually arrived in Via Serbatoio: a stone front door, a small courtyard, a staircase with broken stone arches, and along the wall some revolutionary slogans half covered over with whitewash.

We rang the bell. Vittorio came to open the door for us. Behind him came a youth with large frog-like eyes. Everywhere there were gaudy coloured posters and rolled up red flags propped against the walls.

Vittorio hugged Suna impetuously and happily. He said he knew she would come. He tried to kiss her on the mouth, but she dodged him. He grabbed her hand and covered it with tender kisses.

"Why don't you come to the pizzeria with us? We were just about to go and have a bite."

"Where's Santino?"

"He's at work."

"Where?"

"Why are you so interested in that half-wit? He's a spineless guy, only good for making a fool of himself. He hasn't a scrap of initiative. Okay, he's quite a meticulous worker, but since he's been here with us he hasn't changed his peasant mentality a jot."

"I like him the way he is."

"Do you know what he does every evening? Goes dancing in some totally tasteless nightclub, with the orchestra all dolled up in silver jackets. He's obsessed with this fantasy of posh restaurants and fashionable bars, he's a washout."

"Who does he go to these places with?"

"Some short-arsed chunky girl he's picked up God knows where. The truth is that lad has no balls, he's a wet blanket. If we were fascists instead of Marxists he'd do exactly the same things with exactly the same meticulousness."

"You talk like this just because he's better looking than you are."

"Don't talk bullshit, good looks don't count for a thing."

"It counts for me. When's he coming back?"

"He's gone out to distribute leaflets with Mafalda."

"Who's Mafalda?"

"She's a new member. The daughter of a monarchist lawyer, just imagine!"

1.00 a.m

We went to the pizzeria. Suna was absent-minded and hardly spoke. The other lad whose name is Antonio never opened his mouth either. Vittorio talked all the time about the Movement, about his passion for Suna, about terrorism, about the war in the Middle East, about the Americans, about sex, his father, and many other things.

I ate a pizza that tasted of cardboard and a salad that was yellow instead of green. However, the bill wasn't too much, we paid less than 1,000 liras each. Suna paid because Vittorio's pockets were empty. He turned them inside out for us, all stained with ink and grease, as if they were two flags.

"What on earth do you do? Do you keep pens in your trouser pockets?" Suna burst out laughing. Vittorio took out a biro broken into two and gave us a demonstration of how he could write with both pieces. I burst out laughing too. Antonio watched us all contentedly, his large bulging eyes wide open.

Suna ordered a beer. Vittorio looked at her with comical supplication.
"What's wrong?"
"Not Italian beer, please. It tastes like piss."
"What beer do you want?"

To earn himself a Dutch beer he made a fork appear out of his sleeve, then he made it disappear with quick comic gestures. He embellished the whole performance with monkey-like grimaces and childish whimpering.

We drank eight cans of beer. Then two more. And then two more again. Vittorio was becoming daring, hands and feet up in the air, balancing himself on a chair. Suna laughed, though without much conviction. As a reward he asked her for a kiss. Suna gave him one.

We went back to the Movement's headquarters, but Santino still wasn't there. He didn't turn up at all during the afternoon. Vittorio became as forceful and impetuous an executive manager as ever. He went out, came back, discussed, wrote, gave orders, determined and obsessed, with at times a gentle and at times a harsh tone of voice. The others listened, and did what he told them.

At about six we went back home, tired from having hung about in the heat all day without doing a thing. Suna was in a bad mood. She flung herself on the bed and said she didn't want anything to eat or drink.

"If you want to go to the cinema, Vanna, the money's in my bag."
"I have my own money."
"Go then."
"By myself?"
"What are you afraid of? I'd like to stay here alone for a while, without anyone around. Bye bye."

I went to the cinema even though I didn't feel like it. I chose a thriller, which was on at a local cinema, and as soon as I went in I realized I'd make a mistake: the cinema was full of men. They sat in groups or alone, made loud comments about the film, ate sunflower seeds and spat the shells on the seats in front of them.

I sat in a corner, at the end of a row of empty seats. Five minutes later someone came and sat next to me. I turned my head for a second. It was an old man with a cold. He watched the film with his mouth open, breathing heavily through his nose. As soon as I turned back to the screen I felt his cold hand getting under my skirt. I stood up and changed seats.

On the screen brightly-coloured cars flashed past, pursued by other coloured cars. A hand brandishing a pistol appeared in the foreground. It fired. The car windscreen shattered. A blood-spattered face stared at us with dead yellow eyes. The car took a bend at great speed and launched itself down a steep slope, hitting the rocks, losing its wheels and bumpers. It somersaulted three times and ended up in a pool of stagnant grey water with a splash.

I let out a sigh and leaned against the back of my seat. I felt a naked hairy arm. I turned and bumped against the face of a middle-aged *pater familias* with a twisted greedy mouth. I stood up and went out.

I had only been away from home for three quarters of an hour. Suna had told me she wanted to be alone, so I strolled along the narrow streets of the neighbourhood. I crossed a square. I bought myself an ice cream in a café just as it was putting its shutters up. I emerged into a larger road flanked by acacia trees encased inside cages. I was walking slowly thinking of Orio and his worried anxious face.

Suddenly I was assailed by a screech of brakes. I turned and saw a large flashy car coming to a standstill by the kerb. Out of the window appeared two ugly young heads. They asked me if I wanted to go with them and how much I charged.

I walked on without looking at them, hoping they'd realise they'd made a blunder. A minute later I heard them start up the car, and gave a sigh of relief.

But after walking twenty paces or so, I heard them pull up again. The car stopped alongside me and proceeded at exactly the same pace as I was walking, its rackety engine revving noisily.

I carried on resolutely, as if I hadn't seen or heard them, hoping they'd weary of it. But a moment later I heard the car mount the pavement with two of its wheels just behind me. An arm stretched out of the window and tried to grab my blouse.

I began to run, but this only spurred them on and they started zigzagging noisily, driving on and off the pavement. I was scared. The road was empty; there wasn't a single person in sight. I stopped by an entrance, protected by a kerbstone.

The car slid near me and out jumped a young man with thick long sideboards, a sly face and pot belly. He wore a pair of tight-fitting strawberry-coloured trousers and a black shirt open to his chest.

"Are you scared, pussy cat?"

I knew it was better not to answer. I started walking towards home.

"Why in such a hurry, babe? Come on, hang on a minute! If you get inside the car with us we'll give you a nice present."

I walked with my head down, sweating, panting, biting my lips. I hoped that my refusal to answer would eventually make them give up.

"Just listen, you dope, I don't have a knife or a pistol! I've only got a beautiful throbbing cock and you, what do you have? No money, I can see that, you're a poor sod like me. You've got a beautiful arse though."

His friend burst into raucous laughter. I saw a bus coming and waved my arms frantically to make it stop. The driver looked at me for a moment perplexed and then continued his merry rush along the empty road.

I started walking again with long strides but the youth with sideboards continued to follow me. Behind him came the low, dirty car with the noise of its powerful clapped-out engine. Every so often they would rev up the engine and the empty road would resound like a train going through a tunnel.

"Well, then, when are you going to show us this arse of yours?"

I had thirty yards to go before the turning into the street that took me home. I wondered whether I should take out my keys, but I decided not to. They would have noticed. I had to do it at the last minute, surreptitiously.

I started walking faster, keeping close to the wall, though without running. I felt they weren't too sure what to do. Maybe in a minute or so they'd jump on me, or they might drive off laughing. The youths in the car were watching to see how their friend with the sideboards was getting on.

"You're wearing a wedding ring, I see. So you're married, eh? God, what a swine of a husband you must have! To let a pretty young wife like you roam the streets at night, all alone."

"Get a move on, we're dying of boredom in here," shouted one of his friends from the car.

"A beautiful arse means a beautiful cunt, isn't that so? Can I lift up your skirt, may I?"

His hands took hold of my skirt. I turned around and kicked him on the shin. He bent down swearing. We were only a few yards from the door and I ran the last few steps, slipped the key in the keyhole and went in. But I didn't have time to close the door and the youth with the sideboards reached me and thrust his foot in the opening. He pushed it open with his shoulders and followed me in. The others were laughing at him, waiting with curiosity to see how he was going to behave. Fortunately they didn't get out of the car as I had feared.

I had already run up the flight of stairs taking the steps two at a time, when the youth caught up with me. For a moment we stared into each other's eyes. A flash of hatred passed over his childish face, I saw him lift his clenched fist and felt it crunch heavily on my nose. He bent towards me, gave me another punch on my temple, grabbed my handbag and ran off.

For a moment I couldn't see a thing. There was a black wall in front of my eyes, a hammer beating inside my head. I touched myself, I was bleeding. I sat on a step and rested my burning face against the wall.

When I got my breath back I went downstairs to close the door. I had a nasty feeling they were about to come back. Then, holding my nose with my fingers as best as I could, I went up to the third floor.

Fortunately I still had the keys in my hand. The house was dark and silent. I went to the bathroom and washed myself. Then I went to my bedroom but found the door was locked on the inside. I knocked.

"Giannina, do you mind sleeping on the sofa? I'm with Santino, see you tomorrow."

I wanted to tell her what had happened, but her cold voice discouraged me. I heard Santino's soft, gentle laugh. I couldn't understand why they were in my room. Provoked by a sort of childish curiosity I bent down to look through the keyhole. I could see a bit of Santino's naked body, his limp penis the colour of corn, and Suna's head resting tenderly on his thigh.

My head ached and my nose started to bleed again. I went into the kitchen and drank some cold milk. Then I made myself up a bed on the sofa in the living room.

3rd *September*

I must have screamed in my sleep, because all of sudden I woke up to see Santino's face above me. Suna stood there in her long nightdress, leaning on her crutches.

"What have you been up to? You're all black and blue, and you're bleeding."

I told them of my adventure. Santino laughed softly and sleepily. Suna told him off and he became more serious. She listened full of indignation and kept interrupting to ask for more details.

"You did fine to kick him, but you should have aimed at his balls, that would have paralysed him."

Santino sat on the sofa and stared at me in a daze. I asked him how Orio was.

"So so," he answered, opening his beautiful hands in front of him.

"But when is he coming out?"

"Who knows? They keep saying tomorrow, tomorrow, but he's still there. He asked about you."

"I'll go and visit him tomorrow."

Suna drenched my face with hydrogen peroxide and made me gulp down some cognac. She was pleased that I was there to witness her reunion with Santino.

"He came at eleven, I thought it must be you, but it was him. That cretin Vittorio hadn't told him I was looking for him, a real shit, isn't he?" Santino was looking now at me, now at her. His pale blue eyes were dilated with sleep and he laughed apologetically as his eyelids fluttered together.

"This neighbourhood is changing," said Suna. "It wasn't like this before, I used to go out at night by myself without any worry. But tell me, what was this guy like, describe him to me, I know all the lads in this neighbourhood."

Santino fell asleep, his head dangling on his chest. Suna drank some cognac too, as I retold the story for the third time.

"What was in your bag?"

"15,000 liras and all my documents."

"Tomorrow we'll go and report it."

"I don't want to make a report, I've still got Ciancimiglio's one on my mind."

"Don't worry about that, I'll tell Hasan and get him to have it quashed. You'll see, he knows lots of people at police headquarters."

I was falling asleep on my feet too. I saw my face reflected in the glass of a painting: my left cheek and eye swollen and greyish-blue, a black bruise just above my cheekbone. Luckily I had at any rate stopped bleeding.

"Isn't he handsome? Look at him!" said Suna, gently putting her hand on Santino's sleeping face. She bent down to kiss him, tenderly sucking his upper lip. Santino woke up and put his arm round her shoulders. They went back to bed.

4.00 p.m.

I found the documents together with my empty wallet. They had been thrown on the pavement just outside the entrance. A neighbour had found them as he was taking the chain off his motor-scooter. He handed them over to me with a self-assured look, sleeking his greasy hair down with his other hand.

I asked him if he had heard anything last night. He denied it over-confidently, his eyes looking down and a false jarring note in his voice. I realised that he had heard, but he had purposefully taken care not to interfere.

At two, while Suna was asleep, the bell rang. I went to open the door and found myself confronted by a massive solid man with a handsome gypsy-like head and cheerful grey eyes.

"I bet you're Giovanna."

"Yes, that's me."

"Let's take a look at you. Well, you're pretty, black eyes, curly hair, long eyelashes. You're married, yet you look like a girl. Who beat you up?"

He couldn't have been anyone but Suna's father. His large, strong body, his long arms, his whimsical mouth, even the scent of carnation and the jersey of soft, expensive wool, emitted a feeling of calm self-confidence.

"I'm Suna's father, the Turk, I guess you've heard about me already."

"Well yes..." I was about to add something, but he cut me short with his warm nervous voice.

"Don't listen to what my daughter says about me, she's quite a liar. But you are not from Naples, I gather?"

"I live in Rome."

"Nasty, dirty town that. I've always been had there, once they even sold me a house that had been demolished a month earlier. Thank you for escorting Suna. A disabled daughter is a real burden. How's Oliver?"

"He's well."

"Don't tell me where you're from, I want to guess. You've got a vaguely Roman accent, but underneath that there's something else, let's see: Apulia?"

"My mother is from Caltanisetta, my father from Marsala."

"Why did you tell me, I wanted to guess myself, anyway it's obvious you're a Southerner, your legs are six inches too short, and your eyes are so suspicious. But why didn't Oliver come with you?"

I was about to answer, but this time too he interrupted me with a mischievous look.

"Of course, yes, it's too hot, that's right. Anyway, here's 30,000 liras for your expenses. Now I must be going because I'm very busy."

As he started to take the money from his wallet Suna came in, leaning wearily on her crutches, her eyes puffed, her face haggard, her hair unkempt. They embraced each other tenderly.

"Now Suna, go to the doctor straight away, today, ask him to take new X-rays, bring me the bill, then go back to Addis. It's too hot here. What about you, Giovanna, are you going back to the island with her?"

"No, I can't, I must get back to Rome."

"Who's going to accompany Suna then? You won't leave her on her own, will you? If it's a question of money, I'll pay for the journey of course."

"It isn't because of the money, my husband is waiting for me at home."

"Well, let him wait. You accompany Suna, then you can go back to Rome, I'll pay for that ticket as well, of course."

I was about to reply, but I noticed that he wasn't listening to me anymore. He had stopped in front of one of his pictures and was contemplating it with fascination. His face had softened, his lively grey eyes had become sentimental and dreamy.

"Daddy, will you have lunch with us?"

The gypsy didn't answer. He stood there in front of the painting, enchanted by the elegance of that domesticated family scene. [...]

    4th September[10]

"You could be doing something in that school of yours."

"Like what?"

"You should work out a 'softening-up' process; you could talk to the boys, do some propaganda for our ideas."

"Yes, of course, so that they kick me out straight away."

"You're scared, aren't you? Now I know what sort of person you are, I've got it figured out, Giovanna: you're honest, I can't deny that, sensitive to other people's problems but shit scared, and it's this fear of yours that fucks you up."

"You're right, I'm scared."

"It isn't an ordinary kind of fear, I can see that. I look at people and I suss them out right down to their guts. Yours is the fear of someone who lacks confidence. You don't believe in yourself, do you?" Vittorio looked at me sternly with his clear, insolent little eyes. Suna was eating an ice cream and didn't seem to be listening to what we were saying. Santino was operating the duplicator with Mafalda.

"I don't think I could do anything good in that school, I'm helpless. Besides, I find my colleagues too disagreeable, and the pupils too, they're cocksure, idle, sadistic, I just hate them."

"It's your own fault, and of people like you. You dish out these half-baked ideas, dead-as-mutton teaching and repression and you make the kids just like their parents, if not worse, just morons. If you only had some enthusiasm, passion and also of course a clear capacity for historical analysis."

"I just don't have the enthusiasm."

"You say it as if you were saying: 'I have no saliva'. Your fear is cultural and social, a typically evil result of your fucking petit-bourgeois background."

"It's a fear which results from thousands of years of servitude, you arsehole."

"You always have to defend women, Suna. According to you no woman ever has any defect; she's just a pathetic victim with no responsibility and no blame."

"Fuck off, Vittorio."

He was about to make an angry reply, but something made him hold it back. He grabbed Suna's white nervous hand and pressed it against his cheek.

Suna rudely drew her hand back and carried on licking her ice cream. Her eyes were fixed on Santino who was fiddling about with the duplicator with slow, indolent movements.

Next to him Mafalda looked like a bear. She picked up the sheets, put them in order, cleaned the grease off the machine with a rag, turned the handle, doing everything with careful, heavy, clumsy gestures.

The two didn't look at each other, but there was some secret bond which drew them together, a complicity they couldn't completely hide.

Mafalda is 28. She's tall and dark, she has thick legs and large breasts, and her face is dark and heavily lined. At first it appears almost ordinary and anonymous, though slightly brutal and introspective. But when you look more closely you discover something sensual and tender which lights up her heavy features.

"One of our lot teaches at a grammar school in Pozzuoli, you should talk to him. Until a few years ago he was a slavering drifter like anyone else. Then he met us and joined the Movement and now he's a good militant comrade. I want you to meet him, but just now he's on holiday with his girlfriend."

"As far as holidays go he's still a drifter."

"Faele, you've always got something to be critical about."

"I'd like to know why we should be here working our arses off while he's having fun in Yugoslavia with that pest of a girlfriend."

"Just watch it, and mind your own business. Have you made that list of what we want?"

"What about the money?"

"I'll see to that. You just make that list and shut your mouth."

Meanwhile Santino and Mafalda had disappeared. Next to me, I felt Suna stiffen. I turned and saw that she was biting into her ice cream with bare teeth, sullen and gloomy.

"The trouble is that the fascists are carrying out 'softening-up' missions too, so how do we distinguish ourselves from them?"

"Don't talk bullshit, Renzo."

"What a bore."

"It's you who's the bore, you're never satisfied with anything. What the fuck is it you want?" interrupted Suna. She stood up and, dragging on her crutches, went towards the door to the balcony. Vittorio, Faele and Renzo carried on quarrelling, but I couldn't follow their argument. I wondered whether I should follow Suna or wait for her.

She came back a minute later, her face stony, and sank into her chair. One of her crutches fell to the floor, and Vittorio bent down solicitously to pick it up.

"What's wrong, are you sick?"

"Let's go, Giovanna, I'm fed up with this shitty place."

I helped her get up. We walked to the door, but Vittorio ran after us.

"Where are you going? Wait, Suna, what's wrong with you? You promised to come to the pizzeria with me."

"I don't feel like it."

"Are you coming back later?"

"No, I'm not, in fact tomorrow I'm going back to Addis. Bye bye."

"What, what are you saying? But listen..."

Suna took his head in between her hands and kissed him passionately on the mouth. Vittorio tried to clasp her in his arms and she bit his lip violently. He staggered back in astonishment, and she ran off limping, her long black skirt and large fringed sleeves ballooning out behind her like a great black bird dragging itself along on its wings. I remembered Giottina's words: "beware of the evil wings of the one who can't fly."

I found her at the bus stop, leaning against the lamp post. She was staring in front of her, her muddy grey eyes clouded with rage. She told me she had found Santino and Mafalda in each other's arms on the balcony.

I helped her get on the bus. I didn't know what to say to comfort her and we travelled home in silence.

I was hungry and cut myself two slices of bread. Suna refused to eat, and went to lie down on her bed. I had lunch by myself on the table crawling with flies: cold potatoes from yesterday, milk, a banana.

While I was eating, I suddenly found her beside me, her face sweaty, her lips pale.

"I can't sleep, Vannina, I'm too hot. Have you ever been jealous?"

"Yes, once three years ago when Giacinto had a fling with a girl called Lillina who worked as a cashier in a guesthouse in Monte Mario."

"What did you do?"

"Nothing. I saw this girl once when I went to visit Giacinto at his garage, and she was there having her Fiat 500 repaired; she had hair down to her waist and her trousers were so tight they could have split on her bum; from the way they looked at each other I realised they'd been making love, I understood it straight away."

"How did you react?"

"I stood there like an idiot with such a terrible gut ache I thought I was going to shit myself. Later I asked him if he was in love."

"What did he say?"

"That he didn't know."

"And you? What did you do?"

"I threw up, then I didn't feel like eating anymore."

"And then?"

"I started spying on him, I followed him like a half-wit, I'd go and visit him at the garage all the time, to put it in a nutshell I became an unbearable nuisance. I realised that from the way he started treating me, like a stupid boring little girl. He continued to see her anyway. Then just as I was getting used to it, they left each other."

"I get so mad at Santino standing there like a sack of potatoes, anyone who wants him can have him, he's got no character, he doesn't even know what he likes and what he doesn't like, he makes me sick, he disgusts me. If he comes, tell him I don't want to see him any more. No, don't tell him anything, just kick him out, throw him down the stairs, tell him he's a tod, that I hate him, that he can go and hang himself, and now I'm going to go and masturbate, when I feel depressed that's the only thing that cheers me up. Bye bye."

She went banging her crutches on the striped floor-tiles. I poured some more milk into my glass. I peeled a peach.

While I was eating I heard a sob, and I went to see if she needed anything. I found her lying on the bed, naked, one hand on her groin, her eyes full of tears.

I didn't know whether to go in or stay. I asked her if she wanted something to eat. She lifted her beautiful troubled eyes and smiled at me with seductive sweetness.

"Come here, Vannina."

I drew closer. She beckoned me to sit next to her. I did so. She took my hand and placed it on her belly.

"Can you caress me, do you mind?"

It was the first time I'd touched a woman's belly. It felt disagreeably soft. I played a little with her hair in the way I sometimes do with my own.

She closed her eyes. She stretched her arm and pressed my hand on her damp flesh. My body was icy, my throat blocked up. I touched her more deeply and her soft tender sex opened timidly to my touch. It relaxed between my fingers like a small open sea-anemone down in the depths of the sea.

A few second sufficed. I felt her spring, stretch and all of a sudden relax with a small stifled cry.

Her warmth roused me and I would have liked to kiss her, but she pulled the sheet over herself and with an abrupt gesture turned her back on me and huddled against the wall.

I stood up and went back to the kitchen.

Midnight.

I went to see Orio in hospital. He looks better. I took him some comics and this made him happy.

Giacinto rang me up at about nine to ask when I was going back. I said: tomorrow, if Suna goes to Addis, otherwise in a few days. He says I'm letting myself be mesmerised by a witch. I laughed and he slammed the receiver down in a temper.

At dinner Hasan showed up wearing a summery lilac shirt through which one could see his lean muscular chest. He was cheerful and self-assured.

"Use 'tu' with me, Vannina, okay? Has Suna been to see the doctor yet?"

"I don't know."

"In my opinion this doctor business is just a cover-up, I think underneath it all there's something else, a love affair perhaps. Do you know anything about it?"

"No, I don't."

"You're afraid of spying on her, aren't you? Well, you're a discreet girl. You're quite right, remember that in this life the less you talk the better. Where's Suna?"

"She's asleep."

"Okay, let her sleep. How old are you, Vannina?"

"Twenty five."

He fixed his unsmiling grey eyes on my face. His large red mouth is of a course, striking beauty.

"Do you think Suna will ever be any good for anything in her life?"

"What do you mean by 'good for anything'?"

"Well, find a decent husband she won't split from after living together for a couple of months; have children, become a good mother. I'm afraid she'll always be a misfit."

"If she carries on studying medicine she could become a doctor."

"Bullshit. Can you imagine a crippled doctor? And on top of everything a woman doctor? I'd be happy if she doesn't end up in a home for the subnormal."

"Why should she end up in a home?"

"I shan't live forever, and I haven't saved enough for her to live on the interest. I've got all the others too, wives, children, the fact is I just can't give her enough to live on without working. And left to her own resources I just know she'll never make it."

"She could work."

"There's no work for cripples, besides haven't you understood yet what sort of person Suna is? Intelligent, talented, I don't deny that, but fickle-after a while she gets bored with everything."

His voice is deep and caressing. When his grey eyes light up they flicker with sharp, steely reflections.

"If I were in her shoes, I'd kill myself," he continued. "True, she's only a woman, for a man it would be much worse. Let's hope she finds a husband who will take her as she is, with a good dowry perhaps, and then she could have children. She's beautiful, she should make the most of that."

"But Suna can do everything, she can walk, travel, work."

"She can do everything all right. She can make love, too, I know, but that's the problem because to convince herself she's attractive in spite of her legs she makes love left, right and centre."

I was about to ask him why she shouldn't make love when she chooses but he cut me short with a sharp affectionate gesture.

"It would have been better if the paralysis had affected her up to her navel, then there wouldn't be any problems and I wouldn't worry. What's she going to do if she gets pregnant, can you tell me that?"

"She won't get pregnant, she's careful to take precautions."

"I can see you're an emancipated girl. I'm all for women's emancipation. When I think of all those poor Turkish women shut up at home I feel like crying. All the same, a woman shouldn't try to behave like a man or she'll lose all femininity, she'll become vulgar and promiscuous. For me a woman must more than anything be shy and mysterious, like you for example. I'm sure you don't go around making love to all and sundry."

I didn't feel like answering him. I knew just what he was after–to drag me in and get me to talk about myself and then about Suna, giving away all her intimate secrets.

"You think I'm being moralistic, I know that, but you don't say so because you're a kind girl. You know, amongst all Suna's friends you're the one I like most, you're not arrogant, you're not over-confident, you're not conceited. Besides, a woman doesn't need to make love as much as a man, so why not preserve the discretion that is so beautiful in a girl?"

To answer him would have been equivalent to giving in to him. I looked him up and down. He arched his slim graceful body in front of my eyes, showing his narrow hips, his crotch and his long shapely legs.

"When I was in Turkey I knew women who'd only made love two or three times in their lives, just after their marriage, and that was all till they died. They didn't have a clue what sexual pleasure was, yet they were healthy, plump, happy–much more cheerful and content than girls like Suna who take the initiative as if they were men, make love day and night, and then have nervous breakdowns."

"Daddy, why are you tormenting Giovanna with your stupid ideas?"

"Ah, you're awake then!"

Suna came forward, limping, her muscular arms bare to her shoulders, a yellow towel wrapped round her neck, her wet hair hanging in shiny compact locks over her frowning face.

She went up to her father and kissed him on his cheek. I noticed that in front of his daughter he loses a lot of his confidence. He still talks arrogantly but can't avoid showing a certain embarrassment.

"Have you been to see the doctor?"

"No, I haven't."

"What are you waiting for?"

"I'll go, Daddy, just leave me in peace."

"It's not good for you to be in town in this heat, in this sweltering house. Besides, what's the point of my renting a house by the seaside?"

"You should give me some money, Daddy."

"What for?"

"I want to buy myself a rubber dinghy."

"A rubber dinghy, with your legs? Are you crazy?"

"So that I can go into the sea."

"Aren't you ashamed of showing yourself in a swimming costume in your condition?"

"No, I'm not."

"How much do you need?"

"300,000."

"I'll buy it for you for half as much."

"But I want a special one, a large one, with an engine and everything."

"I'll see to that, my darling. I must go now, Emma's waiting for me."

"I'll ring you at your office tomorrow."

"What for?"

"For the money."

"Well, we'll see, I'll think about it."

He hugged his daughter, and me too. The scent of carnation and lavender water penetrated my nostrils, cloying and sensual. He left, gently closing the door behind him.

"He forces me to tell him a whole lot of lies to get around him. I hate him, did you see how suspicious he is? He prefers to waste his time buying all the stupid things I ask for rather than give me the money direct, the swine."

"Have you decided to give some money to the Movement?"

"I haven't decided yet...well, perhaps I will. I think they're doing some good. I like Vittorio, he's sincere, even if he does have a bee in his bonnet, especially about women. I think I will, yes, I'll give him some money, that is if my prick of a father forks out." [...]

9. Ibid., 151-163.
10. Ibid., 165-173.

Colomba

Preface and translation by Elvira Di Fabio
Harvard University

A writer hears someone knocking at her door. It is a character who is asking to be heard. Zaira, known as Zà, a mountain woman from the Marsica region of Abruzzo, is looking for answers to the disappearance of her granddaughter, Colomba, 'Mbina, whose bicycle was abandoned on the edge of the majestic woods. The search for the girl, whom she raised as her own child, unlocks memories of her family's past, stories that had been lost, just as 'Mbina, and she now hopes will be uncovered and immortalized with the help of the "woman with the short hair," a writer who lives in the solitude of those very mountains.

The novel begins as follows.

***

Colomba*

When someone asks her how a novel is born, the woman with the short hair answers that everything begins with a character knocking at her door. She opens the door. The character enters and sits down. She makes some coffee; sometimes there'll be some freshly-baked cookies, or some bread and butter with a bit of salt sprinkled on top, for those who prefer salted to sweet. The character will drink the coffee that's been offered to him. He will munch on a cookie or two. Some of them shyly admit that they prefer a cup of tea at that hour in the afternoon and that they would like to taste that apricot marmalade for which she is known among her friends. The author will prepare some tea, which could be either mint or jasmine, with lemon or with milk, depending on their tastes. She will open the jar of apricot marmalade and will slide a spoon into it so that the visitor can help himself as he pleases. The character will sip his tea glancing about, and then he will tell his story. Some presume to light a cigarette. And the woman with the short hair, so as not to be rude to her guest, will simply limit herself to shifting her chair away, or opening the window a bit.

---

* Original title of the book: Dacia Maraini, *Colomba* (Milan: Rizzoli, 2004), 9–16.

After having drunk, eaten and told his story, the character usually says goodbye and leaves. As he dissipates, the woman with the short hair will scrutinize him with a precocious nostalgia for his absence. But something did not gel in that encounter, and she will simply limit herself to thinking, "Too bad, I could have gotten to know him better!" She won't get sick over it.

If, on the other hand, her visitor, having finished drinking his tea, eating his bread and butter and his apricot marmalade, will ask her permission if he can stay a bit longer; if, after having stretched out his legs by walking about the room, he will ask her if he might lie down on the sofa; and if, after having rested for a half-hour or so, he will request a glass of fresh water and then take up once again the details of his story; and if, around nine o'clock in the evening he will find it completely natural to sup at her table, and therefore, after having shared with her a plate of spaghetti with olive oil and fresh parmesan, having drunk a glass of red wine, and having peeled and nibbled an apple, he will even ask her for a bed to sleep in, well in that case, it will mean that that particular character has firmly taken up camp in her imagination and has no intention of going away. The next morning, in fact, he will lay claim to a cup of milk with coffee, to some bread with that marmalade that her friends like so much, perhaps because it is not too sweet and has a delicate flavor of apricots and juniper. He will continue to narrate the details of a story that will gradually become more complicated and intricate. At this point it will be quite clear that the time has come to write a new novel.

A character knocked at the door of the woman with the short hair. Timidly tapping knuckles, entering without making a sound. It's a modestly dressed mountain woman. Sturdy boots on her feet. She has sat on the edge of the chair and has remained silent, letting her coffee grow cold in front of her. She seemed embarrassed and ashamed but determined to stay. Then, slowly, toward evening, after having swallowed some soup and drunk a glass of wine, she got around to talking. She's self-conscious because she thinks that her story is not interesting, that no one would feel like listening to it.

Zaira, known as Zà, that's her name, considers herself nondescript, commonplace, and, besides, she is beyond the age of the heroine of a novel. So then what is it that motivates her to infringe upon long-standing habits of silence and tact to go knock on a novelist's door? From the timid and self-conscious person that she is, she becomes determined and resourceful when it comes to her granddaughter Colomba, known as 'Mbina. She raised her as a daughter, she explains hastily, and now she has disappeared. Her face contracts like a Barbary ape's when she pronounces the word disappeared. What do you mean disappeared? Disappeared, disappeared, no one knows where she went, or with whom, or why, or even if she's dead or alive. But her less-than-submissive expression suggests that she hopes to find her alive. And after having treaded many paths, she thought of asking a novelist's help in discovering the clues to her lost granddaughter. Everyone believes that she has died somewhere in the vicinity of her town, in the mountains of Abruzzo. But she, Zà, does not. And she is certain that the author will lend her a hand in her quest.

The narrator politely explains that she does not feel like recounting the tale, very commonplace truthfully speaking, of this Colomba who has gone missing from home. Other stories are unraveling in her imagination. For example that one about a mother who is trying to make her adult memory appealing to her little girl by telling her about women and men in other times. Can a mother hide behind fairy tales so as to talk about grand topics of life with a curious child who is so fond of plots and subplots, even the most rambling ones?

Go home, Zaira, and keep the story of Colomba, known as 'Mbina, to yourself, she's not interested, says the woman with the short hair a bit brusquely, pushing the character out the door.

That very night the author dreams of slipping into the boots she saw her visitor wearing and of entering into the Ermellina woods to look for a missing girl who left a white and blue bicycle on the forest's edge. In the dream she is surprised: hadn't she turned away that character who was a bit dull, self-conscious and predictable? And yet, that woman is now there in her dream and she is moving about with confidence that does not suit her. Who gave her such daring?

It's funny how her body, ignoring the will that inhabits it, should be imagining itself taking up the semblance of a character that she judged to be of little interest. What a tangle! Segismund had never found himself in more difficult straits. How many times had she taken along that dog-eared book by Calderón de la Barca, on the train, on the bus, on the subway, all through her teenage years. Seated among people, she would forget that she was alone. That process of apparent dissolution, she knew, meant being "overtaken by bewilderment." But was it Segismund, prince of a double life, that pale, imprisoned cave-dweller with a will not his own, to arouse her curiosity? And was it a vague sense of identification that was drawing her to the Polish youth, cloistered in that hovel, platonically yearning for a luminous palace, a garden full of flowers and flowing waters? Was the dream that Segismund has, retracing the great welcoming halls of his father's palace, based on experience or desire? The boy's feelings are torn by the awareness of an irretrievable loss. A loss tied to the memory of an estate never definitely possessed. And yet that estate exists, and it is the entire world, something radiant and intoxicating that he is rightly due. Everything seems to come back on itself, like the agony of time that goes neither forward nor backward. But are not the intense feelings of a pale and tormented prince, who continually confuses the reality of imprisonment with a not too certain memory of a smiling and caressing garden, are these passions not like the plight of a writer?

"Colomba Mitta went missing from home the morning of June 2," reports a clipping from *Eco della Marsica* that Zaira has her find on the table. "The young woman who lives in Touta with her grandmother, is twenty-two years old. Her bedroom was in order: the bed made, her slippers lined up on the mat in front of the door, damp towels hung on the window sill, a book on mycology lying on the nightstand. In the kitchen, a cup full of coffee, untouched. The sugar jar just unscrewed with a teaspoon full of sugar, as if she were about to sweeten her coffee. But that teaspoon never reached the cup. Her purse, with money, documents, cell phone, license, was left on the dresser by the front door. She was wearing a pair of brown pants and a pink sweater. Wrapped around her waist, a turquoise K-way waterproof jacket. That is how the shepherd Gvannitt saw her when he spotted her as she jumped on her bike, speeding off toward the mountain.

"Her grandmother, Zaira Bigoncia, reported getting up at eight, going to the kitchen and finding the coffee still warm in the cup, the chair shifted and two crumbled cookies on the table. She thought that perhaps her granddaughter had gone back to her room, so she instinctively placed the saucer on the cup to keep the coffee warm. Then she went to the bathroom. When she returned fifteen minutes later, she noticed that the cup was still in the same spot, with the saucer on top. She then rushed to her granddaughter's room, but she found it empty. She assumed that she had gone off in a hurry without having taken her coffee. Every so often it happened that she was late for work and would run off on her bike without even saying goodbye. She immediately phoned the Post Office, just to be told that she wasn't there. She waited another half hour and called again. But there was no sign of Colomba. Yet it only takes ten minutes from the house to the Post Office."

Her hands on the keyboard. Her feet resting on a footstool, the woman with the short-hair wonders whether writing is a way of investigating, as Zaira leads her to believe. Or perhaps a form of medicine, as a young girl had once explained to her as she handed her a packet of poetry, "I am healed by writing." A teenager, fifteen or sixteen years old. What does she need to be healed of? Love-sickness? Family discontent? A bad night's sleep? She seemed to be looking at her with eager curiosity, as if she would have liked to open up her walnut-shaped brain to understand what type of kernel was hiding in there.

On the other hand, a retired man once announced to her, while handing her a wrinkled manuscript so that she, as expert, might glance through it, that one writes only out of gratification, "as if enclosed within a garden of delights," he had concluded quite contentedly.

The word garden surprises her, as a desire for escape when faced with the austere forests that are before her eyes, woods that overlap other woods in a sequence of azure and green treetops that suggest the indecipherability of a mountainous landscape.

Garden as reassurance? Literature made it a place of sensuality and mystery. There are many gardens enclosed in the impenetrable walls of *A Thousand and One Nights* and in those gardens the most extraordinary adventures are carried out: mistaken identities, loves overturned, forebodings, revelations, expected and unexpected encounters, unfortunate loves, requited loves.

Yet, in today's news, the word garden has taken on a more sinister meaning: dreaming of a happy oasis where rivers flow with milk and sweet-smelling fruit grows spontaneously on trees, where seventy-seven virgins dance to the sound of a sublime flute, young Muslim men go and have themselves blown up from waistbands filled with explosives and hidden under a very normal looking shirt, freshly washed and ironed. They don't care that their bodies are mangled and blown to bits, as long as they can blow to bits and mangle other bodies, the enemies of their religion.

Recently there's been an increase of young women who have themselves blown up. The two hands of a loving mother tie around the waist of a daughter chosen by God the waistband loaded with TNT and, rigged in this way, with a veil that covers her hair and part of her forehead, the girl will go off secure and determined, optimistic and solemn, to kill so many innocent victims, sacrificing herself on the altar of religious fanaticism.

But how will these heroic women be rewarded once they enter the gardens of delights? What will happen to the seventy-seven virgins? Will they turn their backs on her? Or will seventy-seven seductive young men with slender hips, long arms and sweet dreamy eyes come out from deep within the thicket? Or will they perhaps discover, yet again and even in their death, that theirs is a destiny of silences and desires destined to rot in their hearts?

When she least expects it, the character Zaira leaves a photograph or a letter for her to find on her writing table. This time it is a black and white portrait of a couple. He is dressed in a groom's suit with an incongruous railroad cap pulled down on his head, a thick moustache, a closed umbrella pointing toward the pavement. She, arm-in-arm with her groom, has on a long dark dress, two dangling circle earrings of gold, an embroidered collar discretely and modestly opened on a short, wide neck. Her hair is pulled back. In her right hand she holds a rose that she has awkwardly raised to the height of her bosom. Behind them you can make out a dark curtain artfully draped. It's clear that they are posing in a photographer's studio and they are not used to being portrayed. He has a wide, stern face; she seems bewildered. She stares at the camera, her mouth slightly pouting. She's probably about sixteen year old. He seems a bit older, though not more than twenty-five.

"This is the shepherd from Abruzzo that gave rise to our family," explains the character Zaira with a mellow voice, "I have gathered papers, letters, photographs. At least Colomba's disappearance has served me well in this regard, that is, to get to know my family about whom I had taken little interest in before now. Where do the roots begin and when? And how do those little recurring characteristics that distinguish one family from another reveal themselves? Only after having lost 'Mbina did I take to rummaging through those long-forgotten house papers that were lying about in the basement. I didn't manage to go much beyond this photo. The rest is lost in a void."

A diligent character, thought the woman with the short hair, an industrious character who attentively looked behind her, without waiting for the writer to do it for her. Her voice rings of something soft and ingenuous, but at the same time precise and meticulous that kindles a curiosity in the writer. She keeps on saying: Zaira's tale and Colomba's disappearance do not interest me. But then her ear, almost instinctively, listens for that voice, for that story, even if her thoughts circle around in rebellion.

Clare of Assisi: In Praise of Disobedience

Preface and translation by Jane Tylus
New York University

Chiara di Assisi: Elogio della disobbedienza (*Clare of Assisi: In Praise of Disobedience*) is a fascinating blend of genres. Novel, diary, notebook, historical study, it takes up topics as varied as the long illness that kept Saint Clare of Assisi (1194-1253) in bed for 28 years, to the time the author spent as a young child in a Japanese prison camp, to speculations on changes being made by the new Pope Francis. But perhaps the best way to describe the book is a conversation. *Chiara di Assisi* opens as a dialogue in the form of an email exchange between a young Sicilian girl named Chiara who is proposing to a "cara scrittrice" that she write a book on her namesake, Clare of Assisi, and the "cara scrittrice" who is Dacia Maraini. The *scrittrice* finally gives in to the young girl's persistent requests to write about this strong-minded 13th century woman who fought to have autonomy within the church—and who, briefly, won. But at that point, the young interlocutor inexplicably disappears, and the rest of the book consists largely of Maraini's conversation with herself, and thus with us as readers. That a young Sicilian girl named Chiara really did write to Dacia Maraini and really did convince her to write a book on her namesake, says a great deal about Maraini's openness to interventions from without—the same kind of openness, one might hazard, that characterized the historical Clare.

Dialogue indeed represents one's openness to "voci"—not insignificantly the title of another book by Maraini and not insignificantly the very lifeblood of the theatre, for which she has written over thirty works. In *Elogio della disobbedienza,* Maraini is as responsive to the voice of the young Chiara Mandalà of Sicily as she is to the voice of Clare of Assisi, reachable not through email but through letters to Agnes of Bohemia and the rule she wrote for her Clarisse and the testimonies given by the women who lived with her when she was considered for canonization, a short two years after her death in 1253. Thus Maraini does not project an image of the writer as God, that overdone Renaissance trope of a Dante or Ariosto manipulating the threads of their texts from a dizzying height of mastery, but the writer as an altogether human and humane figure who listens to voices that come from the fringes of the community. Beaten down by Chiara's demands, the "cara scrittrice" Maraini finally agrees to write the book, saying she's submitted to an act of "scivolare": "of falling into a far-off epoch, the Middle Ages, but one closer than we might think."

The novelist as vulnerable, compassionate, and in a less ethical register, curious: about the world around her, its past and its possible futures, and especially its varied and always unsettling present. This is the posture that Dacia Maraini occupies in *Chiara di Assisi* as in other recent works, as she probes episodes of violence against women, the difficulties of growing up, and protests against unjust authorities, keenly listening for and to the voices of the unchosen ones. But such work is always in the framework of telling a story—the work that novelists and writers do. *Chiara di Assisi* continues to probe the very issues that have mattered most to Maraini throughout her career, as it breaks new ground with its experimental form and engaging conversations.

The following excerpts draw on the beginning and the very end of the book, as well as on several passages where the "cara scrittrice" is wrestling with some of the more complex aspects of Clare of Assisi's life: Her fasting, her commitment to poverty and to chastity, her fascination with her neighbor Francis, her stubbornness, her paralysis. As the dialogue with the contemporary Sicilian Chiara suggests, these are by no means issues, and interests, locked in the medieval past. They have distinctively modern resonances, and for that reason the story of this tenacious Umbrian woman has an at-times disturbing relevance for today. Finally, in this "praise of disobedience," it is only fitting that Dacia Maraini reveals herself to be disobedient too, as she departs from "received" ideas about a meek, patient, suffering young girl overcome by a charismatic Francis, and pieces together a story about a passionate and strong-willed woman who was intent on recovering Christianity's revolutionary fervor.

Clare of Assisi: In Praise of Disobedience

Dear writer,[11]

I'm a student from Sicily, from a tiny village on the slopes of Mt. Etna called Santo Pellegrino. It's at the end of a miserable but very beautiful island, an island you know well. I love it, but I always feel its defects gnawing at me, like hungry fleas.

My name is Chiara. This name will mean nothing to you, but for me

---

* Original title of the book: Dacia Maraini, *Chiara di Assisi: Elogio della disobbedienza* (Milan: Rizzoli, 2013).

it means a great deal, possibly everything. For a long time, I've been racking my brain over this luminous, crystalline name, a name that speaks with pensive radiance. The choice was a simple one, almost banal; my pious mother wanted to name me Chiara because I was born on Clare's feastday, August 11—the day of her death, since we don't know the day of her birth. In fact, we don't even know the exact year she was born, perhaps either in 1193 or 1194.

Banalities of coincidence. If I was born on the feast day of Santa Genoveffa, would my silly mother have named me Genoveffa? A stupidity of the calendar, let's say. The fact is that my father wanted to give me his mother's name, Giuseppina—a name that made my mother want to vomit. It actually makes me want to vomit too. So to pacify my mother they agreed on choosing the saint's feast day. Does this seem like something we should take seriously? So I am just the result of a compromise. Albeit with a nice result. Though I'm someone who has always felt compromises like the point of a knife digging into my flesh.

For years I've asked myself who I am, because I honestly don't know. So I started with my name, hoping that you might help me figure things out. A few months ago I took a train to Assisi. En route I read a little book about the Saint from the library in my village. I have no money, as you might have figured out by now. My father is a surveyor, and he built some horrible little illegal villas on a mountain where, when it rains, the side of the hill tends to slide down toward the valley. And for this he was sued. But he's not guilty. He built them only because of a certain gentleman—though to call him a gentleman is a joke. Let's just say that he's one of those types who wanted to save the money it would have taken to hire a real architect, someone who would have forced him not only to spend more money but to bring his project before the official body of the Comune for approval. Something he had never done. And at the end the fault was my poor, timid father's.

My mother is half illiterate: a girl from town who thought she'd made it big by marrying a modest if ugly little man. The son of ignorant farmers, with considerable effort he had learned to draw lines on a piece of paper, to count and to work with bricks and mortar. The gentleman, instead, who had enabled us to survive for years—until they condemned my father for illegal construction and fined him and sent him off to jail for four months—owned farmlands he converted into homes, with the complicity of a friend who was an assessor. He built lots of these illegal condos, but right before they put a stop to it, he sold them off at a high price and in the end bought an enormous mall. But he sold that too, and transferred all his money to Romania where he runs a big furniture factory. The responsibility for the illegal construction fell to my father. He's called Alfio, just so you know. He's a good father, in the sense that he's supportive and doesn't ask questions. He let me continue my studies, and he's not like other men in the village who beat their wives. He has blue, innocent eyes and is always sad. I love him.

The city of Assisi amazed me: maybe because I saw it first through the eyes of the book that I am reading, or through the imagined reconstructions of a historian of the middle ages. Steep winding streets, mules and horses that go up and down, palaces with heavy, buried doors, huts of wood and bricks, elegant and enormous churches. Hardly had these mules set off, their fast hooves clicking on the road paved with stone, than I seemed to enter into a film by Pasolini. The cobblestoned streets were no longer outside my reach, but right under my feet. The narrow, severe towers rose up right before my eyes. The ancient houses with their massive walls were so close that I could rest my hand on them and feel the sweating of the stones. When I heard a window opening up above my head, instinctively I stepped aside, knowing that in these houses, even the richest ones, there were no bathrooms and that urine was collected in chamber pots that the little hands of a busy servant woman would overturn in the middle of the street the following morning. (But wait! I ask myself, what about the cesspits, as I remember the tale of Boccaccio about Andreuccio da Perugia who fell into the sewer. Did the black holes of the sewers reach up into the bedrooms too? Were they inside people's houses? I'll have to figure that one out.) I even saw mules laden down with wood, edging up the hills just like they do in my village, climbing those impracticable streets. I saw the shops of 13th century Assisi, with jars in some windows and piles of cloth stacked up in others.

But I'll stop here because I don't want to bore you. I would be so happy if you wrote me back. You alone can help me understand; for now, I don't understand. Yours, Chiara Mandalà.

Dear Chiara,

What a bizarre letter. Seriously, what do you want from me? You tell your story with intelligence and verve, but where do you want it to lead? I know nothing about Saint Clare and I have no interest in finding anything out. Perhaps you could explain to me more clearly what you're looking for. Kind greetings, D. M.

Dear writer,

I was so happy when I got your answer I started dancing! I thought you'd just ignore me. I confess (and if we start getting to know each other you'll find out how my forthrightness always has me beating my head against the wall), I confess that before turning to you, I wrote to another writer with the same request. He never answered me. And then, from the depths of my memory came forth the images of a Palermo with its uneven streets on which the wheels of carriages made a continuous, blunted noise that accompanied the life of the citizens throughout the whole day and maybe during the whole night too. I remembered Marianna Ucrìa and I realized in a flash that I had approached the wrong writer. The right person is you. Please forgive me if I didn't write you first, but only after I failed to hear anything back from the other famous writer from my island!

What do I want from you? It's not easy to explain. However, I swear to you, I don't want to be introduced to an editor, or have someone write a preface for a book I might write, or be propelled into the world of literature. I have no literary ambitions. What I would like is for you to escort me on this journey into historical memory, in search of a woman who no longer exists. That's how I see myself: invisible, without a name, although I have a name and an address and even a family, unhappy as it is. I am passionate about the story of Clare of Assisi. Why that's so isn't clear. I'd like you to help me understand. I know that the more I learn about my namesake, the more extraordinary she'll become. To put it bluntly, I want you to write something about the Clare of 800 years ago to help me understand something about the Chiara of today. Am I asking too much?

Dear Chiara,

You are certainly a strange creature. You're dragging me into something that doesn't interest me in the least. Why don't you write the life of St. Clare? I'm sure you'd do a wonderful job.

Dear writer,

I read in an interview with you something that really struck me. You said that your characters come to seek you out. They knock on your door, they come in, they sit down, and they tell you their story. You offer them tea, sometimes biscotti with aniseed. You listen patiently to their stories and then you walk them to the door. That's it. Off they go, these characters with their tales, and you never see them again. But then you added something. "Every now and then after drinking my tea and eating my cookies, a character will ask to stay for dinner, and after dinner he asks me if he could spend the night, and the next morning he asks me what's for breakfast and then he takes up his story where he left off the night before. That's what I know that it's time to start a new novel."

I know I'm being presumptuous, but I really think that this time I'm the one who's knocking at your door and asking you to tell a story, trying to lure you into writing about Clare. Don't worry, I won't be content with just lemon tea and biscuits with aniseed. I want to stay for dinner, and to spend the night.

Dear Chiara,

It's true that I wrote those words, but you are not a character telling me your story. You're proposing to me the story of someone who is not you, who lived eight centuries ago, about whom you know very little, and I nothing. Why don't you approach a scholar? I do know that there's a vast literature on this saint from Assisi who was close to Francis, the holy protector of our country. I'm certain you'll find someone who will listen to you with attentiveness and generosity. Among other things, now I remember having read some years ago a beautiful book by Chiara Frugoni that discusses the saint from a lay, historical standpoint. Why don't you ask her? [...]

13 February[12]

For weeks I haven't received a letter from Chiara Mandalà. I find myself in murky waters, taken by the hand of a fictional character, as she says, but I have no idea what to do with her. I'd even tried to reach her by the email address she gave me, but nothing. As if I'd been in dialogue with a ghost. Strange, strange Chiara, why aren't you answering me? I've looked on the map of Sicily for Santo Pellegrino and it seems there is no such town on the slopes of Mt. Etna. Perhaps a girl named Chiara Mandalà doesn't even exist. But then with whom have I been corresponding over these last few months while books about Clare of Assisi are piling up on my desk? There was a brief interruption in her silence when she asked me for the list of books that I'd gathered and I was plunged into a system that allows for an exchange between computers, without going through email—something I had no idea you could do. And since then I've heard nothing more from her. I'll have to continue on alone, keeping a diary, and maybe that will help me. But I'm missing my interlocutor, my desperate Sicilian. I'll have to make necessity

into a virtue, and learn to converse with myself. [...]
>	2 July[13]

Some time ago I read with much pleasure and tenderness the theatrical work of a nun who lived around the year 1000, called "Abraham." The author is Roswitha of Gandersheim, who lived two centuries before Clare in a German convent and who wrote plays that were performed in the convent by the other nuns. There is such wit, such a delicate sense of maliciousness in these texts, that it's astonishing. How could an enclosed nun tell the story of a friar whose young pupil escapes from the convent and ends up as a prostitute in a whorehouse? The friar goes to find her. She thinks he's a client, and he plays along with the trick—up to a certain point. Then he tells her who he is and gives her a sweet and paternal sermon, reminding her that it was not she who chose that profession but her poverty and her solitude. At the end he brings her back to the convent and everyone winds up being happy. What kind of courage did it take to write about this encounter between a friar and a prostitute? And how much did it take to portray a girl forced into prostitution because of hunger when everyone singled her out as a woman possessed by the demons of luxury and libido?

One of Chiara Mandalà's letters mentioned "the happiness of the body." I ask myself what a "happy body" might mean to a woman. If happiness comes through mortifying and attacking one's own flesh, can we really speak of freedom of choice? From what we understand of her through her writings but also from the way that she lived, Clare of Assisi—with her stubborn faithfulness of a lifetime, forever tied to the choice she made as a girl—would never have reneged on the promise she made to her divine spouse and to herself. And yet the other nuns say of her that at a certain point she talked about wanting to go to Morocco, where several Franciscan friars had been martyred. They said that she dreamt of the voyage as a way of achieving martyrdom. But would it be irreverent to imagine that there was something else in that wish to go to Morocco?

We know that at the beginning of her vocation Clare imagined herself taking the word of God out to the people, like Francis. Which meant she would have traveled through towns, busying herself with the sick—not just the sick nuns of the convent whom she cured with such affection, but the lame, the blind, victims of plague who all moved around the peripheries of the world of the rich in the city of Assisi. There was nothing heretical or unwholesome in this profoundly sincere vocation of a nun. Do I hazard too much if I suggest that she might have even enjoyed jumping on a boat and traveling to the Holy Land to see with her very own eyes the grotto where Christ was born—as her mother Ortolana had done? To kneel down before the manger in which the Christ child had been warmed by the breath of a donkey and a cow? What would it have meant to her, to turn her gaze on horizons that were not those of the restricted, closed spaces of the little convent of San Damiano? Was this a lawful, human desire, or a diabolical temptation, as the Fathers of the Church would have us believe?

Can we rule out the possibility that Clare wanted to leave that prison that she chose and desired, but that perhaps over time became too familiar, impeded only because as legend has it she was paralyzed and deprived of bodily movement from when she turned 30 until her death at 59? Freedom is not just about the will, liberty is not simply refusing to obey the rules or making mischief. There's also the freedom of curiosity, of discovery, of knowledge, of exchange, of wandering. This is where doubt sets in. Isn't it possible that her sickness was a pitiless and overly harsh act of renunciation, suppressing a sentiment that is completely legitimate, but considered at the time dangerous and illicit, diabolical and presumptuous? Is it disrespectful to think that? Why were her legs immobilized? Why not her heart, her brain, her hands? As if she wanted to punish herself by way of the very limbs that had prodded her to disobey.

Disseminating and preaching the word of God. Was this only the wish to express thoughts already enclosed in prescribed formulations, or that marvelous and most human of desires—to meet new people, frequent unknown places, enter into dialogue with strangers and perhaps convert them to one's own faith using examples and reason? Doesn't the liberty of man consist in movement and dialectic as well? Exactly, I seem to hear the voice of Chiara Mandalà saying, the liberty of man, that man who even grammatically constitutes himself as the center of the universe. And not of woman, she who is always derived from him, an appendix, a creature perennially in danger, something to control, guide, take care of.

Clare spent the twenty-eight years of her illness spinning cotton and silk to decorate the altar coverings that she would send to churches in Assisi. Without ever tiring, without ever complaining about that terrible paralysis. Was it all obedience and resignation? Was it necessary penance so as not to succumb to temptation? And what if accentuating the punitive nature of a decision made with such force was the only way to control things? Wasn't there the risk of falling into arrogance? Was it only to keep her hands occupied and busy that she dedicated herself without rest to embroidery? And what if instead it was a way to become deaf to a body that had to be and remain mutilated? A body held at bay with rigorous maneuvers, deprived of nourishment, mistreated, humiliated. What could they have been whispering about, those body parts of a lively young girl who loved life, their normal voices rigorously silenced? What could that mortified and determined little body say in the mute language of desire, a body that she restrained with force, beat down by fasting and penance? What was it saying that she didn't want to hear? Why did she carry this mysterious illness around with her for 28 years?

What if instead those legs had demonstrated their autonomy, and those feet accustomed to taking a thousand times the steps that led from the kitchen to the chapel, the chapel to the cloister, the cloister to the cells, the cells to the chapel, what if they had calmly taken themselves toward that great door, closed and barred? And if those bare, calloused feet had suggested to her that she defy the cold and the rain and go out, looking in the face the world that she had chosen to serve? Is this an impertinent thought when speaking of a saint? It seems to me that her maltreated body said something that the saint didn't want to understand. And if these legs still robust and young were turned to stone so they couldn't talk? Because the cloister is an inalienable destiny, it was necessary to choose that destiny and make it one's own in the most ferocious and glorious of ways, transforming constraint into a virtue, imprisonment into sovereignty. Is that what Clare of Assisi wanted for herself? [...]

5 July[14]

The popes that succeeded one another during Clare's long stay in the convent all avoided confirming her rule. The first Rule ever written by a woman. One that while timidly declaring its resistance to hierarchy within the convent, asked to refuse all donations and all money, regardless of whether they came from the pope or a lay benefactor.

The popes' rationale made sense: if nuns were supposed to be enclosed, prohibited from leaving for any reason, prohibited from working and even from requesting alms, how would they have survived? Who would have furnished them with the food and necessities of life? Hence the need to give them income, and hence money and property. But property, as Saint Francis has taught, needs to be defended: with gates, keys, strongholds. And with guard dogs, barbed wire, sentinels. Property must be protected, and that's exactly what Clare didn't want. No property and no defense. A nun should own only the clothes on her body, and that's it. Not even food. She should support herself by working with her hands and asking in exchange just a bite of food. This was the freedom Francis proposed for his friars, and that Clare wanted for her nuns, the marvelous, terrible liberty of being naked in the world. [...]

12 July[15]

[...] Clare's rapport with the popes was curious and contradictory. She was obsequious, respectful, devout, but also disobedient, subversive, independent. "She could never be persuaded, neither by the pope nor by Bishop Hostiensi that she should own anything," Sister Philippa, as always, tells us in the records gathered for her canonization. But the pope was referring to the Fourth Lateran Council that mandated that new religious orders should adopt Rules that already existed, such as the Benedictine Rule that admitted the possession of goods such as dowries into the convent. But Clare didn't want to distance herself from the words of Jesus, who says, "Go, sell all you have and give it to the poor, then come and follow me!" From here originate the contradictions that endured as long as she lived.

How many popes tried to get her to change her mind! Innocent III, Honorious III, Gregory IX, Innocent IV. To say nothing of all the cardinals. But Clare "could not be persuaded," and she finished with a victory, at least a victory that lasted as long as she was still alive. It was Pope Innocent III himself, "a great pontiff open to the signs of the times, capable of understanding and blessing this novel Franciscan evangelism," as Chiara Giovanna Cremaschi has written, to grant the *Privilegium pauperitatis* [Right to poverty]. Though he didn't approve the Rule *Ordinis Sancti Damiani*.

Something new was happening in Italy around 1200: "Groups of women called to a life of contemplation and characterized by a strong emphasis on communal poverty sprang into being," explains Chiara Giovanna Cremaschi. "The phenomenon was particularly strong in north-central Italy." The proliferation of these women's groups nonetheless created problems for the Church. In 1218 Pope Honorious III entrusted Cardinal Ugolino di Segni, his representative in Italy, to launch an inquest in the hopes of channeling all those "scattered rivulets into a great river of female convents, thanks to the solicitous and timely concerns of the Cardinal, who would immediately seek to bring order to spontaneity and difference."

The choice of these women, as the cardinal would go on to inform the pope, was based on a few fundamental principles: a commitment to communal poverty and a refusal to "own anything under the sun"; the privilege of exemption, and thus "independence from bishops and the right to appeal directly to the Apostolic Seat, which agrees not to hold them responsible for paying duties, tolls, tithes, and any other taxes unsustainable because of their poverty. In compensation they would guarantee their loyalty to the Rule of Saint Benedict according to the orders of the Fourth Lateran Council, that obliged new forms of religious life to observe one of the rules already in existence."

Ugolino di Segni, who would become Pope Gregory IX, was a learned man and a good strategist. But he worried about the norms and was preoccupied by the growth of movements dedicated to poverty, particularly by the large number of women throughout Europe who were joining together to live, chaste and impoverished, beyond papal control. Nonetheless, he was very solicitous in his research. So much so that he felt the need to go personally to Assisi to understand exactly what was going on. And thus on Easter Sunday of 1220, he presents himself at the convent of San Damiano to meet Clare. Cardinal Ugolino "was fascinated by the personality and spiritual stature of the young woman who spoke with him with such simplicity," as Chiara Giovanna Cremaschi describes. Despite his visit, in the years following his visit, the cardinal did everything he could to "channel those monasteries created with the specific intent of living in radical poverty into the riverbed of what he would call his own order." Hence begins a mad struggle, full of injunctions and refusals that would endure for years...

Even today, in an Italy that has forgotten the prophetic words of Clare, the popes continue to practice the politics of a great power that both appeases and controls. But lately a pebble has started clogging up the gears. Pope Francis I, the new pontiff who's come from faraway Argentina to stick his nose into the Vatican Banks and into the powerful systems of the Holy See. And he does so with irony and impertinence, bringing in some fresh air in a way that makes one think of Francis and Clare of Assisi.

Pope Francis kneels to wash the feet of the young prisoners of Naples. I look at the photos that show him bent down, gentle and patient as he takes into his hand the inmate's clean heel, a boy stunned by this unusual gesture. I see a tattooed foot and the pope delicately raising it to immerse it in fresh water. I can't make out the tattoo. Is it a dragon? A moving train? A butterfly? The pope doesn't stop to consider the small design tattooed onto the inmate's skin. He's delicately immersed it in the shimmering waters of the basin, taking it into his hands. I can imagine the boy's timidity, his surprise, but also perhaps his feeling of empowerment. Might he have been also a little ashamed of that tiny drawing on his skin? Was it a siren or something like it? Can a pope hold in his hands a siren in the form of a tattoo? A siren with naked breasts and a tail in the form of a fish? But the pope, in his gesture of Franciscan humility, has pretended not to notice it. Bent over in such gentleness, he drew the bare foot from the water and dried it off with a clean towel.

Madonna Clare would certainly never have encountered a siren tattooed onto the foot of one of her sisters, not even one of her servants. These were girls from the countryside, with muscular arms, faces reddened by the sun, their feet big and tough, accustomed to going without shoes. The young abbess could certainly have seen a scar close up, whatever might be left of a finger almost completely sliced off by a poorly-handled scythe. But certainly not a siren. Though I'm sure that had she seen one, she wouldn't have been scandalized. She would have kissed that foot with the gentle graciousness of a soul welcoming of and responsive to the humble. So severe with the wealthy, so tolerant of those who had nothing. [...]

7 August[16]

[...] The miracles of Saint Clare are sometimes moving for their simple quotidian nature. Like that of the stray cat. In the testimonials given by the nuns who lived with her, I find this: "It was also said by this witness that once when Clare couldn't get out of bed because of her infirmity, she wanted a piece of linen to be brought to her, but there was no one to bring it. Suddenly one of the convent cats leapt up on onto the table and started yanking at the cloth, struggling to bring it to her as best as it could." So even the cats loved her, and when they could, they helped her. Would there have been other cats in San Damiano? What would such an intelligent creature have been named? And did it have license to jump up into the sick woman's lap to purr?

We don't know about other animals, but we do know about this cat. In the convent of San Damiano there once roamed a cat, nameless but incredibly smart, who understood Clare's words so well that he grasped her request for a table linen and dragged it to her bed with his teeth. Was it a miracle, or only the intuition of an affectionate animal? It's not important. It's nice to know that despite her constant pain and enforced immobility, Clare had an affectionate relationship with a cat. Were there other cats in the convent? Did they have names? Were there dogs, goats, geese, chickens? It's likely that since they refused all property, even possessing a domestic animal would be considered a sin. Francis thought that way. Especially hens, I imagine, or goats that gave milk. Cats were admissible, on the other hand, because they had no use, other than catching mice. Is this why cats frequented San Damiano? Were there mice in the convent? I would think so. Little country mice that got into everything, leaving their droppings in pans, among the laundry, as still happens today. They're the most difficult to chase, because they get out through a crack under the door. They nest in a ball of cotton, forgotten under a stair. It's happened to me, such as when I found one in the refrigerator in my country house. It came in through an aeration vent, grabbed some food in a hurry before it could freeze, and went right back into the tube. Another time as I was putting on a jacket that hung in the entryway, from both pockets—left and right sides—two mice leapt out, scared out of their wits. How could I permit myself to come and disturb their refuge after a month of absence?

Who knows if Clare was afraid of mice, as is the case with so many women? A fear that probably goes back for centuries, since it was mice that were carriers of plague. But thinking about it, I'm convinced that Clare wasn't afraid of these tiny creatures of God that scurried throughout the convent. Perhaps the alley cat captured them. But Clare certainly wouldn't have killed them herself. Generous and attentive as she was toward all creatures and their needs, she would have had respect even for mice, who can't be blamed for being mice and for being hungry. Just like fleas or mosquitoes or lice or ticks—they're not to be blamed. But we do know that Clare valued cleanliness, and that when one nun had lice it's likely that she rubbed into her hair a paste made of tar and oil that they used to get rid of parasites. Up to what point is it mandated that we must co-exist with God's smallest creatures? I would have liked to ask this to Saint Francis. Isn't an ant also one of God's creatures? But if an army of ants invades the kitchen in search of food and assaults a plate with a piece of bread soaked in a bit of oil and that's the only meal of the day, what is one to do?

The relationship between Christians and animals has always been a mystery to me. Sometimes it appears to be a thing of great tenderness, sometimes absolutely nonexistent. It's true that Francis loved animals. One grasps this from his beautiful "Laude," even if he doesn't mention beasts specifically. The love that he directs to the sun, to the moon and the stars, doesn't exclude forests, trees, animals, creatures of the Lord, like everything else. There's the episode of the wolf of Gubbio, certainly, which many historians have wanted to interpret figuratively, as an encounter with the enemy. In fact, though, wolves never travel alone. They're animals who go about in packs, and who only attack when they know they're stronger and more numerous, surrounding and driving their prey into a corner. But there's political significance too, in the most elevated sense of the word, in the story of the wolf of Gubbio. In fact, legend has it that Francis spoke to the wolf and proposed to him a treaty. He didn't change his nature or transform him into a lamb with a magic word, which he could have done as a saint. Francis always held fast to reality, and sought to act in order to bring peace, not war; justice, and not handouts.

Francis spoke with this fierce wolf and convinced him that he should no longer attack sheep and men. In exchange he guaranteed him that every day the inhabitants of Gubbio would provide him with food. It was a pact, almost a contract. The extraordinary thing is that Francis thought that one might be able to arrange a contract with an animal, considering him worthy of respect. Such was the originality and novelty of his attitude. I like to think of it not as a sentiment of benevolence bestowed by a master on his servant, or as alms given by a rich person to a poor one, but as a treaty between equals.

Thus the revolutionary nature of the exchange with the wolf. Above all, Francis believed in the equality of all living beings. He put his faith in dialogue, in example, in bargaining, in tolerance, in sum, in true politics, the kind that seeks out a way to enable people of diverse thinking, diverse backgrounds, diverse ideas, diverse political sensibilities, even diverse species, to live together through trust, reason, and mutual understanding. For those who believe only in the law of force and the destruction of one's enemy, this kind of discourse can only irritate, like smoke in one's eyes. Francis and Clare were, in fact, considered by a great many people to be an irritant, like smoke.

"As the blessed Francis went towards Bevagna," Bonaventura of Bagnoregio recounts in his *Legenda Maior*, "he preached to many birds; and those exultant beings extended their necks, spread their wings, opened their beaks, touched his tunic; and his companions who waited for him on the road saw all these things." Giotto has given us a painting of the saint when he was already aging, turning towards these winged creatures the same gentle disposition with which he spoke to human beings.

I want to imagine that Clare had this same kind of affectionate and indulgent relationship with the cat. At times, however, cats bring embarrassing gifts, carrying to a beloved human their tortured prey. How would our infirm Clare, her hands eternally busied with embroidery, have reacted to the cruel gift of a mouse mauled by the cat and left at her feet? I think Clare would have chided the cat for his ferocity, but with a sweet voice, and then she would have given it a caress because she well knew that this was the nature of felines, and that the bloodied prey was a gift given to her with love. [...]

Dear writer,[17]

I don't know how to express my gratitude. I know that you've done an enormous amount of work. I hope you're not sick and that your ribs are intact despite the pain. I feel a little guilty for having dragged you into this, but I hope it was worth the effort. I fell in love with Clare, so much so that I followed her into the convent. And I thank you for that. Only now do I think I understand what it means to have a body that's happy. I won't constrain my breasts with a cord made out of horse hair, and I won't tie around my waist a girdle lined with pigskin. But I believe that I'll sing in church, where finally my voice can take on wings. I'll sleep in a modest little bed, not on the ground and not on a sack filled with straw or vine shoots. I won't be using a rock from the river for a pillow. I won't have to chase the fleas out from under the covers—I'll have sheets, and I won't consider them a diabolical temptation. Nor will I think of the devil as a little spider with sticky paws, as St. Catherine once wrote. Something of the interior force of Clare and her sisters will continue to flow through these rooms that have not forgotten the tenacity and joyous warmth of those nuns. Perhaps we've learned that the body can exercise chastity without subjecting itself to torture. We can be chaste out of the sheer joy of love.

---

11. Ibid., 9–16.
12. After another 15 or so exchanges, in which the "cara scrittrice" is increasingly drawn to this story, Chiara suddenly stops writing. The next section of the book, pp. 61–62, consists not of letters but of diary entries, beginning with this one.
13. Maraini, *Chiara di Assisi*, 126–131.
14. Ibid., 131–132.
15. Ibid., 136–141.
16. Ibid., 185–189.
17. Chiara Mandalà eventually resurfaces and the book closes with her final letter to the "cara scrittrice" (Maraini, *Chiara di Assisi*, 249–250).

III

Short Stories

A woman and a man in a train station in Japan (1967). Photo by Dacia Maraini.

A Christmas in the Snow Globe

Preface and translation by Michelangelo La Luna
University of Rhode Island

In this short story Dacia Maraini recalls, through the magical effects of a snow globe, the end of WWII in Japan. Maraini's family, who spent two years in the concentration camp of Nagoya, is invited to celebrate Christmas Eve 1946 in a hotel in Tokyo. Dacia and her two sisters could not participate in the party organized by the US Government at the Imperial Hotel, because "'They are too little'...as if they had not also been in a concentration camp, together with the adults, for two years." It is a privilege to unveil this unpublished typescript since it is the first time that we can read a story on what Dacia and her family did right after the end of the war in Japan and before returning to Italy. Therefore, we can consider this short story a precious tile of the mosaic of Dacia's childhood in Japan, as it is recounted in books such as *The Ship for Kobe* and *Bagheria*, where the author speaks about the journey to Japan, her incarceration in the concentration camp and the return to Bagheria, Sicily. I would like to finish by mentioning the following book on Maraini's period in Nagoya, Japan, recently printed: Noriko Mochizuki, *Dacia and the Japanese Concentration Camp* (Tokyo: Kabushiki Kaisha Miraisha, 2015).

A Christmas in the Snow Globe[*]

I have in my hand a snow globe, one of those in which—around a house, a city, and a tree—thousands of confetti are set in motion with just one hand movement.

In the middle of the snow globe there is a miniature city, with its pagodas, its tiny houses with wood roofs, its glass palaces. TOKYO is written on the wooden base. It reminds me of a film by Orson Welles, in which the avalanche of memories begins from the observation of a small, insignificant, and perhaps even tacky, object.

I shake the transparent, little half-dome and I see a cloud of silver grains rising. The glass fills with unexpected lights. The city starts to turn on itself. Tokyo: a Christmas of fifty years ago...The city amplifies under my eyes; it becomes dark with warlike powders. The bombs have reduced it to rubble and a little girl who looks a lot like me is playing among those piles

---

[*] Original title of the short story: Dacia Maraini, "Natale '46" (unpublished typescript).

of rubble. It is curious to find out that the destroyed city, which today has been rebuilt and is completely transformed, it now stays alive and theatrical inside the snow globe.

The mind's eye enlarges an image: a long corridor with red carpets, thick and soft, on which the shoes of a little girl move soundlessly. This is not a house but a hotel. I understand it from the smells rising from those carpets: of unknown shoes, of rose-scented moth killer, of seaweed powder. Here is the Imperial Hotel, the largest hotel in Tokyo from those times. It miraculously survived the bombs and fires, then was seized by the Liberation Army soldiers. The officers lived there: handsome young men with blonde, short-cut hair, ivory colored pants and shirts with little stars on the shoulders, who were running up and down the stairs of the hotel with a bold attitude.

The jeeps that roamed through the cities, dodging rubble and beggars were stopping in front of the main entrance. All around, the blankets of snow were unable to hide the desolation of a city conquered and reduced to ashes.

The little girl is playing hide and seek with her sisters among the rubble: a cracked house with walls still intact, the "tatami" (rectangle shaped raffia floors), jumped into the air like dirty wooden pallets. The youngest sister, who has long blonde hair down to her shoulders, is looking for her. The oldest sister runs to hide behind a corner of a building that has miraculously remained standing. But she does not notice a piece of iron protruding from the broken stairs of the ghost house. The little girl bumps into it and falls, injuring a knee on some broken fragments of glass.

The snow becomes tinged with blood. The sister quickly arrives. "What do we do now? Can't we play hide and seek anymore?" "But no, let's continue." The cold alleviates the pain. But the knee starts to swell and the blood is dirtying the shoes. They are forced to go back to the hotel.

Soon after, a doctor with almost invisible eyes behind thick glasses, leans on the little girl's knee and starts stitching the wound with a needle and thread, as the young mother would have done at home for a tear in her dress.

The pain is unbearable. Such a pain does not fit into a snow globe and it erupts furiously. She finds peace only when a gentle nun with an opaque voice says to the little girl: "Think of the wounds of Christ." But perhaps this happened many years later, in a boarding school in Florence, where the energetic nuns were moving between the kitchen and the study rooms, clinking the rosaries made by huge glass beads.

"Tomorrow He resurrects," continues the nun with the dull voice, "Christ died for the wickedness of men, but he will be reborn because he is the son of God. From those wounds on the feet and hands many flowers will spring."

For years I waited to see the flowers jump out from the wounds. But I just saw blood and pus. It was Christmas Eve, which is why my memories are confused. That night in Tokyo something extraordinary was celebrated: the first postwar Christmas Eve…In the high-ceilinged dining room of the Imperial Hotel, a dinner was prepared with the precious things that the Americans had brought from their country: powder peas, canned crabs, mountains of vanilla ice cream, and sweet hardtacks.

The ignominious fact was that the little girls that night were not invited to that wonderful Christmas Eve dinner in the great hall of the Imperial Hotel. "They are too little," was the tautological explanation of the adults, as if they had not also been in a concentration camp, together with the adults, for two years; as if they had not been starving too, with the others; as if they had not spent days talking about food, together with the adults.

With tears in their throats the three sisters climb the endless stairs of the Imperial Hotel, they bury themselves under the sheets and wait for the adults to turn off the light, so that they can unleash the great pillow fights.

Now, on the ledge of the hotel room, in the twilight of the iridescent glass dome, appears a female figure. It is the young mother of the three little girls. She is wearing a beautiful, all black dress, with hundreds of sequins shimmering like many stars. But perhaps this is not so. Perhaps there are the usual phosphorescent nuggets, which are glued onto an uncertain memory.

The young mother enters the little girl's room in that hotel, after the war, almost dancing on high heels. How will she stand poised on those heels? Her arms are bare, very white and shining. On her lips she wears new lipstick, a coral color that makes her look like Rita Hayworth. Her eyes sparkle radiantly. But was that true or was it the same unhealthy effect of the silver specks that flicker through the air after a happy hand shook the snow globe?[18]

Yet it is possible that the eyes of the young mother glitter because it was Christmas, because the war was over, because she could move freely without running into barbed wire, because she was no longer wearing the rags of the camp full of bugs, but was in a magnificent hotel at the center of a big city, destroyed but still regal, with its stone gardens, its temples of painted wood, its wide streets, its theaters, its restaurants that slowly resumed living.

Certainly the young mother had sparkling eyes in the beauty of her thirties, and also because she was in love with her husband, and with him she thought about pursuing a future made of dreams and conquests. Dreams that later vanished into nothing. But certainly back then she counted on it and her clear face was smiling with confidence.

These were the last days of the year 1946, and as soon as a ship was available, the whole family would have returned to Italy. For the time, we were stuck in Tokyo and my mother worked as an art expert for the Liberation Committee of the Allies.

Perhaps the black sequined dress belongs to the family's life from another time, to another snow globe that lies motionless among the most dusted memories. Who knows? Probably it is another Christmas, in Sicily, or in Florence, another Christmas after the war. Perhaps the beautiful starry eyed mother that Christmas Eve was simply wearing a G.I. military shirt donated by the Americans and a pair of men's pants cinched at the waist by a wide belt.

"Tomorrow is Christmas, mom," I believe cried the little girl with hair so light that it appeared white, while the young mother pulled the covers up to her neck. "Stay with me, please," begged her daughter. The scent of lavender Yardley caressed the little girl's nostrils. She wanted to hug her mother and did not want to let her go down to dinner with the soldiers. But the officers were waiting for her in the dining room, which had been decorated for the party. And she could not miss it, together with her handsome husband. The little girl already imagined how the young mother would have descended the stairs, pulling up her skirt with two fingers to uncover and free the two little shoes encrusted with rhinestones.

But here he is, the seductive young father, who was also on the doorstep of the little girls' bedroom. He's wearing a white shirt and a new khaki jacket that is too large in the waist. He approaches the bed where the eldest daughter lays next to his wife. He pulls the woman's head with an affectionate gesture, and bends over to kiss her on the temple.

They would never kiss that way again, with so much tenderness and abandonment. Never again would the little girl have seen them in the future embrace with such grace and happiness. From that Christmas night everything started to fall apart and deteriorate. What could have happened? How could those two lovers have been able to lose each other and separate without regret? It is impossible to know. This was part of the secrets of the adults.

While the snow blends festively in the snow globe, the two young parents opened the window of the hotel room, they pushed the red velvet curtain a little to the side, did a little jump and disappeared into the night, flying intertwined. The last thing I saw in the dark were her starry little shoes gleaming like those of Cinderella.

The next morning there was a surprise at the bottom of the bed: a big red woolen stocking full of precious gifts: mandarins, condensed milk, almond biscuits, wool socks.

At one o'clock a jeep came to take them in front of the Imperial Hotel. The Christmas party for the children took place somewhere else. But where? Maybe at the Navy "Headquarters." It is hard to say. The snow globe does not explain it.

The table was set for about twenty children. Next to each place was posed a strange cylinder of crepe paper tied with a red bow. The little girl was wearing a green dress with some bees drawn on the front, and seemed to sense the buzz of those small creatures under her chin. In a plate, steaming soup of powdered peas reminded her that it was party time, that they were guests of a great victorious army that had already established a new and disciplined relationship with food. Perhaps even her dress was made of powdered peas, had thought the little girl, comparing the grass and lake water colors that connected the pea soup to her dress.

Raising her head the little girl saw a bloated turkey coming, lying on a huge metal plate, headless and legless. But is it not the same bird that now knocks against the frosted glass with its beak and asks to come in and party with them? I will not eat that beast even to please my mother, had thought the little girl. And what if the guards[19] get angry and close me in a dark closet for a whole day? But there are no more guards, we are no longer in the camp, stupid! We are in American barracks, along with many other blonde and well-fed little children. No one will take away the food from your mouth.

Out of the corner of her eye she saw her father and her mother standing, holding hands. A gesture that reassured her. Everything scared her then. That little, absolute certainty meant more to her than anything of what she thought she could have available: the indissoluble, interlacement of the family. She looked at them: that father and that mother so thin and so pale. They were beautiful, they were exposed, and they needed all her loving protection. She would have never left them alone, she said to herself, never.

Yet later, she was distracted and something had happened that the two started to consider themselves strangers, almost enemies. But what had happened? The little girl never knew.

A soldier now leans on her to show how one can blow up the paper cylinder that splits in two, by pulling out a metal tab. He had asked for another and yet another. These were not the same bombs one protected himself from running in a cave dug underground, but a playful, triumphant explosion.

Soon after some red and white striped sugar sticks arrived and a pile, a real pile of chocolate bars. "Eat, it's Christmas!" And she had bitten her lips because her instinct instead was to hide the food, the way dogs do when they get a little piece of bread. She wanted to bury the good things[20] so that she could go and find them in times of famine. She had learned this in the concentration camp.

Meanwhile, accompanied by cheerful music, all the children had begun to sing in the choir before the tree that towered in the middle of the hall. It was a giant pine, smelling of resin. The branches, covered with white cotton, were shining upon the red bows and silver glass balls. At the top of the tree, on the tip of bristling needles, was hanging a foil star that turned on itself like a weather vane on a roof. But there was no wind, so how could the star turn? The little girl had understood that every wonder happened through the influence of some hidden skills of those soldiers who chewed gum and rolled their shirt sleeves up their arms, as if it was summer. Everything was possible to someone that had won a major world war.

But here, now, the snow globe sits on my table and seems to say, in the mute language of objects: enough, I am tired. As much as I shake it, I cannot recreate the magic of the memory. Nothing, not even the swirling snow, will revive the old city of Tokyo in that sad and happy postwar 1946.

---

18. Here the original Italian says, "la cupola di vetro," which was translated into "the snow globe."
19. The original Italian has "guardiani," which refers to soldiers in the concentration camp.
20. The original Italian "Ben di Dio," was translated into "good things;" the expression means "great prosperity."

Little Aylan

Preface and translation by Michelangelo La Luna
University of Rhode Island

"Little Aylan" is the dramatic story of a family who escaped from the Syrian war in search of a better life and freedom. The picture of the three year-old Aylan Kurdi, who drowned on September 2, 2015 on a Turkish beach, touched the world. According to Maraini's short story, however, this was not enough to push governments and people to do more for the refugees.

For Maraini the drama of emigration afflicting today's world is worsened by the indifference and greed of Western society. In fact, the figure of the engineer Polipi—who doesn't feel any emotion in looking at the picture of little Aylan, and thinks that he and his family should have stayed at home—represents the personification of a society "where the job is becoming more precious than life itself." I would like to thank Dacia for giving us the opportunity to translate this unpublished typescript, and to unveil its strong message.

***

Little Aylan[*]

"Look at this photograph," my partner said. I was warming milk for breakfast in my robe and slippers. I was about to tell him not to bother me as the milk was close to boiling. It was going to spill over onto the stove if I didn't pay attention. But from the tone of his voice I realized that I had to look. I looked at the newspaper picture with half-asleep eyes, but I didn't understand. What was strange about a young boy sleeping on an empty beach? "The waves threw him on the sand," Giordano said with a tone of cold anger, and then I realized that I was looking at a dead little body.

"What's his name?" I asked, to try to give him some importance. Giordano got up and slammed the chair. He walked away as though it were my fault that the child was dead.

I picked up the newspaper, and I read that this young boy lying on the beach like a piece of driftwood, was called Aylan Kurdi, from the town

---

[*] Original title of the short story: Dacia Maraini, "Il bambino Aylan" (unpublished typescript, 2016).

of Kobanî, in Syria. He was headed, with his parents, to Canada, to an aunt called Tima Shenu Kurdi, fleeing a war that had destroyed their home and their city. The Canadian Government rejected their application to join the aunt in Vancouver. So they paid a private agency $5,860, to take them to the Greek island of Kos, from where they would be taken on a larger boat to reach Vancouver.

And so, on a designated day, they filled a sack with blankets and with the little money they still had, they set sail at night, from the Turkish beach at Bodrum. They crowded onto a raft with twelve more people, an inflatable raft that at maximum could hold eight.

The phone starts ringing. Someone from the office wants to know why I'm not at my desk. I realize I am late. I reply that I'm coming. I dress quickly, put the newspaper in my purse and rush toward the office, forcing the old scooter.

The office manager goes on a tirade in front of all my colleagues, "You're a goat, a silly little goat!" He shouts. I don't understand the excessive resentment. Just for being a few minutes late? Okay, he's probably in a bad mood. It's been happening more and more often—for reasons outside the office. He gets angry and starts screaming and insulting us. I showed him the photograph of little Aylan. I do not want to justify my delay, but I would like to get my colleagues and office manager to talk about that death, which seems to me a symbol of the horrors that we are going through. Engineer Polipi casts an angry glance at the photo and makes a bitter comment, "This is what happens to people who leave their home and presume to camp in other people's houses."

I know I should not respond, but I can't resist it. I yell at him that in front of the dead body of an innocent child, he should have more respect. He replies coldly, without emotion, "Consider yourself fired! Not for the delay, but for arrogance." My colleagues were very careful not to defend me.

When I get back home, Giordano is not there. That's strange, because usually he comes home before me. I put some water on the fire to make an herbal tea. I'm cold and I feel a fever, though probably it is just due to anger and to a sense of desolation for which I don't have a name.

At about eight o'clock, I start to worry. I dial the number of the restaurant where Giordano works, but they tell me that they haven't seen him. I call his mother, but she replies evasively that she doesn't know anything. What to do?

I wander around the house, hesitant and worried...should I go out looking for him...go to the police...call his friends...then I see something white on the pillow of the queen-size bed. It is a sheet of paper folded in four. I take it and open it.

My beloved Giordano, with whom I have shared the apartment for two years, decided to leave for Scotland, where he found a job "worthy of my degree." Direct, laconic, brutal. But why not tell me anything? Why do not warn me? Not even a word of explanation, is it possible?

I sit in the kitchen and pick up the newspaper. I start to read more about the young boy, Aylan. The inflatable raft departed at night, while the sea grew rough. Before leaving the coast, a young man handed out life jackets, said one of the survivors. Many in that raft did not know how to swim. But they faced the sea and the danger of death, in order to save themselves from another death, that of their country in ruins, of the killing bombs, of Assad's soldiers torturing, shooting, hanging.

At five in the morning the Turkish police were notified that there were deaths at sea, at the mercy of the waves along the south coast. A young Turkish woman, journalist and photographer, Nilufer Demir, rushed to the scene and found the baby face down on the beach lapped by the waves. He was wearing a red shirt and a pair of blue shorts. The young woman photographed the child, then the cops who came to get him. She immortalized that soft, light little body, abandoned as a wreck on the empty beach, she fixed it forever in the geography of our mind as he was picked up by a tall young man, dressed in black, wearing a red vest with white hem. In those muscular arms the baby seems even smaller, almost like a newborn just entered in the world.

The photographs by Demir have gone around the world. In Canada, many accused the Minister for Immigration for having refused a visa to the Kurdi family and causing the death of the child. The minister replied that the asylum application was incomplete, that only the name of the father was given, while family members were not listed. Someone defined it as a "bureaucratic monstrosity."

The whole world is moved by that picture. In the arms of the Turkish policeman Aylan seems simply asleep. On his tiny body there are no wounds, bruises, traces of blood. And indeed his loneliness, his sweet grace, his abandonment to death, that is breathtaking. More eloquent than any atrocious story, that lonely little body—miraculously intact—tells terrible things about the growing phenomenon of migration.

Giordano also emigrated, running away from a humiliating job and a partner he doesn't love anymore? With less despair, with less risk, of course. But is it an escape or what? Fleeing from his own country, from his own home, from his own city, from his own woman?

I know that pain will attack me later. For now, I continue to read about little Aylan, and I feel in control. The tears stopped on the brink; the edge of the eyelids completely dry. If Giordano would tell me, "Come on, leave that shit-work job you have and join me here in Scotland," would I do it? But he didn't ask me and probably won't. It's clear from his silent escape, his disappearance. He has fled like a thief, which probably means that in addition to the work, he also found another companion.

But my thoughts go back to little Aylan, to his death at sea. To his parents. But right, what happened to his parents who were also on the raft? I read on the Internet that one of the survivors accused the father of the child of driving the inflatable raft. Abdullah Kurdi, reached by a journalist, admits that it's true, but he tells his version of the story: as soon as the raft was filled and after taking money from everyone, the organizers ran away. Before leaving, however, they entrusted the helm to the oldest man of the group, the mature Abdullah Kurdi, father of Aylan. He, who had never piloted a boat in his life, refused, but they threatened to jettison the children if he did not. And he was forced to accept.

So they got off on the overloaded, inflatable raft. They traveled for barely a few hours, then, just before dawn, the inflatable raft started to sag. And in the craft a brawl started. Everyone clung to what was left of the raft, trying to push the others into the water. The first victims were the children. The father of Aylan abandoned the by then useless helm and held his son, but someone gave him a blow that knocked both of them into the sea.

"We have life jackets, we can survive. They are already searching us with a ship!" Abdullah had cried, trying to stop the fight while trying to recover his son who fell into the sea with him. But the darkness made it impossible to see. Some bodies shone in the night under the moonlight, but there was no sign of little Aylan.

Meanwhile, Abdullah had managed to find his wife, who was swimming swallowing water and crying voicelessly. He told her to lean on him—he knew how to stay afloat. Meanwhile, the sea had calmed and the sun was about to rise from the bluish horizon.

"My life jacket is soaking up water" shouted a young man who was struggling in the waves. Abdullah put a hand on his life jacket and realized that it was completely deflated and filling up with water. He quickly took it off, just as his wife sank under water with a gurgling sound. He tried to grab her, but without success. The life jackets, which had been bought at great cost, were fake.

Eventually, three were saved—among them the father of Aylan. To him, the Turkish President Erdogan, with great fanfare, gave a certificate of Turkish citizenship. This is the story.

I will leave, I tell myself, I'll go away, too. I don't know where, but I have to escape from this country, where the job is becoming more precious than life itself.

Viollca the Albanian Girl

Translation by Elisabetta Mariotti
AIIC—International Association of Conference Interpreters*

Viollca is standing behind the windowpane, holding her teddy bear in her arms. It's raining outside. Cars drive by slowly, splashing water and mud along the way. Her mother is in the other room, packing her suitcase for her. Her father is sitting in the kitchen holding the daily paper without reading it. Every now and then, he mechanically stirs his coffee with a spoon, even though, by now, it has become cold.

A horn is honking repeatedly.

"It's him. Xhuvan. Grab your raincoat. Quick."

The mother hands her daughter the suitcase. The father walks to the door to say goodbye: "Take care, Viollca, vogelushja ime, my sweet little girl."

"Let Xhuvan take care of things. He knows what to do. And write us as soon as you have a chance."

"Here, take some money for the trip." The father puts a few dollars in his daughter's hand. Then he walks away, blowing his nose.

Her mother hugs her on the doorstep and she then reaches out to grab Viollca's teddy bear before she walks away, but the girl holds on to it for dear life. No one, for any reason in the world, can ever separate her from her beloved Malek. She has never slept a single night without him for as long as she can remember.

Xhuvan is kind. He opens the door for her like a gentleman. He gestures her to get into the car while he places her suitcase inside the trunk.

"An hour ride and we'll be on the ship in no time..." He is cheerful. He tries to snatch the bear away from her, but Viollca spasmodically clutches it against her chest.

"You are a good girl. No crying at all. I like that. A brave young lady, on her way to conquer Italy, aren't you?"

On the boat, Xhuvan lets her out of the car and wraps an arm around her shoulders. *"Do të hash bukë?* Are you hungry, Viollca? would you like a ham sandwich?"

Viollca shakes her head no. She is tweaking her bear's right ear with her two fingers.

---

* Original title of the short story: Dacia Maraini, "Viollca la bambina Albanese," in *Buio*, BUR Scrittori Contemporanei 8 (Milan: Rizzoli, 2012), 23-39.

"This teddy bear is filthy. Shall we throw it into the sea?"

Viollca starts shaking. Tears pressing hard against her eyelids.

"That's okay. If you don't want to, forget it. I was just thinking of buying you a new one, you know? Do you want a soda?"

Viollca keeps tweaking the little creature's ear without answering. Her legs are cold because they are naked. The pumps her Mom bought for her make her lose her balance.

As soon as they get back inside the car, she takes her shoes off and stuffs them underneath the seat.

"What are you doing? taking your shoes off? you are not a wild little girl playing in the streets anymore. *Je një zonjushë*, you are a classy young lady now, in your short skirt and high heels."

Viollca smiles thinking about the look on her sister Anjeza's face when she saw her in those high heels. She started yelling that she wanted to go to Italy with Xhuvan too. But Anjeza is only eight years old and she hasn't had her period yet. Teuta, her youngest sister, started crying for her. Her brothers, instead, didn't look too happy. The eldest, who works as a crane operator at Durres harbor, was cussing and swearing. The other brother, Anton, shouted that they were all crazy, all crazy.

"Go make some money and then come back. You'll need it to get married. And then, the roof needs to be redone. Go, Viollca and *Zoti të shpëtoftë*, may God keep you safe."

"If someone asks your age, you must say you are seventeen, *kuptove*?"

Viollca is nodding while she is looking at her skinny legs and knobby knees. It's kind of hard for anyone to believe you are seventeen years old when you haven't even turned twelve yet.

"You look older, listen to good old Xhuvan. Ok, so, remember: seventeen years old. Here are your new papers. Your name is still Viollca but your last name has changed. It is now Mrozek; don't forget!"

The girl gives him a thumbs-up. She saw someone do that in an American movie and it stuck in her mind.

At Brindisi harbor there is another big, dark car waiting for them. Two Albanians and an Italian shake Xhuvan's hand. He hands the girl over to them and leaves.

No one asks her any questions. They don't even greet her. They get her in the big dark car which takes off, with screeching tires, heading towards Rome.

She feels like peeing but, from the expression on the three men's faces, it's easy to realize it might be better not to ask them to stop anywhere. They are fighting over money, using a weird mixture of Italian and English.

The apartment where they take her is huge. There are two bedrooms, one just for her and the other one for another Albanian girl named Cate.

"This is where you sleep and this is where you eat. No phone calls, no going outside, no windows, no talking to strangers. Just wait for us to come and get you. *Gjith mire*, alright, *kuptove*?" And immediately, as if to show them what would happen if they disobeyed, she gets slapped in the face so hard that it makes her head turn.

Viollca holds her breath. For no reason must she cry. She dropped her teddy bear. Through the corner of her eye, she is checking whether Cate is being slapped too. Instead, she sees that the eldest guy, the one with the muffin-top belly, is pushing her against the wall, lifts her skirt and starts yelling.

"What's this? tattered underwear, broken elastic band! slut! you can't be wearing stuff like this! what are you, some kind of animal? Put on something decent and clean. This is gross: I don't want to see this ever again!" She got slapped too, after the man was done yelling at her.

Now the two men are gone. The house is silent. The sound of an accordion is rising from the street. Viollca looks out the window to see who is playing. But one hand pulls her back immediately. It's Cate, who has grabbed her t-shirt: "no window!"

Viollca wanders around the apartment admiring the brand new floors, the tiles with their eggshell colored edges, the ample white curtains, the dark and massive furniture, the roomy kitchen with light green cabinets. Back home, in Shijak, she used to sleep in the kitchen on a mattress thrown on the floor at night. There was only one tiny bedroom for her parents and youngest sister. The other sister would sleep in the living room with their grandmother, while she shared the kitchen with her two brothers. To use the bathroom, they had to go out on the landing. The same sink and toilet were used by four families. It was called the "goose fight place." Screams could always be heard from the landing, behind the door that had been locked shut from the inside. Everyone accused the others of leaving the bathroom dirty, or staying in there for too long, aggravating those who were waiting outside. Children had learnt to hold it in, like everybody else, waiting for their turn to use the toilet.

Instead, here there is a large bathroom, all clad in pink tiles, just for Cate and herself. Viollca has fun opening all the taps. Not only cold water gushes out in abundance, but hot water too.

Then she skips towards the kitchen. She opens the refrigerator door and it's filled with food: milk, eggs, cheese, peaches, grapes, cookies.

"You can eat all you want. If you need anything, just ring this bell, *kuptove*, understand? a lady will show up from the apartment below. You will never stick your nose out of this door for any reason. If you need anything, just ring the bell." When he was saying this, the youngest guy, the one wearing the orange leather jacket, hit her leaving a lump behind her ear.

"We'll come and get you tomorrow evening, at eight. Wear the clothes we have laid out for you. See you tomorrow."

Viollca heads back towards the living room, munching on a cookie. As she is walking by, she sees Cate crying, laying face down on her bed, barefoot, and with disheveled hair. She is thinking of going in. But then she shrugs. After all, I don't even know that girl.

While she is eating, lying on the couch, her eyes riveted to the TV screen, she sees the door opening through the corner of her eye. On the threshold, a stocky middle-aged woman appears, her black hair tied in a bun at the nape, with huge hands and a half-moon smile.

"Ah, you girls are here. Is there anything you need? you understand some Italian, don't you? you must be Viollca, am I right? and she is Cate. Good. Have you checked your bed yet? would you like an extra blanket? it has been cold lately. Are you hungry? you can heat some bread in the oven. I bet you want to call your folks in Shijak. I'll do it for you. There is no phone here. I have one. I'll tell your parents you are fine...Why is she crying?"

Viollca shrugs. What the heck does she know! by the way she looks, she seems to be too tall for her age: thirteen years old, the two men had said. She has big feet and a droopy nose. And she is constantly sobbing.

The woman grabs the phone number and leaves, locking the door behind her. Viollca walks to the window. She would like to look outside. But it's forbidden. Perhaps she could stand back and look out. She had heard so much about Italy and is curious.

But beyond the window there is only a wall. A building with no windows. Maybe a factory, who knows. No one can look inside where they are, maybe that's why they chose that apartment. The kitchen window is the only one from which you can see rooftops and, in the background, the street with a line of cars of all different colors.

From a small narrow opening in the bathroom wall, she can catch a glimpse of a beautiful sky, sprinkled with white clouds, that remind her of her country.

"Make a lot of money, Viollca, do te jesh e pasut, you'll get rich." She had never heard her mother's voice so excited before. "Keep close to Xhuvan, trust him."

But Xhuvan had handed her over to the two men and disappeared.

Sleep fills her eyelids while, on the couch, Raffaella Carrà greets her from the screen. She is wearing a white, ample dress, which turns into a milky wave at her every move. She would like to have a dress like that. Instead, the clothes the two *patrons*—as the woman downstairs calls them—

have left them to wear are two skimpy leopard-print skirts, midriff-baring tops, fishnet stockings and black and red lace panties. Tomorrow evening the two men will be back to take them to the circus. So she will be able to see dancing seals and talking doggies up close.

The following morning, they are dragged out of bed by the lady from the apartment downstairs: "wake up, girls. Let's get to work. Enough sleeping! I have to wash your hair first. Here are the hairdryers, shampoo, make-up kit...did you have coffee? by the way, my name is Mà, that's how you should call me."

Cate's eyes are all red, hair stuck to her cheek and she is just about ready to start her endless crying again. Viollca looks at her scornfully, holding Malek, the bear, tight to her chest. As long as he is with her, she will not cry.

"Nasty hair. Nasty hair. We are going to wash it, dye it...come on, get up!"

Viollca would like to ask her what they are supposed to do but the words stick to her palate, unable to take shape.

The woman rolls up her sleeves, takes each one of them to the bathroom in turn and washes their hair, adding disinfectant to the shampoo, as if their heads were filled with lice. But where does she think we come from?

"Viollca, you hand me the rollers and you, Cate, stop crying otherwise you won't go out tonight. And for every day of work you miss, you get ten lashes."

Cate gazes at her from underneath her platinum blonde curls, baffled and imploring. Is this woman serious? She doesn't look like a jail warden. Although there is something sharp, deep down her faded blue eyes, her broad smile and double chin lend her a reassuring look. But at times, when she says "understand?" bending her head to one side, her gaze becomes piercing and stern.

"Done. Now it's your turn, Viollca. Take your shirt off so it doesn't get wet."

She was washed, disinfected, curled and made-up too. When she emerges from the hairdryer she looks at herself with amazement. The girl in the mirror is not the Viollca she knows but a different one, a weird and bewildered little woman, leaning out of the glass as if from a movie screen.

In the evening, when the two men come to pick them up, Mà takes them down the stairs, holding them by the hand as if they were two dolls to be put on display.

With their butts hanging out of their short skirts, their veiled legs in fishnet stockings, the red garter belt peeking from their panties, their glittery tops and cropped velvet jackets which make their blond curls stand out, the two young girls appear at the doorway, bewildered, like two porn characters in a comic strip.

"Wow!" the youngest *patron* shouts and slaps Mà's butt-cheeks. "Get them in the car. We'll be right there after we have coffee." The two girls are made to sit on the back seat, covered in synthetic fur.

It has stopped raining. It's a warm evening, although it is December, there's a faint smell of coffee in the air. Now they are racing through Rome's brightly-lit winter streets. The store windows are overladen with Christmas decorations. Too bad the car is driving so fast. The two men are talking to each other and, if they have anything to say, they tell Mà. As if the two girls had no ears.

"The kid must get rid of that bear. She can't show up with that horrible mangy animal."

"If you try and take it away from her she starts screaming...but maybe they will find her even more attractive this way, holding on to her toy. It makes her look more girlish."

They laugh. But then they start quarreling over money again.

They see a check point. The driver steps on the gas. The other guy raises his voice: "slow down, you idiot! take it easy. Don't go any faster, drive normally."

The cops are busy chatting. They don't even bother to look at the car with the two little girls.

Then they reach a square, with a bunch of locked up green wood kiosks at the center.

"Tell them to get off from that side. Hurry up, fast!"

The girls rush up the stairs as they are told. Mà is right behind them, huffing and puffing. The two *patrons*, wearing canvas shoes and dark glasses on their pale faces, are way behind them.

A door opens. A woman's arm reaches out. Mà says hi and then leaves. The two men whisper something to the younger and well-dressed woman behind the doorway and then take off.

Viollca and Cate are shown into two different rooms. The woman, who introduces herself as Gabriella, sprays them with something that smells like pine needles and insecticide.

"Now wait here. And be nice. These gentlemen pay a lot of money. Big money" she makes an eloquent gesture with her fingers, "they want little girls. Say that you are ten years old even if you are twelve and you, Cate, almost fourteen. They won't stay too long. Close your eyes and think about something else. It won't be too bad. Never scream, never cry, never flee. *Kuptove*, is that clear?"

Viollca lifts her eyes and looks at her. This woman, Gabriella, reminds her of her Mom: the round, freckly arms and tiny snub nose perhaps. What would she do if I hugged her? but probably this is not allowed either. She clutches her Malek against her chest as the door closes and she is left alone inside the room.

There is a bed with a floral pattern cover in front of her, with an armchair upholstered with the same pattern next to it. Further down, there is a glass top coffee table with a whisky bottle, water and a bowl filled with chocolates. Viollca grabs a couple and brings them to her mouth, after having thrown the crumpled wrappers underneath the bed.

The window shutters have been left ajar. On the nightstand, a lampshade edged with crystal tassels is shedding a pink, sugary light.

Viollca sits on the bed and waits, cuddling Malek the teddy bear.

She has almost fallen asleep when she hears the door open.

"May I?" A funny-looking dwarf peeks through the doorway, wearing a hat that is bigger than his head, propped on his ears.

Viollca smiles. He tiptoes towards her and kisses her hand. Then he takes his hat off and gently places it on the armchair. There might be a bunny rabbit in that hat. She actually has the impression of seeing a white cottontail. But now the man grabs her and smothers her by holding her head against his head.

Gabriella said: never scream, never cry, never flee. Viollca keeps her mouth and eyes shut. She wonders where Malek has fallen, since the man wrenched the bear out of her hands and threw it somewhere as he was hugging her.

But what is the funny-looking dwarf with the bunny rabbit in the hat doing now? he is rubbing up against her and is panting while he is crying. I wonder where Malek might be? she opens her eyes to look for him and notices that the man has pulled a dark sausage out of his pants. Then he grabs the girl's hands and wraps them around the sausage, which feels as soft as cotton balls.

"You are my little girl," he whispers in her ear and starts crying again. Maybe he lost a daughter. He looks so fragile. But he suddenly starts laughing and tickles her exposed navel with his finger.

"What did they make you wear, poor girl. Take this for yourself. Keep this. I know that those thieves steal from you. Don't show this to anyone."

Viollca is looking at the two hundred thousand liras he is holding in his hand. But then notices that the man is twisting, shaking and white spit comes out of his sausage, soiling her fishnet stocking.

"Hide this in your bra," he suggests with an unequivocal gesture. "This money is yours, don't let them take it away from you."

Viollca sticks the two hundred thousand in her bra. The man is standing up and is putting his hat back on. Then he steps lightly towards the door. Before closing the door behind him, he blows her a kiss.

Viollca gets down on all fours to look for her Malek, who landed underneath the bed. She brushes him off, kisses him and cuddles him while she is singing the same lullaby her Mom used to sing to her.

The door opens abruptly. Gabriella is standing in front of her, stretching her hand out. What does she want? her other hand is firmly planted against her side, and her whole motherly body is tense with impatience and rage.

Since the girl does not budge, the woman comes closer, sticks her hand in the girl's bra and fishes the two hundred thousand out. She presses the money inside her pocket. With the same hand she slaps her, and that really hurt since her hand is covered with rings.

"Never steal! Never keep the money for yourself. Or I'll beat you. You can't hide anything from me, anything, *kuptove*?"

In the mean time, the door opens again. There is a young man on the doorway, holding a raincoat on one arm, frowning.

"Where is the virgin?"

"Here she is, one second. Wait for me to get her ready. Why all this rush? Can't you wait, for Christ's sake?"

"For seven hundred thousand I am not in for any niceties."

And he starts unbuttoning his pants. Gabriella glances at him for a second, to figure him out, then decides not to make any comment and leaves, gently closing the door behind her.

The young man has taken his pants off and has meticulously folded them on the armchair. Now he takes his shirt off and hangs it on the back of the armchair, then he yanks his socks off and places them in his shoes, after having folded them four times.

In his underwear and a white tank top he walks towards her: "Are you the virgin?"

Viollca bends her head clutching her tattered Malek to her chest.

Without uttering one more word, the man gets on top of her and starts fondling her. Viollca closes her eyes and clenches her teeth. She turns into stone. Malek fell on the floor again and she can't see him. I wonder if he can see her, from down below, while this brute is crushing her under his weight.

"Come, come, come" she hears him yell. But where?

She opens her eyes for a second and she sees him on top of her, his head bending backwards between his arms, stretched out against the bed above her head. Drops of sweat fall from his naked chest, smelling of wet dog. Maybe he is a dog who has turned into a man. Viollca tries to check out his feet to see whether they are shaped like paws. And she sees something dark and hairy. "Did I hurt you?" he says, panting over her mouth.

She can't even speak. The pain is so strong, sharp, as if someone ripped her innards from within. The dog bit me, the dog bit me. I wish he stopped dripping sweat over me.

Now her legs feel cold, frozen and motionless on the bed sheet. Her belly too feels cold and stone-like.

At around one o'clock the two men show back up to get them. Gabriella is counting the money. And complains about Cate who has never stopped crying.

"How was it?"

"Fine. Here's your money. Except for my cut."

"Both fine?"

"The little girl was good. The other girl cried the whole time. A customer left without doing anything."

"Did he pay?"

"No, how could I..."

"Bitch, bitch, bitch!" The youngest *patron* grabs Cate, kicking and punching her. Cate falls to the ground. Viollca watches her without making a peep. She has almost ripped Malek's ear off to avoid crying.

"Do you know how much money I gave your father for you, do you know? three million and you scare customers away? slut, bushter, bitch!" he kicks her head, her belly.

"She is young, she doesn't know, leave her alone." Gabriella says with a faint voice.

"She is young and she must learn. She is young and she must learn!"

The older guy grabs his arm. "Don't spoil the goods, Gheo, you are going to ruin her if you keep this up."

"Tomorrow I want to see you smile, or you are gonna get it!"

But Cate can't stop sobbing. She kicks and screams, her face covered in blood and snot, then seems to suffocate in her own sobs.

"I swear I am going to kill her."

Tomorrow she will have calmed down, I'll take care of this, leave her alone. She is new in this business...She has to get used to this" Gabriella says in a more determined voice, knowing that one of the two men is on her side.

It's three in the morning when the two girls finally get home. Viollca collapses in her bed but cannot fall asleep. In the darkness of her room, she is waiting for her stone body to turn back into flesh. But stones don't melt. They will be stones forever. This is how she is seeing her arms now, far away from her and as heavy as rocks, her legs feel like stone, and she is unable to move them. Her belly is a boulder that lays motionless and indifferent like stones, on that alien and ice-cold bed.

Maybe she is already dead and her body and mind are slowly blending into an endless rocky landscape.

But something insistent brings her back to life: it's the sound of Cate's howling that does not seem to stop. Viollca puts her hands on her ears and plunges in a frigid, mineral slumber.

During the following days everything becomes easier. Cate stops crying. She lets herself be guided by Mà's rough and loving hands who dresses her, combs her hair and takes her to work, without complaining anymore. Her face has become expressionless and absent. Mà, to help her out, secretly sneaks a few tranquilizers into her pocket.

When Cate gets back home, she locks herself up in the kitchen to gobble down the whisky bottles that are kept there for the customers. The two *patrons* know what is going on but they turn a blind eye.

Thanks to pills and booze she is feeling better, and sometimes she even laughs. In the morning they sleep late. Take a bath. Then they sit and watch TV. In the afternoon, the two *patrons* pick them up and drive them to the brothel. Customers show up in droves, since finding girls that young on the sex market is not easy.

At night, Gabriella counts the money, keeps 3% for herself and gives the rest to the two *patrons*. The girls get nothing. "We send the money to your folks, don't you worry."

Once the business is up and running smoothly, surveillance becomes less tight. Lashes and beatings are not mentioned any longer. Sometimes the young guy even offers them a cigarette. Every now and then, the older guy lifts their skirts up to check their panties. But nothing more than that.

One day, Viollca catches Gabriella peeping through a hole in the wall while customers are having their way with her. That shiny and nocturnal eye she glimpses behind the hole gives her the creeps. She decides to block it by placing a mirror against the wall. But the next day the mirror is gone and the dark pupil is still there, liquid and sparkling, spying on her every move.

Viollca shrugs. What difference does it make? The hard thing for her is to carry all those stones from one apartment to another at two in the morning. Each night they become bigger and heavier. Malek's hugs do help, who smiles all alone every now and then, and Cate's muffled laugh, when they pig out on chocolate.

"How old are you?" It's a new customer, all dressed in dark clothes. Sitting on the bed next to her.

"Ten." This is what they instructed her to say.

It doesn't look like the customer wants to get undressed. He looks at her with pity and keeps asking question.

"How long have you been coming here?"

"Three months, I think."

"Where do you come from?"

"Shijak, Albania."

"Do your parents know you are here?"

Viollca bends her head. What should I tell this intruder? no one ever asked her all these questions before.

"How many customers do you see every day?"

"I don't know. Eight, perhaps."

"Now we are going to get you out of here. Don't worry. We'll take you home. Don't say anything. Don't tell anyone about me, God forbid, keep your mouth shut. Tomorrow I'll come back to get you. Is that ok?"

Viollca holds Malek tight. To go where? With whom? and what about Cate? but she doesn't dare ask questions.

The man puts his coat on and leaves without adding a single word. She can hear him raising his voice while he is quarreling with Gabriella. He is asking for a discount to avoid giving rise to her suspicions.

The following morning, Viollca is awakened by blaring sirens. Maybe an accident happened? But the sirens stop in front of their building.

Steps can be heard running up the stairs. And then someone knocking frantically on the door. Viollca opens up. The young man from the day before is standing in front of her, wearing a police uniform.

"I told you." And winks at her, smiling. He is holding a gun and walks around the apartment with other men dressed like him.

"Where are the two men?"

"Not here."

"Where?"

"I don't know."

They search everywhere, but they only find Cate curled up in her bed, in a stupor induced by whisky and pills. She stares at them with her mouth open and scratches her dyed and disheveled head.

The two young girls are taken to the local precinct. Fake papers get thrown away. The parents, who are contacted on the phone, swear they knew nothing. Questioning begins. Viollca, sitting at the edge of the chair, replies hesitantly, in the broken Italian she has learnt watching television. Before she starts answering she only asks, in a soft voice, whether she can keep her bear Malek with her.

Adele Sòfia, the police commissioner, gently strokes the girl's head. "We will get those two scum bags" she says looking at the girl who is sitting in front of her with her stony gaze.

A Number on Her Arm

Preface and translation by Virginia A. Picchietti
University of Scranton

Dacia Maraini has long endeavored to bring to light concealed and marginalized experiences. Through her body of work, she has created a multilayered representation of those to whom society and its institutions deny power, authority, and agency. Among her protagonists are the socially invisible, ostracized, and traumatized; the disenfranchised, abused, disabled, and victims of prejudice and discrimination. They cross gender, national, and generational lines.

Maraini's works serve as venues for voices, thoughts, and experiences that historically have not occupied the central focus of cultural representation or that have been outright censored. The play *Dialogo di una prostituta con un suo cliente* (*Dialogue of a Prostitute with Her Client*, 1978), for example, presents a prostitute's own thoughts on womanhood, her profession, the sexual objectification resulting from the patriarchal devaluation of women, and her own desires as a woman. The novel *La lunga vita di Marianna Ucrìa* (*The Silent Duchess*, 1990) recounts the life of an 18th century deaf and mute duchess who overcomes abuse and social invisibility to develop independence and authority over her self-expression, both sexually and through the written word. The mystery novel *Voci* (*Voices*, 1994) uses the investigation of a murdered actress to expose violence against women. The historical novel *Il treno dell'ultima notte* (*Train to Budapest*, 2008) features a young female journalist who unveils two histories: the personal turmoil lying behind the Iron Curtain in the narrative's present-day setting of 1956, and the unknown fate of the protagonist's Jewish childhood friend Emanuele, deported to Auschwitz during World War Two.

The short stories comprising the collection *Buio* (*Darkness*, 1999) share the impulse to bring to light the human actions and experiences that lie in darkness. As stories about the relationship between victim and oppressor, they expose acts of physical and psychological violence, exploitation, and intolerance. Child abuse, prostitution, domestic violence, rape, and homophobia, the stories reveal, result in the victim's trauma, loss of agency, and even death.

The story "Un numero sul braccio" ("A Number on Her Arm") breaks another type of silence—that between victim and perpetrator of the Shoah. Through the encounter between victim and perpetrator, the story participates in the dialog on guilt, accountability, victimization, and retribution stemming from turn-of-the-21st-century investigations of the Shoah and its aftermath. Even more significantly, as the narrative engages the Shoah victim's voice, it performs an act of witnessing: it testifies to the long-term psychological trauma resulting from the concentration camp experience and from the tactics used to control, dehumanize, and annihilate camp prisoners.

Set in Buenos Aires fifty years after the end of World War Two, "A Number on Her Arm" recounts the chance meeting between Mara Grado, an Italian survivor of Auschwitz who was fifteen at the time of her internment, and Hans Kurtmann, an SS camp official now known by the pseudonym Georgy Ricciotto. The story's exploration of suffering, culpability, and justice lying at the heart of considerations of the Shoah, uncovers several layers of "darkness." Darkness is represented by the number on Mara Grado's arm, which she keeps under a sleeve as many camp survivors did after the war, when the world was less willing to face this difficult history and its questions of guilt, complicity, and acquiescence. Darkness is also represented by the memory and trauma that have lain underneath Mara's reconstructed life in the postwar; by Hans Kurtmann living behind a pseudonym and concealing his crimes while hiding in Argentina; and by the encounter between victim and executioner taking place inside a small shop, rather than in a public space or before the justice system.

It is in the symbolic darkness of the closed shop that past meets present, victim meets executioner, and truth meets fiction. Within this darkness, Mara Grado's narrative is illuminated by images that constitute the visual codification of the Shoah experience. References to concrete elements allow the reader to make a connection between Mara's experience and the documentary and cultural representations of the event. Thus, Mara remembers Hans Kurtmann's gun, his whip, and his clean boots and manicured hands. She remembers her own mud-laden clogs, the yellow Star of David Jews were forced to wear, and the trains used to transport prisoners. She mentions the barracks, the showers, and the heaps of dead bodies. Matched with their place within the survivor's recounting of the Shoah experience and the suffering that comes to light through it, these elements provide us with explicit markers for our own witnessing of Mara Grado's darkness.

A Number on Her Arm[*]

While on vacation in Buenos Aires, Mara Grado window-shops along the elegant De Gama Street. This is not actually a vacation: She is in Argentina to help her pregnant daughter, who will soon face a difficult labor. The ultrasounds show that the baby is curled up in his mother's belly and that the umbilical cord has tied him up like a sausage.

Her daughter's husband, an Alitalia Airlines employee, is always away on business. Though her daughter has a young housekeeper from Paraguay, there is so much to do and always so very little time to do it.

And yet, while Teresa naps and her two small children are out with the nanny, Mara has found time to go for a walk.

Her feet carry her lightly as a delicate breeze makes her skirt flutter around her knees. The sky is a crystal-clear blue, like a sparkling windowpane filtering a placid and warm sun. Mara Grado takes a deep breath: She has not felt this free and serene in a long time. Problems at work have become small and insignificant, lying beyond thousands of ocean waves, and she is alone in an unknown city among people who speak such a modulated, musical language.

But there, in front of her, is a bright shop window displaying dozens of agate objects, from pink to lilac, light blue to blue, green to black. There are bowls, plates, ashtrays, vases, turtles, elephants, parrots, all made of a transparent stone.

"I should buy my daughter a gift," she says to herself, looking at a light blue agate jug with midnight blue concentric circles.

She opens the glass door, making a handful of small metal tubes chime. Without looking at the person behind the counter, she points to the small pot-bellied vessel. She finds it in her hands and examines it. While thinking that it seems made of the very sky she left outside the door, she hears a voice ask, "*Le gusta?*"

It strikes her like a lashing to the legs. All of a sudden, a mass of dark clouds invades the bright shop. But why? What has alarmed her? The voice of the man before her—yes, that must be it: a faintly foreign accent, a drawn out "s," a distorted vowel. She lacks the courage to lift her eyes, for fear of seeing what she does not want to see.

She panics. Though tempted to leave quickly without looking at that voice's owner, she makes a courageous decision: "I will look at him. I will

---

[*] Original title of the short story: Dacia Maraini, "Un numero sul braccio," in *Buio*, BUR Scrittori Contemporanei 8 (Milan: Rizzoli, 2012), 137-145.

look at his face. I have to know if it's him!"

Mara Grado lifts her wary eyes and meets those of a kind, smiling, elderly man. No, it cannot be him, she thinks, and once again focuses on the sky-colored agate jug. But her heart spins like a top, as the unwitting man praises the agate's qualities: "This ancient stone comes from the bowels of the earth... It is called moss agate. The Indians say it has the power to heal wounds..."

By now, there is no doubt: That voice belongs to Hans Kurtmann, the most brutal SS officer in the camp. Mara lowers her eyes to look at the object in her hands. She could not move her legs if she wanted to, and they are about to give out.

The man gives her a friendly smile. He sees her turn pale. He asks if she wants water. Water? Water? The word is hammered into her brain like a nail: Water!

"No, I do not want water," Mara Grado says. "Would you tell me your name, please?"

What a stupid question! He must have changed it if he lives here. But he cannot hide that strong German accent. She looks at his wrinkled, but manicured hands with nails cut short. How could she forget those hands?

Images come to her mind against her will. Hans Kurtmann in an SS uniform, his hair always slicked back perfectly, his neck slender and stiff. An elegant man who would walk on his toes to keep from getting his boots dirty with mud from the camp.

Hans Kurtmann strolls by with a whip in his hands and *Whack!* when you least expect it, he strikes your legs, or your breast, or your face. "Your clogs are not clean this morning! Shame on you!" How could she have clean clogs in that mud?

She had tried to say something, but he would not let her finish: A whipping cut her off. Blood gushed from the wound on her mouth.

It is morning. Hans Kurtmann, neatly shaved, leans over a boy. The boy has just gotten off the train that has traveled three days and three nights with a load of hundreds of Jews who have not had any food or water the whole trip. The boy is bundled up in a coat that is bigger than he is, and wears a visible yellow star on his chest. His cap fell off when he stepped off the train. The official bends down to pick it up and put it back on his head. "It is cold. You need to cover up, little man," he says, and the boy smiles appreciatively. But a female voice calls. The boy turns and is about to go towards his young mother. A female guard's sinewy hand pulls the woman towards a line directed to the barracks. Hans Kurtmann holds the boy's hand in a tight grip as the boy kicks and flails in an attempt to reach his mother. The man snuggles up to the boy, and with a sweet voice, tells him that everything will be all right, that his mother will return shortly, that in the meantime he will bring him to take a bath. "*Weine nicht...Alles ist gut,*" he whispers in his ear. "Do not cry."

It is that same kind, slightly well-mannered voice that is now describing the virtues of the Argentine agate to her. After having consoled the boy and still holding him by the wrist, Hans Kurtmann escorts him to the showers. He places a piece of soap in his hand and nudges him towards the changing room. The boy is scared; he reassures him. "*Weine nicht,*" he says. "Your mother will wait for you. You will take a bath and she will be waiting for you when you return."

The boy is now naked. He has a small protruding belly, big ears, slender shoulders, a thin, dirty neck. Hans Kurtmann takes his hand again and brings him all the way inside the shower room. Behind them is a heap of bodies, hundreds of Polish, German, Dutch, French children. The door closes on those small naked shoulders, on those fists gripping the deceitful soap. Instead of water, Zyklon B gas will soon fall and kill them all in a matter of minutes, amidst screams, sobs, vomit emanating from their suffocated throats.

Whether he was dedicating himself to the interminable procedure of the outdoor roll calls, whipping an inmate bloody, or consoling a boy just before sending him to the gas chamber, Hans Kurtmann always fulfilled his "duties" as a soldier with the same obsequious courteousness.

Mara Grado was fifteen years old at the time. She survived because she had a hardy constitution. Upon her arrival, they put her to work in a munitions factory. She was captured late, in November of '44, betrayed by a friend who had revealed her hiding place in Torino. By then, the Germans had needed so much labor, that they had postponed the complete extermination of the Jews until after their "victory."

"Ma'am, do you not feel well?" says the courteous, slightly worried voice of the man behind the counter.

"Hans Kurtmann," Mara Grado whispers. She is overcome by panic. What if he kills me? What if he starts kicking me? What if he grabs the whip and strikes my face?

The man turns pale. But he immediately stiffens and continues with a polite voice, "My name is Georgy Ricciotto. I am Tyrolean. Who are you looking for?"

"You are Hans Kurtmann. I recognize you. You don't frighten me.

You don't frighten me."[21]

"Ma'am, you are mistaken. I am Georgy Ricciotto."

"It's you, it's you. I recognize your voice, your hands. I still remember the day you leaned over the boy who had just arrived from Amsterdam and asked him his name. 'Hans,' he answered smiling. 'Like me,' you said. And you led him by the hand to the showers."

"You are mistaken, ma'am," he repeats in a monotone voice, trying to convince himself more than her.

"I remember when my friend Marlene became ill at roll call one day. She let herself fall and you ordered her to get up. She couldn't, so you shot her in the head. Do you remember how her legs moved? She couldn't die, but you wouldn't even waste a second bullet. We were terrified and cold, but you continued the roll call while she was dying on the ground in front of us. She was the only friend I had in there. She was fifteen years old like me, and you killed her. And now you're here, just like any other contented citizen enjoying his savings..."

"Ma'am, I guarantee you that..." he continues patiently.

"It's useless to pretend with me, Hans Kurtmann, because I'd recognize you even after a thousand years."

He'll kill me now. He'll throw himself on me and beat me to death, said the other Mara Grado, the one who in some part of her head was still walking in the dirty camp snow dragging clogs heavy with mud, in that November of '44.

She had done all she could to forget, or at least to keep from being devoured by that sinister past. She got married, had two children, got a job, found fulfillment, and at present she was preparing to help take care of her daughter's child as part of the normal exchange between generations.

But now this man upsets all internal order: Her calm has vanished. Memory has become a dragon in her soul and a wolf that pursues her mercilessly.

The man falls into an offended silence. He acts like he is standing before a crazy person and does not know what to do. He opens his arms and eyes wide, and sighs as if to say, "I can't believe what's happening to me this morning!"

Mara Grado rolls up her sleeve and shows him a number, her own: 4448327.[22] The man gives a start, as if the mere sight of the tattoo has given the unexpected visitor a historical consistency, true visibility.

"Maybe I was that man once," she hears him say in a weak and mortified tone, "but not anymore... People change, they become transformed. Old age has taken possession of me, dear woman, I mean, dear Auschwitz survivor, like it has taken possession of you. Why are you here? Why does your life cross paths with mine? What do we have in common, except for that long ago and now dead memory of war?"

Formal as always, he offers her a chair, which she refuses with disdain. "He's changed tactic," she says to herself. "Now he wants to trick me."

"I am no longer Hans Kurtmann. That young man is dead and buried. I am now Georgy Ricciotto. This name suits me perfectly. Even if it is made up, it is mine by now, it belongs to me, it has become flesh of my flesh. Why do you not try to forget, too? It is obvious from your serene face that you lead a happy life. Why do you want to ruin everything with a stupid and senseless charge?"

Mara Grado did not say anything about a charge, but he apparently thinks that that is her intention. Yes, she will report him, she thinks, but to whom?

"In any case, I guarantee that even if they did believe you, they could not catch me. I will disappear tomorrow just like I disappeared other times before. And you will not gain anything from it. You will only have kept an old man from living his final years in peace."

"I'll find you, Hans Kurtmann, because I want you to be punished, even at this late date. We looked everywhere for you after the war. Someone said you had died, but instead you were hiding here. I don't want your death, Hans Kurtmann; I want you to be locked up in a prison so you can meditate on your criminal past."

"Why are you so determined? Do you not have a little pity? Can you not forgive a poor sick old man? I have already been operated on twice for cancer, and I only have a few years left to live. Why do you want to inflict pain on my children, who are not guilty of anything?"

"Was that Dutch boy you led by the hand to the gas chamber guilty of something?"

"It was my duty. The war forced us to defend ourselves."

"Defend yourselves from what? From children?"

"Defend ourselves from Communist aggression."

"So Hans Kurtmann grew old, changed his name, changed country, changed language, changed profession, and learned absolutely nothing, not even to tell himself the truth once in a while instead of spouting lies."[23]

"I learned to mind my own business, not bother anyone, and keep my thoughts to myself. And my memories, too. You cannot come here and destroy everything out of a stupid desire for revenge."

"If only just once you had used the word 'regret'...."

"And what should I regret? To each his own destiny. Go and report me if you want. Besides, many in the police force and army see it the way I do. Go, and leave me in peace."

Mara Grado feels her eyes fill with tears.

A terrible, overwhelming pity for herself, for that boy named Hans, for this stupid, arrogant man grips her heart like a vice. No conceivable words can be exchanged between executioners and victims, she thinks, not even after fifty years.

She fills her mouth with saliva and spits at the old Nazi with contempt, then heads towards the door with dignity.

---

21. In Italian, the formal register is used when speaking to someone who is not a family member, friend, or acquaintance with whom one has a degree of familiarity. In Maraini's story, Mara Grado changes register from formal to informal at this point in her exchanges with Hans Kurtmann; that is, after positively identifying him. In her first exchange with Kurtmann, Mara uses the formal, which is formed by employing the 3rd-person singular and plural forms of the verb, "No, non voglio acqua ... *può* dirmi il suo nome per favore?" / "No, I do not want water ... Will you tell me your name, please?" In the second exchange, by contrast, she switches to the informal, formed by the 2nd-person singular and plural forms of the verb. My translation represents the informal through use of verb contractions, "Hans Kurtmann *sei tu*, ti ho riconosciuto. Non mi *fai* paura. Non mi *fai* paura" / "Hans Kurtmann is you. I recognize you. You *don't* frighten me. You *don't* frighten me." Mara will maintain the informal register from here until the short story's conclusion. Kurtmann, by contrast, maintains the formal register throughout.

22. Only prisoners designated for work in the Auschwitz concentration camp complex were tattooed with numbers. For detailed information, see the United States Holocaust Memorial Museum website at http://www.ushmm.org/wlc/en/article.php?ModuleId=10007056

23. The original "formule mistificatorie" is translated literally as "euphemistic formulas." The original Italian captures well the Nazi practice of using euphemisms to linguistically encode the concentration camp system.

Might as Well Live and Serena the Bride

Preface and translation by Alex Standen
University College London

In her introduction to the 2009 collection of short stories *La ragazza di via Maqueda*, Dacia Maraini likens memories to a genus of houseplant that one cannot hope to keep alive, no matter how much love and care one gives it. Like a flower that Maraini was gifted during a visit to a Vermont university, which was programmed to survive for only a couple of days, so too, she writes, are our memories destined ultimately to die so that more can take their place. In the collection, Maraini—an assiduous nature lover and gardener—attempts to preserve the multitude of memories which assault her, speaking to her with "una voce che non sa tacere," which "ritorna sui luoghi amati, rimpiange, ricorda, allarma" (p. 7).

In another analysis of Maraini's work, I have discussed how in the latter stages of her career there is a perceptible shift towards self-reflection and representation, with the publication of a number of texts that contain elements of life writing and autobiography (Standen 2014). *La ragazza di via Maqueda* both reflects and bucks this trend: Maraini's introduction, the structuring of the stories as a journey from Sicily, through Rome to Abruzzo, the inclusion of a story about Pasolini and another in which Maraini is evident as a fictionalized version of herself, all point the reader towards an autobiographical text, and yet this is countered by stories which stand alone as works of fiction. The collection fluidly interweaves fact and fiction, gravitating towards "identity-supporting structures," as Paul John Eakin would describe it (1999: 20), whilst simultaneously offering a fragmented imagining of the author as character.

The two stories I have chosen to translate are works of fiction, located in the *Sicilia* section of the collection, which both take young women as their protagonists. Throughout her career, Maraini has returned repeatedly to female characters who are on the cusp of adulthood: notwithstanding their differing socio-historical landscapes and cultural contexts, novels such as *L'età del malessere* (1963) and *Isolina* (1985) and *Colomba* (2005) all offer the reader instances of young women facing the challenges and limitations that society imposes on them–often as a result of their gender. By focusing on women as they move into adulthood, Maraini is able to emphasise the enduring clash between the hopes and expectations of youth and the cheerless realities of adult life.

Ramona and Serena, the protagonists of the two stories presented here, continue this legacy. With her high achieving background culminating in two degrees, Ramona might have expected an ambitious and fulfilling career. Instead, she finds herself unemployed, living back with her mother and facing the monotony of a fruitless job search in a society brought close to breaking point by the financial crisis and offering opportunities only to the well connected. She has tried sales, care work and—at her lowest—a modeling role that descended quickly, and predictably, into pornography. The options open to a bright and hard-working young woman are depressingly familiar in an Italy where multiple young lives are defined by such precariousness. There are moments of bitter humour in Ramona's depiction of her struggles and isolated flashes of warmth in an otherwise bleak world, both encapsulated in the Dorothy Parker poem which gives the story its title, *You might as well live*.

Serena, on the other hand, is at a point in her life which, convention dictates, should be her happiest—her wedding day. Already dressed in her wedding gown, with hair and makeup done, Serena is ready to leave for the church when a box of chocolates tempts her. As the sensuous pleasure of the chocolates increases, so too does her desire for the imminent betrothal swiftly diminish; whilst as readers we are not told of the motivations for the wedding, it might well be that this is Serena's primary rebellion, a unique and transformative moment in her life. Where Ramona's story ended with the spiritless repetition of a bittersweet adage, Serena becomes ever more joyful, ultimately throwing off her shoes and letting her hair down to sing and dance alone to a childhood nursery rhyme.

Two women with their lives ahead of them; two individuals faced with the out-dated confines of a society resistant to change, both wanting to forge their own paths and be the architect of their futures. In her introduction to the collection, Maraini begins with the trope of a journey, on which, "senza neanche volerlo, ho seguito la strada dei miei passi" (p. 7). The two stories are not autobiographical, and yet, set in Sicily, both expose the paradoxes of the island which dominated her childhood: rigid and archaic, but at the same time capable of inspiring passion, joy and laughter.

The short story is a form which is not unfamiliar to Maraini, and in translating the two stories in this particular collection I have sought to replicate the style she employs so effectively in many of her short works of fiction (and I am thinking in particular of the award-winning *Buio* [1999]). By necessity, short stories demand concision: meaning must be conveyed within the strictest limits of time and space and, as readers, we are not to understand everything; instead, the briefest encounter or gesture must tell us all that we need to know. In addition to that, Maraini's particular skill is in surprising her readers at moments when they least expect it, leading us towards one conclusion and then swiftly pulling us towards somewhere else entirely. So often in her works, beneath a façade of normalcy lies something or somebody extraordinary and, in her short stories, we are given the merest glimpse of this. In the aforementioned *Buio,* these twists all too often lead us to the horrors that lurk just beneath the surface of our daily lives, concealed by a veneer of respectability and, often, the ostensibly authorising nature of institutions. In the stories I have chosen to translate, these moments are not ones of violence or shame, but are instead brief yet cathartic flashes of self-awareness and defiance; the moments which remind her readers that there are no such things as ordinary lives.

Works Cited

Eakin, Paul John. *How Our Lives Became Stories.* Ithaca: Cornell University Press, 1999.

Maraini, Dacia. *L'età del malessere.* Turin: Einaudi, 1996.

------. *Buio.* Milan: Rizzoli. 1999.

------. *Isolina.* Milan: Rizzoli, 2000.

------. *Colomba.* Milan: Rizzoli, 2007.

Standen, Alex. "'Solo le storie sono capaci di colmare gli squarci del dolore. Solo le storie ci aiutano a sopravvivere': Autobiographic Traces in the Narratives of Dacia Maraini." *Altrelettere,* 26.11.2014, doi: 10.5903/al_uzh-26.

Might as Well Live[*]

In threadbare slippers, her hair uncombed and her eyes full of sleep, Ramona sits at the kitchen table, leafing through the newspaper that a kindly hand has pushed under the door of the house. In front of her are a cup of coffee and a slice of toast.

Her gaze falls on a photo of a skeletal boy with flies at the corners of his mouth. Her stomach contracts: he's a child and yet he already seems old. His forehead is covered with lines. Lines from hunger, Ramona says to herself, pausing over the harrowing image. Here is someone more desperate than me. Is it pity she feels? Doubtless, but she also realises that her pity passes quickly from the boy to herself: 32 years old, her father dead, graduated with double honours at the top of her class, and no job. Until now she has lived on her mother's pension, but with the arrival of the euro this has lost half of its purchasing power. She's had to leave the miniscule apartment near university, which had at least given her some independence. She's had to return to her childhood home, where she sleeps on a sofa in the den, because her room has been let to a student.

It's been months now that Ramona has been getting up at seven to look for work and she still hasn't found anything. If she didn't have the warm den to sleep in, if she didn't have access to that little money that her mother shares with her, what would she do? It's been a year since she bought a pair of shoes: both her blue flats and the black heels she wears to go out in the evening are misshapen, the soles peeling away. I'll have them repaired, she promises herself again, even if she's not sure where. In the busy district of Zisa where she lives she has never seen a cobbler. Do they even still exist?

Ramona goes back to browsing the paper, pausing distractedly over the inside pages. A half-naked woman advertising a beer company. For a moment her mind, still slow from sleep, searches bewilderedly for some kind of metaphorical link between the beer and the naked woman, but finds none.

Finally, the employment pages. "Hairdressing salon seeking shampooer." Red circle. Why not? Below this, a request for an errand boy in a bakery. But could an errand girl also apply? Red circle around that one too.

---

[*] Original title of the short story: Dacia Maraini, "Tanto vale vivere," in *La ragazza di via Maqueda* (Milan: Rizzoli, 2009), 83-87.

"Seeking bricklayer," "Seeking home help," "Seeking model for a new line of swimwear *Comfort and Seduction*." Red circle or not? She remembers a recent grotesque experience auditioning to advertise Candy Underwear. She had found herself shut in a small pink living room, wearing nothing but a pair of cherry-pink knickers whilst the self-styled director, bald and pot-bellied, ordered her to bend over, lift her leg, push out her chest. Meanwhile a bearded photographer, crouched on the floor, maneuvered a large camera which flashed and made a noise like a combustion engine. The director had forced her into ever more humiliating positions and she'd complied, albeit reluctantly, hoping that it would all soon be over, with some money in her pocket. Instead things got worse. The bald, pot-bellied director had asked her to remove her underwear, "to better continue the performance" and whilst she complained that it wasn't part of the agreement, she'd found him next to her on the sofa, undoing his trousers. Meanwhile, the photographer had continued to shoot. At this point she'd escaped, cursing them. She'd had to finish getting dressed as she ran down the stairs. No, no red circle. She didn't think she'd be showing up at 16, Via degli Emiri to advertise the Comfort and Seduction swimwear line.

Seeking, seeking..."Door-to-door salesgirl, attractive appearance, own vehicle." No circle even here. She's already done that once and has no desire to try again. She'd had to be ready at the agency at five in the morning, in her old car bought on finance, to take consignment of two cases full of clocks and launch herself into the chaotic traffic, her list of appointments on the dashboard. She climbed thousands of stairs, knocked on hundreds of doors, found herself face-to-face with louts, imbeciles and opportunists. When finally she had come across someone kind, she'd ended up stuck listening to the troubles and miseries of an outcast. If by the end of the week she'd sold two clocks it was a bonus. Besides which, she was spending more on petrol than she could ever earn from those damned clocks. No, she was decidedly not gifted at selling. She was either moved to pity, or duped.

"Seeking caretaker for dependent 90-year-old." No circle. This too she's already done and was left with aching bones. Old Signor Emilio was quiet, he didn't shout or dribble, but he did wet himself five minutes after being cleaned up from the previous time. Just like a naughty child. In fact he would smile contentedly while she cleaned and changed him and then, not even an hour later, she would smell urine again. She would ask him, "Signor Emilio, have you wet yourself again?" and, blushing, he would nod his head.

There was something so childlike and tender about him that she couldn't scold him for it. He had children in their sixties who would come and see him every two or three days, speaking to him softly, bending to kiss his downy head and then leaving. She had to stay, a prisoner in the urine-smelling room, at the mercy of a ninety-year-old child.

After six months she couldn't take it anymore, the continual nappy changes, washing his soiled underwear, and she left without even asking for her final paycheck. He waved her off with tears in his eyes. No, no care work.

Come on, she said to herself, don't be difficult, you have to do something! Is it possible that two hard-earned degrees are really worth nothing? She's put herself forward for every imaginable scheme to get an academic role. But every time she gets to the selection process she's up against two thousand others and the selected candidates are almost always favoured by their connections. She's put out hundreds of classifieds, ready to give private lessons in the den where she sleeps and studies, but no responses. Maybe she's cursed?

She gets up, dresses, pauses to greet her mum who is darning socks for a neighbour down the corridor. She already knows that at the end of the month she'll pay her with a dozen eggs, a box of figs, or a packet of pasta.

The hairdresser from the advert is at 41, Via Generale Cadorna. It's only nine o'clock but the shop is already full. There's a coming and going of girls in green smocks, bending over curls and straight hair. Others, gloveless, are busy smearing toxic dye over the heads of women stretched out, talking to one another, whilst the radio blares out an annoying beat.

Ramona edges forward timidly. A large woman approaches her asking if she wants a smoothing or anti-dandruff treatment. "No," says Ramona, "I'm here about the advert, aren't you looking for a shampooer?" The woman's expression changes instantly. She looks Ramona up and down with a hard, inquisitive gaze. Then responds slowly, emphasising her words, "I've already found someone, do you understand, you're too late," and with a gesture of her chin, makes it clear that Ramona is to leave immediately, that she has no time for her.

Ramona leaves, stumbles, and almost finds herself flat on the pavement. She sits, dispirited, mechanically repeating to herself the words of a Dorothy Parker poem that have remained stuck in her head and that come back to her when, at times like these, death seems like the best option:

> Razors pain you,
> Rivers are damp,
> Acids stain you,
> And drugs cause cramp.
> Guns aren't lawful,
> Nooses give,
> Gas smells awful,
> You might as well live.

Serena the Bride*

A pale hand, its fingers smooth and plump, hovers, uncertain, above a paper tray crammed with chocolates. Which to choose? The white shell which could have arrived from the South Seas, the rosebud sculpted in cocoa, the dark star with its points full of cream, or the little bronze chest topped with a coffee bean? Finally, gliding over the tray like a bird, it delicately seizes, into the beak of its two clawed fingers, the jet-black star. It carries it slowly to her tongue, which is taut and protruding like that of a little girl ready to receive the communion wafer. Her mouth closes slowly, squashing the sweet-smelling chocolate against her palate.

In that moment she hears a voice calling, "Serena! Are you still here? The groom's waiting for you in front of the church, your father's downstairs, the car door's open."

Serena hears words coming from her own chocolate-filled mouth, "I'm coming, I'll be right down!" But it's not her voice, she says to herself, there's something in it which doesn't belong to her.

Her fingers, furtive, once again descend towards the chocolates which glisten with a dark and promising light. They seize the shiny white shell and place it calmly on her tongue. Next it is the turn of the little chest which slides between her teeth and melts, liberating a delicious aroma of freshly ground coffee.

"Serena!" comes the shout from outside.

"I'm coming!"

She wipes her chocolate-stained fingers on her ample organza skirt, leaving two dark stains. The young bride takes a step towards the door. But then she stops, turns around and calmly returns to the tray, this time bringing to her mouth a bronze oak leaf, next an exquisitely scented wheat sheaf, then a little fish, dark like a moonless night.

"The groom is waiting, the church is already full of people!" she hears shouted from the bottom of the stairs.

A mauve-coloured chocolate is calling to her joyfully.

"If we delay the ceremony how will we ever make it to Villa Igea for midday?" it's the voice of her sister. Serena smiles but no longer worries about responding.

Now with an impatient, merry hand she undoes her heels and throws them off, one over here, the other over there.

---

* Original title of the short story: Dacia Maraini, "La sposa Serena," in *La ragazza di via Maqueda* (Milan: Rizzoli, 2009), 136-138.

A chocolate is waiting for her, another delight offering itself up. This time it's a miniature soldier in a red and blue uniform clutching a silver rifle. With a nail the young bride peels off the wrapper and places the naked soldier whole into her mouth; she happily closes her eyes as soon as she feels a spurt of liquor on the inside of her cheeks.

"Serena!" a male voice calls from outside. A desperate voice. But it seems to be coming from a distant sphere; the voice of a star in the sky that soon wouldn't make any more noise. A voice that, above all, would prevail upon her no longer. Could that star be calling to her with a more whimpering tone?

I'll eat another chocolate and then I'll see, she tells herself, picking up a butterfly the colour of burnt earth. On each of its spread wings is a red eye, blind yet piercing.

"Serena, Serena!" the voice loses itself amongst the shreds of a mute sky.

Serena moves barefoot towards the door. She locks it. She then drags a heavy desk over and pushes it against the door. She removes the combs that are holding together her mass of dark hair woven with flowers for good luck.

She throws the combs against the wall. And like this, barefoot, her lips covered in chocolate, her hair ruffled, her long organza skirt in her hands, she begins to dance around the room, singing a song learnt in childhood:

> The little ant in a field of grain
> Sees a cricket and falls in love
> Lalalillelo lalalilleo
> Lalalillelo lillela.
> The wedding feast is
> Four cherries and two roasted chestnuts
> Lalalillelo lalalilleo
> Lalalillelo lillela.
> As the two walk down the aisle
> The cricket falls and cracks his head
> Lalalillelo lalalilleo
> Lalalillelo lillela.
> The little ant
> Overcome with pain
> Takes one leg and pierces her heart
> Lalalillelo lalalilleo
> Lalalillelo lillela.

A Sicilian Nun

Preface and translation by Elise Magistro
Scripps College

"Una suora siciliana" ("A Sicilian Nun") is taken from *La ragazza di via Maqueda*, a collection of short fiction published in 2009. In the volume's brief introduction entitled "La geografia della narrazione," Maraini discusses the genesis of the stories and how memory imposes itself on the creative process: "They were supposed to be stories born of curiosity about the world and the joy of narrating [...] But memory is always peeking out at you, and there is no way to chase it away."[24] Returning to the places of her formative experiences—Sicily, Rome and the region of Abruzzo—Maraini draws on both life and memory to explore recurring themes in her fiction in a more deeply personal context.

Nowhere is this more evident than in the pieces pertaining to Sicily. The island's geography is central, not only in recollections of childhood but as a place seemingly frozen in time with its archaic laws and time-honored traditions. A prolific and astute observer of modern day realities, including violence against children and women, Maraini focuses here on the degradation of Sicily's once splendid cities (prostitution involving minors and rampant building abuse) and the devastation of the island's natural beauty. Against this background, readers are introduced to an array of female protagonists whose lives are bound up in these grim realities.

In "Una suora siciliana," Maraini harkens back to Sicily's past, touching not only on the roots of Sicily's environmental ills but on a historic, less explored type of violence against women—that of *la monacazione* or the placing of young girls into convents, a practice that continued on the island well into the 19th century.

Maraini is recognizable here as the voice of the present, a journalist fluent in contemporary feminist discourse, who is drawn into the unspoken yesterday of a Sicily where such discourse was precluded. In the physical location of an abandoned convent, imaginary yet vividly real shadows depict a life of subjugation and emotional violence. In spare prose and a straightforward style, Maraini traces the arc of Sister Philomena's life through the journalist's musings, leaving readers little doubt as to the harsh existence endured by thousands of Sicilian girls destined for cloistered silence.

As a translator, I found the piece appealing as an example of Maraini's mastery of the short form. The author's distillation of complex cultural phenomena into their most elemental and powerful expressions is deftly executed here via an unrelenting focus on the wounded individual psyche. Tenderness and a child-like naiveté permeate Sister Philomena's thought process, an innocence that is reflected in Maraini's unflinching language. With neither the education nor the tools to fully understand her unfulfilled longings, Sister Philomena must simply accept and endure this life. Yet like many of Maraini's protagonists, the young nun possesses unusual self-awareness and tenacity in the face of her bleak reality, making her a precursor of sorts to the author's interest in female mystics that would appear in *Chiara di Assisi. Elogio della disobbedienza* (2013).

***

A Sicilian Nun^{*}

Town C. 10:00 a.m.

A high school. In a small town somewhere in the mountains of Sicily. So many students, asking the hard-working writer to work even harder. But how is that possible? A boy with curly, carrot colored hair looks at her sternly. "You writers have a voice people listen to, but you don't use it like you should."

Observing the boy with the red curls, Georgia is startled to see two long white wings protruding from of his slender shoulders, pointed menacingly upward.

"Our work takes time," she replies timidly. Out of nowhere, a young girl with her belly exposed appears next to the angel, the silver ring in her naked navel seeming to eye Georgia. She looks straight at her, smiling impertinently. "You have a weapon and you don't know how to use it," she says indignantly. "You let us rot in this corrupt and violent Sicily without so much as a word."

12:00 p.m.

A student wearing red knee socks accompanies the writer on a visit to the convent, perched on the cliffs above C.

"Sister Philomena used to stop here to pray, at the Madonna of the Angel." More angels? And does this one have carrot colored curls, too, Geor-

---

* Original title of the short story: Dacia Maraini, "Una suora siciliana," in *La ragazza di via Maqueda* (Milan: Rizzoli, 2009), 158-170.

gia asks herself, following the student with the red knee socks up the steep steps.

"These are their cells," she explains, opening a carved and etched wooden door. Within the little white room with plaster walls there are a pot, a small bed, a rusted metal wash-basin, a white pitcher, a cross hanging above the headboard and a miniscule kneeler of rough wood. Next to the door, on the floor, is a hope chest with elegantly painted bouquets of yellow and lilac flowers and two parrots with curved beaks and red and green wings.

"And this chest?"

"Each nun had her own. They kept their linens and personal things inside. The same chests would then serve as their coffins when they died."

"Their coffins?"

"This particular chest was unearthed during repairs being made to the convent. The nun's body was then encased in a shrine. They say it was intact. She's on track for beatification."

The student with the red knee socks now moves on along labyrinth-like hallways that lead to a hexagonal shaped courtyard. There, twisted white marble columns support the vaults of a shaded loggia. A neglected garden full of roses and lavender tufts stands at the courtyard's center. And in the middle, a well made of grey stone with a rod-iron arch above it.

Georgia returns to the hotel. She sits on the bed and continues to think of that hope chest painted in bright colors. First a nun would use it to store her sheets, towels, and undergarments; later they would lay her body to rest in it. And since when have coffins been decorated with flowers and parrots?

She tries to imagine a very young Philomena having just arrived at the convent a few months earlier, the chest filled with all her things. She wears a black veil pinned to her head. A white wimple covers her throat and falls across her breast, like a freshly ironed smock. Every two days the wimple must be starched and pressed. Just as the rough cotton nightgowns, worn against her bare skin, must also be washed and pressed. Philomena's small, hardworking hands move constantly, as convent rules demand: a woman with idle hands falls prey to the devil, so it is necessary to keep them busy. At 5:00 a.m. there are sheep to be milked and then milk to be scalded in enormous copper pots. Immediately after, sheets must be laundered and laid out to dry in the garden. Later, the vegetable patch needs tending: weeding, hoeing, and removing dead leaves, watering tomatoes and cabbages. Afterwards, it's off to the kitchen to sift flour, chop vegetables, fry eggs and shell beans. In those brief moments of pause her fingers must find their way to the rosary, hanging at her side, and move across the beads as she murmurs her prayers. Then there is the business of embroidering, and towards evening dedicating herself to the reading of sacred texts, and then again to the dirty dishes after supper. And at night, when her eyes are swollen from lack of sleep and exhaustion, those little, strong hands will have to hold the heavy prayer book, while her knees dig into the rough hewn kneeler, as she says her final goodnight to God before falling asleep.

Sister Philomena knows her duty. When she took her vows—and she was little more than a child–she renounced mirrors, clothes and dreams of love. Her child—like imagination is not even capable of understanding the enormity of the sacrifices she faces. The relentless pace of life, and the constant companionship of other young girls like herself distract her from the thought of how cut off she is. Her earnest hands weave threads of silk as she hums, in near silence, a song she once sang with her sisters when they were little and used to play, hunting frogs in the pond behind the house.

Time: 1:30. At the house of the angel with carrot colored curls.

The boy's mother politely helps Georgia take off her jacket. She invites her to sit down in a living room scented with lavender. There are books on the wall and a television that stands out for its small size. It's clear this is a family of readers.

"Would you like coffee? How much sugar do you take?" The woman is kind. The veins in her neck are taut, like she is holding back some emotion. She is thin, with large eyes that protrude from their sockets a bit too much, as though she is straining to see beyond things within her reach in a perennial effort of mind and muscles.

While drinking her coffee and thinking of Sister Philomena, Georgia can hear the woman talking about her high-school aged son. She tells her that he studies a lot—maybe too much—that he is very religious, that he recently enrolled in a Catholic organization, that he is hard on himself and on others. He constantly reproaches his father for his lack of honesty.

"The truth is, his father had a mistress for over ten years now. But I let it go. He, on the other hand, doesn't. He wants his father to be virtuous. But what's to be done? He's still young, with so many carnal desires."

Curious, Georgia observes this beautiful and humble woman who speaks to her frankly and without shame. What has she done to deserve her trust? It's as though she takes pleasure in baring everything about herself. But what kind of pleasure is that? Some kind of self-validation? A request for empathy? The lucid irony of someone who knows this is all she can ask from life and takes pride in it? She'd like to offer up a kind word, but her lips refuse to move.

While nibbling a cumin cookie, she sees the door open. In the entryway, the angel with the red hair appears. Calmly and politely he excuses himself for his impertinence that morning at school. Perhaps she was offended?

"No, why offended?"

"You weren't pestering our writer, were you" interjects the mother, placing a nervous hand on her son's knee.

"I think I've annoyed you. You know how teenagers are," he says, assuming an ironic and paternal tone.

The following morning. Town C. Time: 9:00 a.m.

The school's principal suggests a drive down to the beach for the writer. But she asks to return to the cloistered sisters' convent. The kind man accompanies her in his little black car, up through the town's narrow streets until they reach the monastery, jutting out from the cliff above.

"What interests you so much about this convent?"

"I don't know, maybe the lives of the nuns, or those chests that were both their hope chests and their coffins."

"Would you like to see the dining hall with the frescoed walls or the underground kitchens?"

"Both," she replies, feeling a bit self-conscious. Not even she quite understands why she wanted to come back to the convent.

They go down to the lower floors where the expansive kitchens open up. There are windows, but they are very high up, unreachable. A somewhat sinister, purplish light filters through the glass panes.

Ceramic bowls, leather bags for carrying water, basins, shells, flasks, glass jars, are all lined up on shelves that have been recently reorganized. Brass pots and pans shine on the walls; forms and molds for making sweets hang in harmonious order.

"They were very good at making sweets. People came from all over to buy them. They would put their money on the rotating wheel, turn it, and a tray with the most marvelous pastries would appear."

"So you did this too?"

"No, by the time I was born the convent was already shuttered and half-destroyed. Now the town has restored it. My grandmother used to talk to me about it. She told me that when she was little she used to come here on Sundays to get sweets for the big mid-day meal. The nuns never allowed anyone to see them, but they were there, hidden behind the grate. It was forbidden to show your face to strangers. And those sweets? Oh, were they good! *La scorzonera*—are you familiar with it? A ball made with strips of candied orange peel; and *frisèlle*, rice fried in honey… *gremolate*, infused with blackberry syrup, and *cuccìa*, a mixture of boiled wheat berries with fresh ricotta and sugar."

Their footsteps echo in the cavernous, empty room. Georgia extends her finger towards a big copper pot that appears to be bubbling on the stovetop. When she retracts her finger, it is covered with dust. Leaning against the door-jam she thinks she catches a glimpse of Sister Philomena. She recognizes her from the miniature portrait that hangs in the convent's entryway, along with so many others. A small, thin girl with two large hands. Her eyes are luminous and clear, her smile dark. Can a smile be dark without turning into a sneer? But there is no trace of contempt in that small compact body. Rather, what strikes Georgia is the resolute and warlike look of the young nun.

Town M. 11:00 a.m.

Another meeting. In the little town, clinging to the rocks with it's back turned to a sea that has always been hostile and rapacious. There are four high school classes that have come from T. and two middle classes from C. The principal introduces the teacher whose responsibility it is to introduce the writer. The students seem distracted and preoccupied with their cell phones that light up, one after another. But then, when she starts talking about matters that concern them directly, the phones stop buzzing and their attention is palpable.

It's difficult to hold adolescents' attention. Their minds tend to wander and their thoughts—always jumping from one subject to the next with lightening speed—scatter like startled pigeons at the clap of hands. Only passion catches them off guard and draws them in. Never underestimate the hunger for ideas in young minds unaccustomed to systematic thinking. Curiosity about philosophical conjecture? Civic passion? Perhaps.

The angel with the red hair is nowhere to be seen this morning. The classes are all from other schools. The teacher with heavy eye make-up looks inquisitively at Georgia as she tries to make herself heard in the classroom with bad acoustics. Her voice seems to bounce off the soundproof walls, coming straight back at her.

Facing her are twins with the identical infantile and stubborn face, and eyes cast down towards their noses. They approach the lectern to ask her something about violence against women. The number of rapes, these "bestial acts" – is it really on the rise, one of the two asks. And why is that?

Georgia tries to explain in a kind voice that rape has nothing to do with nature and bestiality. "In nature, rape doesn't exist; animals don't rape," she says. "Instead, we should consider it a weapon of war. Those who rape don't do so because they desire a body but rather because they want to humiliate that body, to offend it, to dominate it."

The young women listen with a mixture of disbelief and coolness, while their hands toy with heavy rings that weigh down their small, plump fingers. They are comical, dressed identically in long red pants and short red-plaid tunics. They wear headbands to hold their hair back, just like little girls, and the braces on their teeth shine when their full lips break into a smile.

Town C. 1:00 p.m.

"We've made reservations at a beach-front restaurant. Would you like to eat fish?"

"Actually, I'd prefer to return to the convent."

"You don't want lunch?"

"I'll eat tonight."

Although annoyed, the teacher with the long black hair accompanies her to the monastery located above the town, right next to the baronial palace that has been gutted and not yet restored.

"They're going to turn it into a museum for us," she informs Georgia with a solemn air.

"Could I see Sister Philomena's room again?"

"She was a poor shoemaker's daughter, did they tell you?" She was engaged, or at least that's what they say. Her dowry was all ready. For however poor, her parents had made sacrifices so their beautiful daughter could marry well. Her future husband was a baker who supposedly had a house and a fairly respectable business. But a few days before the wedding, the young woman ran away, hiding out in the mountains. Here, among these rocks. She took shelter in a cave and lived there for six months without anyone ever finding her. She was as silent and agile as a mountain goat. Her father gave her up for dead. Her fiancé, too. Until one day a shepherd saw her and told people in town. But he also said there was a halo around her head, and that she was thin as a sardine and that she had been speaking with the Blessed Virgin. Philomena's father brought her home since he hadn't given up on the idea of marrying her off to whomever he wanted. But she said she'd kill herself rather than marry, so the father came to terms with his rebellious daughter. Life in a grotto, no. If anything, in a convent. And so Philomena was forced to prepare her trousseau and to order a painted chest so she could enter the cloistered convent. She didn't have an easy life. She was always kept under special watch. A rebellious girl was thought to belong to the devil. But she fasted and tended the garden and studied and prayed, getting up at dawn, so that in time people left her alone.

3:00 p.m.

Georgia follows Philomena's fluid train of thought that draws her back to a faraway place in time. The nun's gaze is fixed on the hope chest that sits towards the back of her cell, motionless, peaceful and refined. That chest holds her treasures: five tunics made of fine Dutch cloth, eight shirts of Sicilian silk, four pairs of linen sheets, eight embroidered pillowcases, two pairs of pointed slippers made of woven straw and covered in black velvet, ten bolts of white damask, ten linen towels, four black veils—two for summer, two for winter—and five or six devotional books: *The Life of Saint Rita*, *The Life of Saint Monica*, *The Life of Christ*, the Gospels with illustrations by a famous Benedictine monk, and a songbook of Christmas and Easter hymns. There is even a rag doll hidden beneath all those things, though she never takes it out unless she is alone.

The chest also contains nightshirts that she has never worn, sewn with love by her mother Agostina Laminti. She remembers her well, in those first days when she would come up to the convent, carrying little baskets that held freshwater fish, walnuts, and ripe apricots from their garden. Then she had gotten pregnant for the thirteenth time. The doctor had told her that the baby was positioned wrong and that she should abort. But she brought it into the world, and in giving life to the child, she had lost her own.

Mamma Agostina always had the faintest scent of basil about her. And when she smiled, ever so slightly, she would cover her mouth with a cupped hand. She was missing four front teeth. At thirty-eight, she already seemed old, hunched over from doing so much laundry at the river with ash and soap. Her hair had turned gray from all the pregnancies. Surrounded by so many children, she never had time to sleep or eat as she should. And yet she never forgot about that rebellious daughter who had lived for six months in a cave, who had refused to marry and who was now shut up in a cell, high in that convent. She had always said that Philomena was the wisest of all her daughters and that she would certainly make a fitting bride of Christ. That was why she sometimes left her other children and raced to the convent with *focacce*, fresh from the oven. Every time she arrived, out of breath, she would sit down on the hope chest and tell Philomena about her brothers and sisters. But she never stayed long. She was always in a hurry to get home. She would kiss her daughter on the forehead and head back, practically running...What she would not give to hear Mamma Agostina's footsteps again!

6:00 p.m. Hotel Belvedere.

Back in her room, Georgia finds yellow freesias spilling out of a blue glass vase. She bends down to smell them recalling their secret, sweet scent. But these freesias have no scent. Then she remembers having heard somewhere that people actually prefer flowers that don't smell. But why? They last longer, was the answer. But then, they might as well be plastic-coated.

Georgia hangs her blue blouse in the armoire and then opens her suitcase to take out her slippers. She lies down on the bed and gazes out the window at the sea in the distance, its color strangely reddish. Further up, almost on top of the hotel, one can see the cliff where the convent and the baronial tower are perched.

The teacher had told her they would be eating fresh 'caged' tuna this evening. "What does 'caged' mean?" "They farm them in huge enclosed areas in the sea. You should see how big and fat they are. The cages are enormous, of course, and the tuna can swim and race back and forth. Then one day they kill them, shouting all the while. They built a factory right on top of the old tuna packing house. My mother used to work there. Her hands were ruined by the constant handling of frozen fish. As soon as the tuna arrives in the factory, they cut it up into pieces and flash-freeze it. To send to Japan and America."

10:00 p.m.

"I'll end up in that hope chest when I'm dead . . . but there's time. I'm just sixteen."

Georgia follows the young nun's daily thoughts. It seems she can hear the buzzing in that small, innocent head. She sees her from behind, seated, embroidering with skilled hands. She sees her gaze, resting on the chest's painted lilac flowers and on those two red and green parrots, with fluttering yellow ribbons tied round their necks. The chest is really quite beautiful, and just the right size for her body. Once she had even tried it out to convince her cellmate, Amalia, who was sure she could never fit inside. She had opened the lid, pulled out all her things and gently eased herself down. She fit perfectly. Amalia had shut the lid, and then—just to spite her—sat on top of it. Philomena remained inside with her arms crossed, thinking in the dark how it must feel to be dead. But she hadn't been frightened. The darkness didn't seem much different to her than when she closed her cell's heavy, varnished wood blinds at night.

"Aren't you scared?" her friend had asked, raising the lid.

"No," a smiling Philomena had replied.

"You're so brave!"

"Do you know what I am afraid of? Not being able to ever have a child," She had blurted it out, but immediately regretted it. How could she possibly think of wanting a child when she had been promised to God? They had cut her long black tresses, and along with them she had renounced all carnal desires. It's what convent rules demanded. But she wasn't thinking about love, she was thinking about a child. Who knows why, but ever since she was little she had wanted to hold and caress a newborn in her arms. It was why she had brought with her—hidden in the painted chest—a ragdoll she had made with her own hands. Sometimes, at night, she would cradle it, holding it close to her breast, and she would grieve.

Amalia had looked at her in astonishment. Girls in the convent thought of nothing *but* love. They would fall madly, carelessly in love, with a monk they had only seen from behind, in church...with a young farmer who had brought eggs to the gatekeeper. But no one ever talked about children. What was love, anyway, if not that pious and sensual feeling that bound them to their celestial spouse?

"Only one groom for all of us?" Philomena sometimes asked herself, perplexed. But she knew that the Abbess Antonia didn't like it when her "dear daughters" (as she called them) asked too many questions. "Faith is blind, my child, and it is not to be questioned," she would thunder, her fat body trembling. It didn't take much to make the Abbess Antonia smile: a dish of particularly well-prepared beans, a dessert made with carob aspic, a bowl of whipped cream–any would suffice.

Philomena bows her head, turning her attention to a new embroidery piece she is working on. A little blond Madonna with a large belly that presses against her blue garments. She, too, was a virgin. And yet she had given birth to a son.

Georgia tries to shut the zipper of her suitcase that for some reason refuses to close. And yet she had bought nothing. But suitcases are like that: they shut just fine when you're leaving but on the return trip, they refuse to close.

They are waiting for her in the car, outside the little hotel with the promising name where she had spent two nights. She approaches the window and observes the sweeping panorama that opens up before her: the valley scarred by illegal construction; a handful of warehouses belonging to the tuna canning facility; the olive trees; the vineyards; the orange groves. In the midst of it all, stands the ugly and lopsided school building. At this very moment the students are streaming out with their colorful backpacks, smoking and chattering and laughing. High above, to the left, is the cliff with the convent of cloistered nuns and the baronial palace.

Turning her gaze upward, she thinks she catches a glimpse of a small figure looking out one of the convent's windows. It could be Sister Philomena. But then again, it could also be the angel with the red hair.

---

24. Dacia Maraini, *La ragazza di via Maqueda* (Milan: Rizzoli, 2009), 7.

Splendor

Preface and translation by Adria Frizzi
The University of Texas at Austin

Theatre, an integral part of Dacia Maraini's literary production, often spills into her fiction, lending it a unique performative character in its use of space, tempo, and narrative voice. The dramatic, tripartite structure of this masterful short story mirrors, in some ways, the overall organizing principle of *La ragazza di via Maqueda*, the 2009 collection from which it is excerpted. The three sections in which *La ragazza di via Maqueda* is divided are named after three geographical areas—Sicily, Rome, and Abruzzo—which in turn are linked to three acts in the author's personal history as well as in the book's narrative project.

The dramatis personae in this piece are Splendor, an Eastern European child prostitute named after a movie theatre; her nameless client, a respectable businessman only identified by his initials (a practice typically employed in sex offense cases to protect a minor's privacy here ironically extended to the perpetrator instead); and the cynical shopkeeper who watches their dance play out without getting involved.

Their internal monologues alternate and intertwine, embroidering the edges of the tragedy that is about to unfold, shifting its focus from the consummation of the abuse to its wider moral and social implications across a dramatic arc that is delicate and grim at the same time.

An earlier version of this translation has appeared in *ELQ Magazine/Exile: The Literary Quarterly* 36.2 (October 2012).

Splendor[*]

Splendor is wearing heels, so high that her small feet wobble at each step. She looks like she's about to fall, but she doesn't. Her skinny legs are reminiscent of a sea bird skittering about on a rock closed in by waves. Her short skirt is edged with thin black fringes that rise and fall like pensive eyelashes. The leopard print blouse sheathing her slender waist slips off her scrawny, child-like shoulders. Splendor is twelve years old and has just arrived from an Eastern country she doesn't care to remember. At times an image insinuates itself into her thoughts, fast and cruel like a poisoned arrow: she sees her mother, barely over thirty, with a huge pregnant belly, lumbering along with a bucket of chicken feed in each hand. She watches her put down the buckets, raise her skirt, and pee standing with her legs spread apart, indifferent to the urine spattering her skinny ankles. Splendor chases away that loathsome image with a wave of her hand. She frowns. Her eyes narrow as she strains to glimpse another image: Raffaella Carrà, there she is, her favorite showgirl, the gorgeous Raffaella encased in a long, glittery black dress. If she concentrates, she can see her smiling. Is she really smiling at her? Her, little Splendor, named after a movie theatre, because of her father's great love for American films? Another loathsome image: a little man with a blotchy red face who steals the money his wife works so hard to put aside to go hole himself up in the Splendor Movie Theatre! The girl kicks at the air to chase away the image. It's Raffaella she wants to see, not the lying, stealing little man who became her father years later. Raffaella—as she calls her in her thoughts—raises her delicate hands and blows her a kiss that slips through her fingers and soars like a light, diaphanous butterfly, fluttering and coming to rest on her forehead. I've been kissed by Raffaella Carrà, she says to herself, and spins around for joy.

Now her stride in the towering stilettos becomes bolder and happier. She heads for Corso Vittorio, turns on Piazza della Cancelleria, walks part way down Via del Pellegrino, reaches Via dei Cappellari and immediately afterward comes to Via di Montoro. The small head with long blond hair is constantly rising to check the street numbers hidden by the trees' leafy branches. One, two, three, and so on until the end. The street is short. When she reaches the top, she begins counting again, backwards. She stops at a number carved in stone. It should be this one, even though it's barely legible. But wasn't it supposed to be a hairdresser's? She pulls out of her pocket

---

[*] Original title of the short story: Dacia Maraini, "Splendor," in *La ragazza di via Maqueda* (Milan: Rizzoli, 2009), 173-179.

a slip of paper with the street name and number. Yes, this is it. Balancing on her long flamingo legs, the child scratches her head with an almost comical gesture of bafflement.

An older man leaning against a door jamb smoking a cigar watches the girl. He smiles to himself when he sees the kid look around indecisively. He knows what she's looking for. Everyone, here in the neighborhood, knows what's behind that door in Via di Montoro. The constant coming and going of scantily clad young girls with lost expressions, of frightened men who before they poke their heads out, glance around, smooth their coats, sniff their hands for fear that some of the cheap perfume may have stuck to their skin, don't go unnoticed. The shopkeeper would like to stop her, grab her by the arm and shake her. But he knows it would be pointless. That little girl is determined and knows what she's about to do. What if she's one of the slaves the newspapers talk about? What if her passport was taken and she was savagely beaten and forced to sell herself? The man's hand rises slowly, runs through his hair, his nicotine-stained fingers scratch his head, just like he saw the girl do. He smiles to himself, amused. Let life flow, let things be, I'm neither a cop nor a priest!

G.F. looks at himself in the rearview mirror. He smiles at his reflection. He's still young, even though the years go by. Thirty-nine springs have passed already, but so what? He sticks his tongue out at himself mockingly. You're not old, you're over the hill! He laughs. It's not true, you're a kid, and kids like people their own age. He feels strong as a bull. His eyes sparkle, a blue only Andalusian ceramic can replicate. Azulejos. That's what his friends call him. Women have lost their heads over those bright, guileless eyes. "Go on, you're in top form!" he says, grabbing the black leather briefcase from the back seat, which immediately makes him look like a businessman. He steps out of the car, locks it with a click. He balances on the balls of his feet as he looks around. Via di Montoro isn't far. But he'll have to walk a little. It isn't easy to find parking at this time in the afternoon. Vicolo Sant'Eligio. That's right, he needs to remember where he parked his Volvo, the last time he spent half an hour scouring streets and alleys for it. He doesn't know this neighborhood well. He lives in Via Slataper. For years he asked himself who this Slataper guy was. Then one night when he couldn't sleep he looked it up on the web: "Scipio Slataper, born in Trieste in 1888, died in Podgora in 1915. Irredentist and socialist. He wrote *My Karst*, a masterpiece of lyrically evocative prose." Good memory, my friend, you should frequent history more! "He volunteered to join the Italian army in 1915, and was killed on mount Podgora." Amen. I'll have to tell my secretary to buy me this "lyrically evocative masterpiece." Meanwhile his feet are heading for Via della Barchetta and from there Via di Montoro. As he approaches the door his stomach contracts with a sharp pang. A raging emotion, deep like a knife stab. He hasn't felt anything like this since he was a kid. And all for a twelve-year-old girl! Who has the name of a movie theatre, that's what he was told: Odeon, Luxor, Ambassador, something like that. What idiocy! A girl barely older than his own daughter, who's ten. How can the idea of rape put wings to his feet? Wait, let's think about it a minute, this isn't rape, he couldn't do such a thing. If she doesn't want to, he won't force her. In any case if it's not him it will be someone else. That's what logic says. Plus, the girl is a consenting party. Point settled. Point understood. Which he won't compromise on. The deal is clear. It's not the violence that interests him, but the temptation, the seduction, the sweetness of a brand new body, an unfamiliar breath, a womb to discover and a darkness to bury himself in. Nothing more, he's sure of it, he knows himself, he won't force, he won't push, he'll be sweet as honey. The thrill of the forbidden? He ponders, or the excitement of a purchase in the dark, a human purchase, prohibited and therefore exhilarating? If I find out she was forced, bought and sold, I will free her, he tells himself as he quickens his pace. I'll be her liberator! No matter what it takes. I will act honorably! He feels his penis stirring in his pants. A mysterious, unpredictable object that sleeps when it should be awake and wakes when it should be sleeping. His mouth widens into a gleeful smile. Come on, my friend, we're almost there! But the appointment is at three o'clock and it's only two forty-five. Never show up early! You risk strange surprises. Meanwhile I'll stop and call Cetti so she doesn't worry. I'll tell her I need to turn my phone off for an important meeting with a client.

  The man hesitates, phone in hand. He enters the number in a hurry and realizes he's misdialed. Is it possible he can't remember his home number anymore? He looks around, flustered. The street is empty. Nobody but an old man leaning against the door jamb of an antique furniture shop, smoking a cigar. What if he's a cop? Then he remembers he's seen him before. He's the shop owner. Nothing unusual. He's just waiting for customers while enjoying the sun on a warm Roman afternoon.

  The man smoking the cigar watches the approaching customer out of the corner of his eye. A handsome man around forty, he notes. Gray suit, a shock of brown hair bouncing over his forehead. His eyes are blue, a blue that reminds him of the doll his sister used to abuse when she was a child. It had exactly the same beautiful cerulean eyes. When he thinks about Mina, he always sees her as a little girl, who knows why. He can't think about her as an adult, even though from a mischievous and impetuous teenager she grew into an ambitious young woman, married twice, traveled all over as a wine expert, developed a brain tumor and died in a matter of months. The pain is always there, sharp and distinct, between his ribs, and it turns his lips down in a bitter grimace. The cigar drops from his hand to the pavement and he slowly grinds it out under his foot, with relish, as if he were stamping out the pain he still feels when he thinks about the sister who died young.

Now the man with the blue eyes walks past him with a spring in his step, swinging the large black briefcase, as if he were going to a business meeting. But he knows where he's headed. You don't fool me, young man! He takes a better look up close and senses his excitement. It exudes from every pore of his youthful skin, smooth and tan. Does he go to a tanning salon before he comes to the apartment of the lady on the fourth floor to rape foreign girls? Don't play the moralist now; you cheated on your wife with a prostitute too. His shoe, busy stamping out the cigar butt, seems to sneer at him. What does it feel like to get your hands on a little girl like the one who went by earlier? The leopard print blouse, the towering heels, the short skirt with black fringes like giant eyelashes. Her eyes, he saw them well, are black with dark circles and make-up. The long, straight, blond hair keeps falling over her forehead and she brushes it back absent-mindedly. I don't rape girls! And he spits contemptuously on the cobblestones.

The young man with the cerulean eyes shoots him a disapproving glance: how can anyone spit on the sidewalk! What a lowlife! The two men's eyes meet. He knows, he knows everything, G.F. tells himself with a mix of fear and derision. His light-colored eyes ask for complicity. You smelled a rat too, old man! You know that the world is made of darkness more than light, you know that sexuality knows no rules. You know that I'm taking a risk, but I'm doing so with exhilaration and restraint. I'm not a brute, I know what I'm doing. I'm bringing to life, to self-awareness a young, unfledged body destined to debasement. I'm going to light her up like a Christmas candle. I won't burn her. That's all.

In an excited and buoyant state of mind, G.F. nods to the old man who's been keeping an eye on him from his shop. But the other turns his back, pretending not to notice his greeting. G.F. reaches the door in two swift strides. He leans forward to look at the names next to the intercom as if he'd never seen them before. He goes over each one carefully. Then, as if he had found the right one by chance, he presses the gilt metal button. The door pops open. The young man pushes the heavy door aside part way and slinks into the dark hall like a cat.

The shopkeeper hears a voice call out, "Is anyone here?" and turns. He sees a lady with freshly coiffed hair, who has walked into the shop without him noticing. "Coming!" he yells. But his thoughts are on the other side of the closed door in Via di Montoro. Where something that troubles him is taking place. Yet he can't feel outrage. Just pity. For the girl with the flamingo gait, with the long straight hair, with the lean hungry hips. But also for the young man who acquits himself in the same moment he accuses himself. An encounter like many others, an everyday encounter. A big city lives off this unseen trade. Forbidden by the law, yes. But one that no one cares about. And yet sadness floods his brain, parches his mouth. As if all the evil in the world came crashing down on his shoulders: Atlas bent beneath the weight of a round and monstrously heavy Earth. A sacrificial lamb. Stay the executioner's hand! a small, unfamiliar voice tells him from under his shirt. But he knows he won't. Why? The man realizes his hands are shaking as he shows the lady with the teased hair an elegant coffee table with a gleaming mother-of-pearl top.

The Little Girl and the Earthquake

Preface and translation by Lisa Tortolani
University of Connecticut

January 13, 2015 marked the 100th anniversary of the earthquake in Gioia dei Marsi, Italy. The town paid homage to the victims by hosting a daylong series of events titled "Voci del terremoto," which culminated in a theater performance written by Dacia Maraini and Ernesto Salemme. In the performance, as in the collection of stories that touch upon this same tragic event in her volume *La ragazza di via Maqueda*, Maraini gives a voice to those that were buried beneath the rubble.

In "The Girl and the Earthquake," an author imagines a tale connecting various people she finds in a set of old photographs during her stay in Gioia dei Marsi. As is typical of Maraini's stories, the experiences of the characters are based on actual occurrences, allowing readers to understand more deeply the historical, physical and psychological factors of the day. Through the hypothetical, though credible, story of Addolorata (whose name literally means "the pained one"), we are transported to the horrors that befell a sleeping Italian mountain town on that January morning in 1915.

Addolorata's history is not solely tragic, however. The last photograph that the author finds is of a young, fresh-faced American girl standing on the campus of a New England university. The future embodied by this student, Ingrid, as Addolorata's niece or daughter, translates Maraini's tale into a story of success: Addolorata not only survived the earthquake and its painful aftermath, but persevered so that her descendants could have the freedom to pursue their dreams.

The ponytailed young woman represents the hundreds of American-born children of Italian immigrants who left their native country in order to survive. After enduring years of poverty and hunger in Italy, Italians looked towards America as a beacon of hope, and many gave their children a life that was free of the suffering from which they escaped. The picture of Ingrid surrounded by collegiate buildings and rolling lawns is a stark contrast to the little corner of the shepherd's house where her ancestor lived for four days without food or water or certainty of survival.

I have tried to remain faithful to the text in my translation, and to the style of the author. As you will see, many sentences are written as in a stream of consciousness, reflecting Maraini's nostalgic tone. The magic of Maraini's tale lies in the subtle way that she conveys the emotion of a devastating day in 1915, and it is my hope that I was able to preserve some of that elegance in my transcription.

The following is a story of survival, perseverance, and legacy.

***

The Little Girl and the Earthquake[*]

Gioia dei Marsi, Italy. The writer holds in her hand a faded photograph. There one can see a little girl with light hair, walking on the train tracks with raised arms. She is wearing a pair of dark knee socks rolled around her ankles and a large pair of men's shoes which are full of holes, unlaced, that are clearly too big for her. All around her one can distinguish the ruins of a house destroyed by the earthquake.

"What are you doing?" the writer asks the little girl who vaguely reminds her of herself as a child.

The little girl does not respond. She continues to walk on those tracks, eyes closed, hands stretched out in front of her.

"And if the train arrives?"

The child gives a little jump. One of the shoes looks like it will slip off of her, and she is about to lose her equilibrium and fall forward, but then she regains her balance and continues to walk.

"Are you deaf?"

The little girl gently shakes her head. So she is able to hear her.

"Where is your mom?"

The little girl indicates with her foot a postcard that is lying on the ground. The writer picks it up: it is the picture of a thin, elegant woman wrapped in a black dress. By the way she confidently walks upon that rugged land, by the way she hugs a notebook and two books to her chest, it is clear that she is a teacher. How curious, on her feet she has a pair of shoes just like those that the little girl is wearing in the other photograph.

"I was sleeping" begins the woman with a heavy, raspy voice that contradicts her delicate, wispy figure. "Everyone was sleeping. The earthquake does not announce itself, it happens, it arrives, it takes you by the neck, as it happened to me…in the span of five seconds all of the beams of the

---

[*] Original title of the short story: Dacia Maraini, "La bambina e il terremoto," in *La ragazza di via Maqueda* (Milan: Rizzoli, 2009), 246-254.

roof fell on top of me, I was left a prisoner...I knocked, I called Giovanni, but no one heard me...I did not know what part of the house had collapsed, the houses then were built without a foundation, as the shepherds built them...a shepherd of that time did little to a house, he's always moving...in fact he was in Puglia while we were dying up here among the rocks...I was calling my daughter who was sleeping in the room next to mine, I didn't know if she was dead or alive...I was crying and bringing my hands to my face but then I would pull them away, stained with plaster...I was covered with plaster from my head to my feet, like a statue in construction...dry plaster, plaster dust that would get into the eyes, into the lungs...better not to cry I told myself, the tears quickly became muck and burned my cheeks, but they were coming out on their own and falling, like big white pellets on my hands, on my skirt. I had space to stretch out my legs, I stretched them...I heard screams from far away...suffocating screams, as if on the other side of a mountain of rubble...slowly in the dark I distinguished something: it was one hand, marble-like, near to my foot...but I wasn't sure...how was it possible to see the hand of a woman, white and closed? a fist full of plaster...but it was without an arm...I tried to move it with a foot...it was really a hand...suddenly it opened like a flower and plaster fell out in rivulets...the fingers moved as if it wanted to greet me. It was a hand detached from its body and it was asking for help. I realized that I was trembling from head to toe...I felt the knocking of my teeth that at first had seemed to me the drumming of rain on the roof...but no, it was my teeth, I understood that afterwards...nevertheless I thought about to whom that hand could belong...I tried to kick it, but it always came back, the floor was sloped like a roof...and I was locked in there, stuck in a niche, under a gigantic beam that was split in two, in a trap between two corners of wall that continued to rain down that plaster dust... they will find me, I would say, they will find me...now they are beginning to dig and they will find me...and so I yelled the names of neighbors: Mario! Gerardo! Concettina! Domenica! but no one was responding, I heard the yells of sirens, I heard dogs barking...and that hand that, even though it was dead, wanted to say something to me...and so every now and again it moved a finger, indicating to me the dark, on the other side of that tangle of iron and of planks and of rubble.

"Days and days passed, I cannot say how many...later they told me that it was only four...but to me it seemed forty...I didn't know when night or day was beginning...I understood that evening was falling from the silence that penetrated among those broken beams...in the morning on the other hand I heard the motors on the other side of the ruins...one afternoon, I think it was an afternoon, I felt a great bustling, and my whole corner moved: the floor began to slide downward, the hand rolled down keeping a finger raised to point out the darkness of the destroyed house. I thought that I would end up crushed and goodbye life...with the last of my strength, and from desperation, I began to scream with whatever voice I had left in my throat...but I had little voice left, my throat was dry, full of plaster and I had already called out a lot.

"I think I am dead. Then I found myself alive, but I wasn't able to open my eyes...someone was pulling me by my feet...from the movement and from the noise I understood that I was on a cart that was being pulled with the loud sound of wheels on rubble...next to me I had only corpses... they think I am dead, I thought, they are bringing me to be buried and I raised an arm to show them that I was still alive, but the
arm did not obey me...and the most incredible thing is that I glimpsed the hand, the white hand of the woman that pointed out the dark, that was raising itself from the dead bodies and was flying away, as if it were a big white butterfly...what did it want to tell me? that we were going to the place where perhaps a cruel God who had wanted to punish men for being men was waiting for us?"

The author opens her eyes in a bed that seems to be shaking. In her ears she still has the voice of...but what would the mother of the little girl be called, the teacher with the thin waist and the spiked shoes? And who is Giovanni? the father of the little girl?

Her hands go to the photographs that she found inside the drawer of an old desk. Yes, there is a photograph of a man that could be Giovanni. A shepherd, tall and dark, wrapped in a big black cloak. And on his head he is wearing a hat with a wide brim. Next to him a flock of sheep. But they are painted. The photographer drew them inside his studio, he wanted though to immortalize him among sheep. He seemed more like a bandit than a shepherd with that ugly hat on his head and that cloak that hides all of his youthful body.

And the little girl?

The little girl continues to walk on the railroad tracks, in silence. She is absorbed in secret and mysterious thoughts.

The writer goes to put down the photos in the bottom of the drawer. Of what concern to her is this unknown family that has been dead for almost a century?

But her fingers continue to grip those little squares of paper and her mind insists on posing questions for which it will not find answers.

What became of the little girl? And what of the mother?

Observing the images more closely, she focuses on one that she had not noticed before. It recalls a wedding scene. One can see a young woman that very much resembles the little girl of the tracks and a man with a mustached-face, and a haughty frown. Ok, probably the little girl was raised and got married. That's all. But there is also something that doesn't fit. In another photograph that is found just under that of the wedding one can see a little girl laid out on a catafalque. And looking more closely one can understand that it is the same girl that walks on the rails. She has a face as white as paper and her head and arms are bound. A stiff little mummy, of which one can distinguish only the motionless, serene face. There is no doubt that is it her. Therefore she died under the ruins of the earthquake.

And the mother? The photo of the wedding is of her and Giovanni. But next to it is another photo of the same bride with a different groom. The writer had believed that it was a copy of the first one. And instead, looking closely, she realizes that the man is another. On the day of the nuptials the second husband looks like a poor young man just out of the seminary. A long head, two inverted sideburns, a moustache that is barely visible, near-sided eyeglasses. How many husbands did this young teacher from the country have?

Slowly the writer realizes that she has entered into the story. Her curiosity as a narrator brought her to the middle of a sequence of events that, although difficult to reconstruct, or perhaps exactly because it is difficult to reconstruct, inspires her to do it.

She clears off the big worktable that is covered with paper. She lays out the photographs one at a time on the large wooden shelf. Here is Giovanni. But next to that photo, plainly, the other photo with a different groom. From what the photos say one can deduce that the young teacher with the thin waist married for a first time, maybe at 16 years old—in the photo she appears very young, it is true that the author had confused her for her daughter, that one that walks on the tracks. The mother and daughter very much resemble each other, but the little girl cannot be more than twelve years old, while the mother could be sixteen or seventeen.

Inspecting those little cards, on the front and back, she discovers a caption that she had not noticed: Nestore and Addolorata today man and wife. And the date is almost illegible, that she is barely able to decipher: Oct...19...Here, it is possible that the first husband left as a soldier and died in the war. Giovanni dies and Addolorata marries Nestore. At that time it was unthinkable, even if she were emancipated, that she would leave her husband and live with another. Anna Karenina and Madame Bovary teach what used to happen to adulteresses. And Abruzzo in the first years of the 1900s was not very different from France in the 1800s.

But here it is, another tiny photograph that shows a young man in uniform. He has neither sideburns nor a moustache but he could have shaved them. He has however the quiet, stunned look of the young man pictured during the wedding ceremony. It could not be anyone other than Giovanni, and he left to be a soldier. It is not certain that he died. But one can gather that from the facts.

The photograph of the two with Nestore's dedication "to my loved one Ratina" which would be the diminutive of Addolorata, Addoloratina seems decidedly older. One can understand from Addolorata's hair. That among other things, for as much as she maintained her skinny waist, she seems more mature, with a more noticeable bosom and cheeks which are a little rounder. She is no longer sixteen years old as in the picture of the first marriage. The mourning period for a woman of that time was rigid. Difficult to marry before a reasonable length of time.

Therefore Addolorata, the young teacher of the small mountain center of Gioia dei Marsi, married Giovanni the first time and Nestore the second time. He's not handsome the second husband, but he has a sweet and kind look.

Who knows what happened in those years between one marriage and another. The very young Addolorata was left a widow. Without children? If the little girl in the photo died under the earthquake, and she was twelve years old, she must be the daughter of the first husband and not the second.

Slowly the portrait composes itself. And the writer prepares herself to write the story of this family that was painfully touched by the sorrows of the First World War and of the earthquake of 1915.

But what happened after the death of the daughter? Did Addolorata and Nestore continue to live in peace?

Another photograph comes to help her. In a snapshot as big as a stamp, in black and white one can see Addolorata: a strange hat hides part of her face and she smiles at the photographer. Looking closely one understands that the photo is not taken in Abruzzo and not even in Italy. In the background one can distinguish two skyscrapers and the sign of a shop: *Bread and...* Therefore we are in an English-speaking country. The United States? Probably, in fact almost certainly yes, because the writer knows of a large community of people from Abruzzo that emigrated in 1915, following the destruction of the earthquake. They arrived in Boston by ship and remained in that area of North America.

Once she was invited by the community. She remembers a certain Caterina with shining eyes. Small and muscular, she spoke of relatives that escaped from Abruzzo after having lost their house, their animals and all of their work tools. They found themselves in extreme poverty, without the means to support themselves and they decided to leave. With the sheep there was not much extra but by selling the wool and the milk they had enough to build themselves a house and to eat every day. They also made delicious cheese that they would bring to the little town market. But after the earthquake every point of sale had been interrupted. The sheep were all dead and with what would they live on? At that time there was no tourism, poverty stung, hunger killed. They found out that in Boston there were families from Abruzzo that were helping those that arrived and were disposed to hard work and they left.

Caterina could be a niece of Addolorata who could have had other children from a third husband. But what of Nestore? Can we conclude that he did not want to depart for Boston? That the two of them separated? And the little girl? What was the name of the little girl of the tracks who died under the rubble? this is not written anywhere. Children are often without names. Hey, little girl! what is your name? The response is an incomprehensible whimpering. Perhaps she does not even know. The writer saw impromptu tombs in the cemetery after the horrible earthquake of 1915 that in one night made more than 33,000 corpses, for which the names of the parents were recorded, but not the children. "They are angels, angels do not have names" says the young teacher, slipping herself among those images.

But Addolorata who instead departed for Boston, after having lost her daughter in the earthquake and having seen her school in ruins and her village completely destroyed, what did she do? Did she remarry? Did she have other children? The communities, especially abroad, tended to encourage marriage, so as to reinforce the ethnicity that was threatened by the other larger and more aggressive ethnic groups.

Let's imagine that Addolorata married. Would she have had other children? Probably yes: it was difficult to imagine a marriage without children...and she was still young. Even if she had left a husband in Italy, the community encouraged motherhood, even if the cards were not all lined up. Italy was so far away and loved ones were so important for the continuity of the species.

It is strange that among the photos there is not one of Addolorata's new family. Except this one...the writer grips between her fingers a picture of a girl with a long ponytail and a vague smile just like Ingrid Bergman wore at that time. The background is an American college, its buildings from the 1930s, its lawns traversed by squirrels, its automobiles from the post-war period. Yes, this could be a niece of Addolorata, the one born in Boston and raised outside of the city in a small house such as Caterina's, in the primarily Italian neighborhood where the restaurants, the churches are still run by Abruzzese emigrants.

Let's imagine that her name is Ingrid. Many young mothers were fascinated by the figure of the magnificent actress who enchanted the world. And they gave her name to their daughters. A name that they would have regretted a few years later, when they learned from the gossip magazines that the beautiful and faithful Ingrid fell hopelessly in love with an Italian director of little moral prudence, that after having had children with her he would leave her for another wife, furthermore an Indian woman.

Yes, it is very probable that this young student with the long pony tail, with the bright smile was called Ingrid like Ingrid Bergman, that she was born in the little house in Boston where her parents lived: the young teacher Addolorata escaped from the earthquake after having been buried in her house, under a rafter, for four days and a young son of emigrants who she met in Boston, that likely worked in the Italian school where she was teaching the language of her country. Probable though not certain.

Ingrid has the pure white, healthy face of a young girl raised in a haven from the sorrows of the world. At times she had to hide her Italian origin, because the Italians had for a long time the reputation of a rough people, quick with their knives and intolerant of all laws. But now things are changed and she, although she knows only a few words of Italian or actually the dialect of her town, Gioia dei Marsi, wants to learn more of her mother tongue.

For this reason she enrolled herself in the summer Italian school, at Middlebury University, in Vermont. Where she met the writer who came from Rome to tell the secrets of Italian culture.

Marina Fell Down the Stairs

Preface and translation by Sharon Wood
University of Leicester

In "Marina è caduta per la scale," the first story from her 2012 collected volume *L'amore rubato*, Dacia Maraini addresses once more the question of violence against women and the institutional and social failure to prevent it. Marina Savina, a twenty year old woman who still looks like a skinny child, makes repeated visits to Accident and Emergency; despite her claims that she has 'fallen down the stairs', the nurse who sees to her, Giovanni Lenti, suspects that she has been beaten by her father. Realising both her age and that she is married, his suspicions shift to her husband. He alerts social services and the police. The young woman from social services tasked with visiting Marina's home (where there are in fact no stairs at all) is beguiled by Marina's smooth-talking husband who offers her chocolates and coffee, smiles at her kindly and persuades her that Marina is epileptic and that he loves her too much to keep her at home where she might be safer. Left alone with his wife, cowering on the balcony outside, he does not deliver the expected blows; rather, he caresses his young wife, recalls his own family history of violence and abuse, and promises that while he will never hit her again, he will not allow her to go to A&E but will tend to her himself with plasters and disinfectant.

This chilling story reveals *in nuce* Maraini's thinking on gender and domestic violence, a topic she has addressed repeatedly in novels, plays, talks and newspaper articles for many years, and which has only recently begun to be openly addressed in Italy with the moral panic about the *femminicidio*, a new word for a historical phenomenon. The reasons, if not justifications, which lie behind cycles of abuse are outlined in a few words towards the end of the story: as a child Marina's husband saw his father murder his mother, whom he suspected of having an affair, while Marina, orphaned at a young age, is brought up by an overly-strict and presumably unloving grandmother. Their mutual dependency with its violent outcomes is thus rooted in childhood trauma, doomed to repeat itself, and nurtured by indifference and neglect both personal and social. The husband is the only character in the story to remain unnamed, suggesting both his anonymity and his ubiquitous presence behind the facade of seemliness and social acceptability.

Maraini is harsh on the failings of social and public institutions to impact or even recognise systematic abuse. The bored policeman called by the hospital nurse reluctantly contacts Social Services, who send an inexperienced and naive worker who is easily, and willingly, fooled. Angela Toro fails to understand that domestic violence is meted out not by ogres and monsters living in a cave, but by seemingly normal, neat and charming men. Even when he speaks openly of men tying women to radiators in order to prevent them leaving the house, the innocent Angela does not see that this will in fact most probably be the next stage of Marina's suffering. If her name denotes otherwordly innocence, her surname is an ironic and oblique comment on an enfeebled response to a problem not even recognised or understood.

The one person who does appear to understand is the nurse, Giovanni Lenti, whose task it is to set Marina's broken arm and later stitch her wounds. He is simultaneously touched and irritated by the girl's silence, her lack of gratitude—after all, we might ask, what has she to be grateful for? Again, naming serves a purpose: the nurse is both the 'lens' of the story, and the one person who 'sees' and diagnoses a social and familial rather than physical condition. Yet he, too, is almost inured to the suffering which continues to pour through the swing doors to the A&E department, whiling away his spare time drinking bad coffee, complaining of the heat and dreaming of the Hawaii evoked in the music coming through his headphones. He is, nonetheless, the only person in the story to act, to take initiative and to understand what is happening to the young woman whose lacerations he sews up delicately and tenderly, if, finally, helplessly.

Maraini's story is written in the present tense, in a demotic, edgy prose which summons up characters almost theatrically: we see them, we hear them speak, and rarely do we have the privileged access to their thoughts that we might expect of classic realist fiction. Settings are summoned up like agitprop scenery, or perhaps Brecht's epic theatre—just enough for the reader to reach an intellectual as well as emotional understanding of the events unfolding. In an email, Maraini comments on the "scrittura rapida, sobria, ironica, che ho usato per mantenere le distanze da una materia così scottante" (January 20, 2013). The translation has sought to maintain the rhythm, linguistic level and pace of the original piece, to 'keep its distance' from voyeuristic sentiment in order to focus on a story destined to repeat itself, not unique but, tragically and horrifyingly, as everyday and commonplace as the language with which it is expressed.

Marina Fell Down the Stairs[*]

Giovanni Lenti, one of the nurses in A&E, is sitting on a stool, a polystyrene cup full of coffee in one hand. Clamped over his ears are a set of headphones giving out some sort of smooth, Eastern music, his favourite. It makes him think of those Gauguin paintings he saw in a recent exhibition. Women with bare feet, flowers in their hair, blue horses large on the horizon, palm trees with large, gently waving leaves which you imagine perfumed and soft to the touch.

It's not so bad today, for a change. Just one stroke all morning. Good. I might even go and get myself an ice cream, he thinks. But just then he sees the glass door swing open. A girl with prominent cheekbones and long brown hair walks towards him, a clearly broken arm dragging by her side.

Fun over, he says, moving towards her. What on earth has happened to her, though? Maybe she got knocked over by a lorry. She's covered in bruises and her arm is hanging lifelessly from her shoulder.

"She says she fell down the stairs" is the acid comment of Ada, the nurse. "Can you see to her?"

"What stairs?"

"How should I know? Won't open her mouth. Anyway nobody's asked her how she came to tumble down the stairs. A signature, documents, that's all we've got."

Giovanni Lenti the nurse looks at her closely. He's sure he's seen her before.

"Wasn't it you who came to A&E that other time with a couple of broken ribs and looking as though someone had tried to strangle you?"

Marina Savina—the name on her registration card—shakes her head stubbornly. But she can't meet the eye of the nurse who seems to be saying "Yes, it's you, I recognise you."

"What happened?" he asks, still looking at her intently.

"I fell down the stairs" the girl answers in a small voice, obstinate, distant, her eyes on the floor.

"You wouldn't look like this even if you had thrown yourself out of the window" he insists. "Who broke your arm?"

The girl doesn't answer.

The nurse hands her over to his colleague to get an X-ray. While that is happening he gets the splints and bandages for the plaster cast. Marina

---

[*] Original title of the short story: Dacia Maraini, "Marina è caduta per le scale," in *L'amore rubato* (Milan: Rizzoli, 2012), 8–24.

Savina is brave despite the pain. She grits her teeth and looks the other way when the nurse pulls her broken arm, when he wraps it in the wet plastered bandages, when he touches her nose which is dribbling blood, to see if there is anything broken there too.

"Your nose is fine" he says, his voice kind but irritated at the same time. He's seen far too many women turning up at A&E covered in bruises, claiming they have fallen down the stairs. "You should all try and come up with a new story" he comments, as he sees her to the door. He is touched by this skinny girl with her big eyes. But it's her silence that he finds most worrying. A silence that means complicity, fear, defensiveness, surrender maybe?

"How are you getting home now?" he asks concerned. But she doesn't answer. He watches her walk off down the busy street, her arm strapped to her body, her cheap, fake leather bag hanging from her free hand. She moves quickly, but slightly wooden, like a shy, proud child, thinks the nurse as he watches her disappear into the crowd.

A month has gone by and the nurse, Giovanni Lenti, is sitting near a window grumbling about the heat. Summer seems to have broken out all of a sudden, bringing with it a sultry, sweaty heat. He still has his headphones on and is listening to the same music from far off islands which reminds him of Gauguin's paintings. This morning there have been two car accidents with broken legs and a crushed pelvis, a stroke, two heart attacks and two cases of senile dementia.

"Not a breath of air" he says, watching the A&E door open then close softly with a feeble moan. And just as he tries to concentrate on the Hawaiian music, thinking about the freshness of a blue palm tree with its hanging yellow fruit bathed in dew, he sees a girl come in limping, her nose bleeding.

"Oh no," he thinks, recognising the girl with the broken arm from last month. Her arm isn't covered in plaster any more, just hangs a little limply at her side. But the girl is limping badly and her face is covered with scratches and bruises. Blood is pouring from her nose, and she is trying to stop it with a small blue handkerchief.

"Fallen down the stairs again?" he asks, his tone both petulant and aggressive.

A small smile twitches the girl's purple lips.

"Oh, finally, a laugh. Tell me the truth, your father hits you, doesn't he," he adds, taking her arm and leading her into the small treatment room. But she doesn't answer, enclosed as she is in angry, mute humiliation.

"Oh well, no matter, if you won't answer, that's your choice...Let me see..." With a timid movement the girl takes off her pink t-shirt and on her bare shoulder there are signs of a whip. Her neck is covered in bruises. With a mixture of pity and tenderness the nurse eyes her vest, colourless from being washed so many times, with two worn patches under the armpits.

"Who is doing this to you? You need to talk. You can't go on saying you've fallen down the stairs, that story's worn too thin. Why don't you speak?"

The girl looks up at him, scared and furious at the same time. As if she is telling him to shut up, to keep his nose out, that it's nothing to do with him.

The nurse Giovanni Lenti shrugs his shoulders, as if to say we've got a right one here. Then he takes her arm and leads her gently over to the window. He daren't tell her to take off her vest. She's got nothing on underneath. He moves the strap aside to look at one of the wounds on her shoulder. Then, patiently, he picks up some gauze with some tweezers, dips it into a rust-coloured liquid and brushes it over the lesion.

"But there's another one here, and here too, under your ear. What did he hit you with?" he asks her, knowing full well that he'll get no answer. "An animal, what an animal, you might not have the courage to speak out but this time I'm going to do it for you" says an indignant Giovanni Lenti who would rather be listening to his music with its soft waves than facing this taciturn, mulish young girl.

He looks at her small, clean, unreachable face. A line runs straight down her forehead, right between her eyes, from her forehead down to her nose, like a scar. It's the one sign of what she is going through. Apart from that her face is as smooth and impenetrable as a doll's.

The nurse looks at her. He is annoyed, but he admires her courage because the treatment is painful. Not a single moan escapes that small, tight-lipped mouth. He's finished cleaning the wounds now, and gets some plasters out of a metal drawer to cover them over.

"You're lucky, you don't need stitches. But you're covered in bruises. I'll give you some cream, here you are. Put it on at home this evening, too."

The closeness of her body makes him feel strangely tender. I want to protect her, he thinks. Like a daughter. Strange, that there is no smell of sweat or dirt coming off this ill-used body. She must be poor but clean, thinks the nurse Giovanni Lenti, as his nostrils pick up a slight scent of soap and mint.

"What's this then?" he says, lifting her hair off the back of her neck. Another wound that he hadn't spotted before.

"You need stitches here...wait...I'll make it go numb, but you'll still feel it a bit, ok? Can you manage that?"

The girl turns her head away and presses her lips together.

The nurse tries to be as gentle as possible but this stubborn girl makes him nervous. The needle won't go into the skin and he is sweating in the effort to hurt her as little as possible. She doesn't breathe. He feels his hands slippery inside the latex gloves. He has the impression the needle is alive and it slips out of his hand like a tiny snake with a devil inside it. He has to get another one. He takes off the gloves crossly, wipes his forehead with some gauze, runs his hands under the tap, puts on a fresh pair of gloves and starts stitching again while she sits motionless as a stone on the chair.

"Finished" he says at last, drying his damp forehead with his elbow. He notices that she is looking at him ironically, her eyes challenging. She's pale and tense, but there are sparks in her eyes.

"You can put your t-shirt back on" he says, washing his hands and face under the tap.

The girl stands up, puts on her t-shirt and heads for the door without a word.

"Not even a thank you?" he calls out after her.

And he see her turn around in the distance and make a ridiculous curtsey, like little girls to a bishop.

You're a funny one, aren't you thinks the nurse Giovanni Lenti. But as soon as she is out of sight he heads quickly over to check the patient list: Marina Savina, twenty one years old. Married. She's only about sixteen to look at, tiny, fragile, nothing to her.

If she's married it must be the husband he says to himself, and he picks up the phone. Somebody should go and check. "I'm phoning about a young woman who has been to this A&E department three times already, each time with wounds and injuries that suggest she has been beaten. I've found signs of a whipping too. No, they are not the injuries of someone who has fallen, they are the type of injuries consistent with someone who has been attacked. She even had bruises round her neck, the fingermarks of whoever was trying to strangle her. Last time she was here I had to put a broken arm in plaster. She claims she fell down the stairs. But that's what they all say."

The policeman's voice the other end of the line sounds bored. "I'll send someone round" he says, and hangs up before the nurse has time to say anything more.

Oh well, we'll see, thinks Giovanni Lenti as he heads quickly to the café over the road. He needs something to cheer him up. He's hungry too. Who knows, maybe a ham roll is in order.

The next day an anxious social worker turns up at the Savina household asking for Marina. A young man in blue shirt and red tie opens the front door and looks at her curiously.

"What is it you want?" he asks in a kind voice.

"My name is Angela Toro. I'm a social worker. I'm here because there's been a complaint."

"A complaint?"

"We were contacted by the A&E department where Mrs. Savina has been treated several times for injuries after being hit. She is your wife, isn't she?"

"Hit? Please, don't say things that you don't know. My wife suffers from epilepsy and she has a tendency to fall down, doesn't matter where she is. She's been seeing the doctor but, you know, she stopped taking the medication a few months ago now and she can't control the fits any more. But please come in, would you like a coffee?"

The young and inexperienced social worker looks around her, surprised. This doesn't look like the house of a monster, as she had imagined it would. It's clean, well-kept. Not big, but it has a small sitting room with mustard coloured fake leather armchairs. At the back you could see a tiny kitchen area behind some sort of curtain. Next to that you could see a bedroom, the door ajar. Everything looks in place. And the master of the house, the suspect husband, is sitting opposite her, polite, his suntanned hands resting on his knees, a winning and hospitable smile stretched over his young and handsome face.

"Mrs. Savina said she fell down the stairs, but I don't see any stairs here."

"Well of course, we're on the ground floor." The young man throws back his head and laughs as if he has just heard the most comical thing on the face of the earth.

"How did your wife come to break her arm?"

"I'd rather she stayed at home and only went out when I could go with her, but Marina can't stay still, she likes to go out on her own when I'm at work. She likes walking round the city. Then she gets a fit and falls. She might fall against something hard or sharp. Once she nearly got run over by a car. They brought her back here still unconscious. She'd fallen in the middle of the road, on a crossing, can you imagine that."

The young social worker, who had come to the door ready to do battle, is starting to wonder if she hasn't made a mistake. This young man, so nice and polite, his face so clear and sincere, can't be the woman-beater suspected by Giovanni Lenti. If Marina Savina really is an epileptic, it might even be the case that she has indeed fallen over and hurt herself on the street.

"But why didn't she tell them she has epilepsy? Every time she claims she's fallen down the stairs", insists Angela Toro, but she's not convinced, she just needs to go through the motions of her job.

Her gaze is drawn to the gentle face of the young man who is looking at her, his eyes smiling and almost affectionate. She sees his slender, tanned hands rising as if to defend himself from some offensive doubt, and his face goes serious with the look of a man who is sincerely hurt at the thought of being wrongly suspected.

"Marina is a wonderful wife and I am crazy about her. But she's as stubborn as a mule. She can't bear the thought of not being independent. She doesn't want anyone to stop her going out. And I won't stop her, even if it causes me no end of worry. Every time she comes back covered in plaster or bandages. But what am I supposed to do, tie her to the radiator? She's like somebody I went to school with, I can still remember her, Pinuccia Missirizzi[25] they called her that because she was always falling over then getting up again, like a puppet. Well, when her father had to go out he tied her to the radiator. To stop her going out, you see, so that she didn't hurt herself. But I'm not really wanting to go that far. I won't even lock her in the house. As long as she's careful! Don't you think?"

The handsome young man is so convincing that the anxious social worker Angela Toro feels almost guilty for having suspected him. For sure this Marina must be a stubborn woman. Why go out if she just falls over and hurts herself?

"Anyway, I don't see what all the fuss is about", he goes on smoothly. "We've been married four years and she's been to A&E what, twice, three times?"

"Three times, that's what Giovanni Lenti said, he's the nurse there."

"Well, three's not a lot if you think she goes out and walks several miles every day. She goes and comes back, she doesn't exactly fall over every day."

"Yes, you're right. I'll tell the nurse. And I'll tell the police, since they sent me here."

"Would you like some more coffee? I've got some really good chocolates here too, would you like to try one? Belgian chocolates, look, shaped like shells. The Belgians are really good at making chocolate look artistic. Please, take one, have one at least."

The timid Angela Toro pops a chocolate into her mouth and sees the man's eyes smiling at her, grateful, complicit almost. She can't help but smile at him and thank him for welcoming her into his home.

"Where is your wife just at the moment?" asks the social worker as she gets up to take her leave.

"Marina? I think she went out. As you see, I don't make her stay in. She's probably gone shopping. She loves going shopping. She's almost cleaned me out with all the stuff she buys" he adds with a laugh. The social worker Angela Toro hears a false note in his laugh, as if he was acting a part. But she suppresses the thought, which seems almost irreverent. A man so in love with his wife!

The man seems to be in a bit of a hurry now, even if he doesn't want her to notice. He obligingly goes with her to the door and waits as she gets into her small blue Seicento car which she parked at the street corner. He waves to her before going back inside and kicking the door shut.

"Nosey bloody idiot" he says as he opens the French window leading onto the tiny terrace and grabbing the arm of his wife, who is cowering on the ground. Marina knows what to expect and tries to protect herself, making herself as small as possible.

"You went to make a complaint against me, you fucking bitch!"

"It's not true, I didn't. It was the nurse."

"I'm epileptic. That's what you are supposed to say. How many times have I told you? But not you, anybody would think you were deaf. Why do you say you fall down the stairs when we don't even have any stairs?"

Marina grits her teeth, waiting for the blows that normally follow her husband's angry words. But he seems to think better of it this time. After spitting over the balcony, he goes up to her with open arms, a tender smile on his lips.

"Come here babe! You know I love you. You're everything to me. I won't hit you again, ever, I promise. In any case next time I'll look after you myself. I won't let you go to A&E. They're all crazy there. Crazy and nosey... It's simple, all we need is a bottle of disinfectant, some cotton pads, maybe a bit of gauze. Well, if we need it we can get some needle and thread too. I know what to do. Come here, my little girl, give me a hug. You and me, we're one and the same, you know? You love me and I love you. Nobody can come between us. Isn't that why I married you? We haven't got much money but what do we care! We've got enough to get by, haven't we? Hold me, darling, you're the only person in the world who has every cared anything about me. You know I lost my mother when I was seven. My father killed her, you know that, I've told you lots of times. Right in front of me. Cuckold, criminal, that's what he was. He was put away for a long time and then, I don't know, he just disappeared. I'm alone, you see, alone in the world. If you leave me what will happen to me? Promise me you'll stay with me forever, my love, promise me!"

Marina holds him to her and closes her eyes. She is alone, too. Her mother and father died in an accident when she was very young. She was brought up by a severe, unbending grandmother, who died a few years ago. She has no brothers or sisters, just a cousin, who she's not in touch with.

"I love you Marina" he says, his head on her breast. And he means it, Marina knows that. Even if love won't stop him thrashing her when he feels like it.

"Tell me you love me, tell me, Marina. I need to hear you say it. I promise I won't hurt you anymore. Never again. Never. I swear. Tell me you'll always be with me. Promise me!"

"I promise" Marina repeats, a little mechanically. And he kisses her so sweetly, so sweetly that once more Marina feels her heart melting. He's promised he'll never hit me again, he's promised she thinks, and I believe him, it's the last time I'll believe him, but I believe him....

And she surrenders to the tender kiss of her young, handsome, oh so loving husband.

---

25. "Missirizzi" in Italian means a roly-poly toy, round-bottomed doll, tilting doll, tumbler.

The Secret Bride

Preface and translation by Maria Morelli
University of Leicester

On the occasion of the presentation of her book *L'Amore Rubato* (*Stolen Love*, 2012), from which the short story that follows is taken, Maraini confirmed her role as that of a social commentator: "The writer is a witness who works with physical details, with tangible reality, that is, the human substance. For this reason s/he has to tell the truth, so that s/he can be an incentive to society."[26] Such a conceptualisation of the mission of the writer as one who propels change through observation and criticism has been a cornerstone of the author's production since its very inception. In line with her literary mission, in "The Secret Bride," Maraini breaks the silence around the age-old phenomenon of domestic violence, a crime made even worse when perpetuated, as in this case, against children.

Told in a harsh and sarcastic prose that, however, never falls prey to facile commiserations, the story is a realistic, timeless account of an ignominious abomination—the mutilation of the protagonist's body, left to the mercy of biology by ingrained mechanisms of patriarchal oppression and abuse. Stripped of its own pleasure, Giusi, "the secret bride" who gives the title to the story, becomes, to borrow Maraini's own words, "an empty body, ready to be filled with the untoward and ruinous pleasure of others" ("Corpo a corpo," 50).[26]

Marked by short sentences, which are mostly the transcript of the protagonist's inner thoughts, the bare and concise prose of "The Secret Bride" is a lucid account of what Giusi's young mind records, in a vain attempt to understand it. What emerges is the seductiveness of, and blind adherence to, the "ostile e affascinante mondo dei padri" ("hostile and fascinating world of the fathers," *Storia di Piera*, 10), a recurrent theme of autobiographical undertones in Maraini's production, which is here taken to its extreme consequences in a blurring of the boundaries between love and possession, devotion and self-enslavement.[27]

Works Cited

Maraini, Dacia. "Corpo a corpo." In *Un clandestino a bordo. Le donne: la maternità negata, il corpo sognato*, 37–94. Milan: Rizzoli, 1996.

———. *Storia di Piera*. Milan: Rizzoli, 1997. BUR Scrittori contemporanei.

———. *La nave per Kobe. Diari giapponesi di mia madre*. Milan: Rizzoli,

2003. Edizioni BUR La Scala.

------. *Bagheria*. Milan: Rizzoli, 2005. BUR Scrittori contemporanei.

------. *L'Amore rubato*. Milan: Rizzoli, 2012.

Staiti, Claudio. "Dacia Maraini, l'impegno civile e la scrittura: 'Credo nel cambiamento'." *Tempo stretto*. Last accessed 5/01/2014. http://www.tempostretto.it/news/intervista-dacia-maraini-impegno-civile-scrittura-credo-cambiamento.html.

***

The Secret Bride[*]

A photograph shows Giusi and Rosaria holding the veil of the bride, their young and pretty mother, Carmelina. They truly enjoyed being the bridesmaids that day in May in a church full of flowers, in front of a stuttering priest who repeated each word thirty times. The woman, who had lost her husband at the age of twenty-five, managed to raise two girls by herself and, finally, after so much hardship, had found a man who loved her and who wanted to marry her despite the girls, wasn't it a miracle? An educated and kind man; a refined musician. What more could she ask for?

Giorgio Politi is tall and elegant. He has brown hair falling over his spacious forehead: he is constantly bringing his hand to his head to push back the hair covering his eyes. He has a bashful, anxious look. His eyes, blue-green in colour, bewitched Carmelina when she first saw him.

His hands "are truly beautiful," she would say, gloating. His long fingers flew over the piano keys with a sweetness and elegance that left her in awe. The beautiful brunette from the deep South would never have thought that she would make a sophisticated pianist with a brown fringe and bright eyes fall for her, a man born in Milan, raised in Brescia in a Catholic school, and who was now performing in the Vatican concerts.

He insisted on marrying her, in spite of her two little girls to support. After some hesitation, due to her reserve rather than anything else, she accepted, certain she had won his heart. And so, on the wedding day, they asked the two girls to dress up in bridesmaid dresses, just like the movies.

---

[*] Original title of the short story: Dacia Maraini, "La sposa segreta," in *L'amore rubato* (Milan: Rizzoli, 2012), 115-147.

It was an exciting and amazing day for the two little sisters. The night before they had stayed up late with the groom, who wanted to be the one to dress their little bodies in white sparkling tulle. He braided fresh freesias onto the headbands holding back the girls' hair, pinned the tulle to their waists with makeshift mauve, shining belts and put little red shoes on their feet that peeped out from under the white tulle.

"Hey presto!" he finally said happily, taking the two girls by the hands and walking them to their mother. "The two bridesmaids are ready. The ceremony can now begin."

Carmelina gave them a kiss before putting on, in turn, the white long wedding dress. She did not tell her husband it was the dress from her first wedding. She had no money to buy a new one. The two girls did not know either that it was the dress their enchanting mother, with long, pitch-black hair, full lips and dimples in her cheeks was wearing when she married their father. She looked like her daughters' sister.

She got married the first time at eighteen to a cheerful and lively man who smoked like a chimney, who could dance tango and milonga and who loved pizza with tomato sauce. It had been a great love. There is still a picture of the four of them, the father, the mother and the two girls hugging each other sweetly, one summer at the seaside. He was going bald, but what did it matter? He was very affectionate with the girls and he knew how to "make them die laughing" as she used to say proudly. He was a wise man, a tireless worker, who nevertheless liked to go dancing with his young bride on Saturdays.

They took tango classes together and they were much applauded for their stage performances. Him, in a black suit and yellow moccasins; her, in a tight red jersey dress and high heels. They made a fine couple and everyone looked at them as the model family.

But after only eight years of being married, when the girls had started to go to school, lung cancer carried off the chain-smoker tango dancer and Carmelina was left alone with her two daughters.

That day, on her second wedding, when the priest asked the groom, Giorgio Politi, whether he wanted to take Carmelina Croci as his wife, he answered promptly with a resounding yes. Carmelina, on the other hand, was unable to articulate any sound. The whole church, including the girls, anxiously lay in wait for a yes that was not coming. The priest was looking at her, quizzically. Very pale, she painfully opened her eyes wide and after a very long silence that alarmed relatives and friends, she nodded slightly. But she was so overwhelmed that she could not speak.

After years of loneliness and sacrifices, she had found a man who was right for her: kind, educated, an artist, a cinema enthusiast, appreciated by experts for the refined and light touch of his hands on the piano keys. How could she be so lucky? Yet, some years later she would tell herself that maybe, on that day, in refusing to let that "yes" out, her body, her mouth, her throat, knew more than her heart did.

They had already decided where to place his piano, sacrificing the girls' study desk. But the two little sisters did not complain. To the children's eyes, too, this kind man with invariably neat hands flying rapidly and skillfully over the white and black keyboard, who pressed the foot pedal in excitement, nodding his head to the rhythm of the music causing his floppy long hair to bob up and down, was a pleasant surprise. They were also happy to see their mother laughing, after she had been irritable and whiny for such a long time. Being in love made her look young again, and whereas before she would constantly mention their late father as if he was watching over them from the netherworld, now she would often forget about them and go out with her new husband, leaving them alone and happy to have the house to themselves.

Flowers. There were many flowers at her second wedding. You can still see the pictures taken by a photographer friend who, in exchange for the service, brought along his wife, his mother-in-law and his cousins. Everyone stuffed themselves at the banquet following the ceremony, held in a hotel on the edge of town.

The groom, Giorgio, who everyone called Gigi, proved to be a good husband. He let his wife decide what to do and what not to do. He was nice to his stepdaughters, he would take them to the seaside when she was working on Sunday and sometimes he would even iron his shirts himself. They had a servant but she used to come only twice a week and she did not have the time to iron the shirts of the pianist, who wanted them always clean and fresh.

Sometimes Giorgio Politi would leave for one of his concerts. Concerts were mostly held in churches, because his protectors were a cardinal and a teacher from a catholic college who would come the house all dressed in black, and he raised his pinkie when he drank coffee, which made the two little girls giggle.

Giusi and Rosaria were very close. They were only one year apart and they looked like twins. They played together, went to school together, slept in the same room, in two separate beds. It was their stepfather who decorated their room, and papered it in pink, with Degas paintings on the walls showing dancers in tutus intent on doing their exercises.

Carmelina did not like living off her husband's money and kept her job as a secretary, which was becoming more and more important. Her boss, a highly respected electronic engineer, trusted only her and called on her all the time. Whenever he did, Carmelina had to drop everything else. But she did so willingly because she knew that she was becoming more and more indispensable in the office and, although slowly, her pay was going up.

One time Carmelina had to leave for Genoa with her new boss, and left her daughters at home with her new husband. It had never happened that she had to spend the night out and she was worried that it would annoy him to act like a father. "They can prepare their own food. Just wake them up every morning at seven for school, you need to do that because they tend to oversleep" she instructed her husband, "make sure that they take a shower. And make sure that they have with them all the books and notebooks they need. Is that ok my love? In any case, tomorrow I'm back, kiss kiss."

"Oh, I almost forgot" she added when she rang him back, "in the fridge you'll find cooked meals for two days. All you have to do is to pop them in the microwave for a few minutes, you know how to do that right?"

He followed his wife's instructions. He put the trays with the food that Carmelina had already prepared in the oven, and served it hot to the table. He made sure the girls went to school at the right time, that they had the books and notepads they needed with them. In other words he did all he had been asked to do by his wife, who was monitoring everything from afar. Or at least so she thought.

In the evening they ate popcorn from the nearby street market while watching the TV in the living room. Their stepfather asked the two girls to sit next to him. Then they played a tickle game. The two girls laughed and laughed munching popcorn and rolling over on the couch with this childlike man who was up for any kind of game.

At a certain point he said "Enough! Now it's bedtime, otherwise who is going to get up for school tomorrow eh, sweeties?" He took them to their room and closed the door with a resounding goodnight.

But then, around three, when the two sisters were already sleeping soundly, he crept into their room. He whispered something in Giusi's ear and she followed him, rubbing her eyes.

What had he told her? Giusi was struggling to remember. Something like "I feel awful, I had a bad dream and I feel like I'm dying. Can you stay with me for a while?"

She hugged him in a motherly manner, pressing her head into his chest. He was shaking, but after a while he seemed to have calmed down.

At that point, she made a move to go back to her bed, but he grabbed her with his claw-like hands and pulled her against him.

Instinctively, Giusi tried to wiggle out of his grasp, but a hand covered over her mouth and she felt the man's body getting heavier and heavier on hers.

The girl panicked. But she could not scream, because he was holding her mouth closed. In the darkness she kicked, thrashed about, but failed to free herself. The iron-hard hands of the pianist opened her, quartered her.

The violence only lasted a few minutes, but it seemed to her like an inexorable eternity. While he was hissing and moaning the ceiling crumbled over her, the floor opened up and her small body, torn to pieces, started to tumble into the void, down into a bottomless abyss.

She regained consciousness in the arms of the man who, in a kind and affectionate way, was now licking her face like a kitten and was lavishing fond words on her. "I love you" he whispered to her warmly. "I'll let you in on a terrible secret: I didn't marry your mother because I love her, but because I love you. I've never made love to her, believe me. I couldn't. You're my real bride, my real little bride. A secret, stunning, gorgeous bride. I'm going to give a precious ring to this little bride of mine. I'll give a diamond ring to Giusi-the-beautiful, Giusi-the-strong, Giusi-the-sweet. I know you like jewelry...I saw you the other day in front of the mirror trying on your mother's diamonds like a little lady...Today we've celebrated the secret wedding I was waiting for. And I know you were waiting for it too right, my love, right, my big little bride?"

Giusi was paralysed. Empty, torn apart, aching, she was asking herself weakly: had she really wanted her mother's husband for herself? Coming from him, a grown-up, it had to be true. But it was all so horrible and baffling that she could not wrap her head around it. She doubted herself, like children do when they trust adults unconditionally.

"I'm asking you just one thing, my love: don't tell anyone. Least of all your mother. Ours is a secret wedding. If you talk, I'll kill your mother and you don't want her to die, do you?"

Giusi was wondering why he would kill her mother, she couldn't understand. But she took his threat and his words as the words of a responsible adult. If he, a grown-up, wise and married man, said so, it had to be true. Yet, there were too many contradictions that unsettled her, although she did not dare answer back. This man frightened her.

He kept kissing her face flooded with tears. Then, seeing that she kept crying and closing her aching legs tightly, he went on in a persuasive voice "You're not a child, Giusi, you're a grown woman, age doesn't matter, you're a woman who needs a husband, not like your silly mother! Can't you see she hates you? If it was not for me taking your sides, she would have already sent you to a boarding school. It was me who put her off the idea. Trust me, your mother is a child, she doesn't understand a thing, she got married out of vanity, without getting that the true bride, my true bride is you, my love…Don't you like to think that we are husband and wife and that we have a great and wonderful secret together? Remember, if you talk, your mother will die. Would you want your mother to die?"

Of course she did not want her mother to die. That's why she was crying. Now he was not hurting her anymore, instead he was caressing her with so much sweetness that she felt a bit reassured.

"Where are you hurting my love? Where? Don't you know that these are the little pains of a bride? Don't you know that marriage starts with a little suffering, otherwise what kind of marriage would it be? If you knew how beautiful you are right now, flushed and in love…Because you love me too, don't you? We love each other, but in secret, remember, not a single word, not even to your sister, their lives would be at risk.

Giusi puzzled over those words that sounded oddly seductive and sweet. While her body was screaming with pain, her soul felt caressed and nurtured.

What did it matter if she was in pain, what did it matter if she was feeling sick? Surely, as he said, it was a way, difficult and painful, to enter adulthood. That night she had become a woman. He told her so while he was kissing her on the neck. A man could not lie. Maybe it was true that he had never made love to her mother, that she was his secret bride, that they could dream about a wonderful future together. She would have happily told her mother, but he said her mother would die and she could not risk it.

That's how it happened, and the scheming pianist had succeeded in turning Giusi into his accomplice. The girl did not enjoy sex with him, but she put up with it as the seal of a mutual agreement. He inundated her with expensive gifts and taught her how to lie.

"You have to say that it was your friends' mothers who gave them to you" he instructed her. "Never name names, be vague. Get your mother used to the idea that there are generous people who are spellbound by your charm, and who buy you gifts for the sake of it."

In exchange, the deceitful stepfather was asking for silence; and silence had become a difficult wall to break through.

Giusi kept the secret even with her sister and was bending over backwards for the latter not to take notice of the relationship that by this time tied her to their stepfather.

Rosaria was surprised at those precious gifts: a designer bag, a pair of leather gloves, a pearl necklace. But she always had a ready answer for it. And when her sister insisted, doubtful, she put her off with "you're young, Rosaria, you're still a baby, you can't understand..." and let her stew in her curiosity.

The time Giusi got home with a flaming red coat lined with fur, even Carmelina was speechless.

"Who bought you this?" she asked in a questioning tone.

"It's a second hand coat" she answered swiftly, "it's from the mother of Ludovica, a friend from school you don't know, mom. Since it was small on her, she gave it to me."

Giusi was trembling at the thought that Carmelina could ask around, call Ludovica's mother and check with her. But mothers, as everyone knows, are inattentive, and Carmelina contented herself with that answer. It did not even cross her mind that her twelve-year-old daughter could lie so blatantly. The lie was bought into, as were many other stories that she made up about the expensive gifts that the gracious pianist gave to his stepdaughter.

The relationship went on for almost two years. Then, one day, something happened that left Giusi dumbfounded. It had been a while that her stepfather had stopped wanting her, at night. But she had not made a big deal of it: she thought he was tired from rehearsals, recording studios and concerts. She did not mind, actually. After two years she still could not feel pleasure with him, but she considered herself, as he had assured her, his secret bride, and brides, adults said so, had to please their husbands.

In bed with him she did not feel anything, but she had got used to closing her eyes and thinking about something else. It was the smell of the man throwing himself on top of her, his body fired up with excitement that sickened her more than anything else. Yet, her little heart had developed an unforeseen feeling of love. She felt a sort of sensual compassion for this passionate man whom she perceived as more immature than herself. She knew that inside her unripe body he was seeking the night, blindly, like a mole digging down into the black and unknown earth in search of a safe shelter. She would have liked to just stroke his hair, and whisper affectionate words to him, she wanted to play with his nipples as she used to do with her mother's when she was a child.

One night she woke up around 3 a.m., she turned on the light and she saw that her sister was not in her bed. She called her but there was no answer. She might be in the bathroom, she told herself. Except that she was not in the bathroom. Where could she be at that time of night? She had even seen her slip into bed the night before.

At that moment a terrible suspicion assailed her. So she made her way barefoot towards her stepfather and mother's room. Just that day Carmelina had left on a business a trip.

She tried to open the door, but it was locked. She could not find the strength to scream as she would have wanted and went back to bed like a zombie. She was torn by the idea that her stepfather was doing to Rosaria what he had done to her. What hurt her so deeply? his betrayal? the certainty of deception? Did he not say that they were secret bride and bridegroom? was everything a lie? Her handsome stepfather was lying both to his wife and to his secret bride, and even to his secret bride's little sister? is it possible to have two brides, three, even?

She went to the bathroom to throw up. Nausea had taken over her unripe, yet already corrupted, body. Then she tucked herself into bed waiting for her sister to come back to ask her what was going on. In the meanwhile she was shaking, her teeth chattering in the grip of a sudden fever.

That night she could not sleep a wink. It was not until it was nearly dawn that she abandoned herself to a sort of painful numbness.

She woke up at 7 a.m. with a pang in her heart, and the first thing she did was to look over at her sister's bed. But it was still untouched. There was no sign of Rosaria. So she rushed to the kitchen where she found her, relaxed, making herself a coffee.

"Where were you last night?"

"I slept on the sofa. You were talking in your sleep and I couldn't sleep."

"And Gigi, where is he?"

"I don't know. I think he's gone out."

Giusi was full of doubt. Could it really be that Rosaria, who had always been her affectionate accomplice, was now hiding such a big secret?

Still, she had lied too. Why be surprised about silence? Hadn't they grown far apart by now?

That time she said nothing. It could be true that her sister had slept on the sofa and that he had left at dawn without saying where he was going. Unfortunately the night before she had not checked the living room. And her sister could be telling the truth.

And yet, her concerns didn't leave her. She would observe Rosaria and her stepfather and wonder whether they were sincere, as it seemed, or whether they were two very good actors playing by the script. It looked like they had nothing to hide. Yet, Giusi sensed it was not so.

At dinner one day she noticed a strange movement of hands underneath the tablecloth. Exactly like Giorgio used to do with her. How many times had they taken the risk and grabbed each other's hands while the others were eating, under the nose of her mother who, unaware, trusted him and called him "the good, new daddy?"

Lately, husband and wife had seen each other very little. Carmelina's job had become more demanding. She often happened to have to spend the night out. By then, as she had anticipated, she had become indispensable to her boss and he wanted her to follow him wherever he went. "Luckily, he's gay" she would say to appease her husband's suspicions. She didn't realise he was more than happy that she had to sleep out. On the other hand, though, Carmelina had brought home much more money, which she used to buy a bigger car and some fashionable clothes, for herself and her daughters.

The handsome pianist, too, happened to sleep out for his concerts. And so husband and wife had become very independent from one another. Nevertheless, when they were out together, they would hold each other's hand, and kiss in public. It mattered to him that public opinion considered them a happy couple in love, but most of all, he cared that Carmelina considered herself the lucky wife of a loving and affectionate husband.

One morning when he was about to leave for a concert, he absent-mindedly said to his wife: "What do you think if I take Rosaria to Arezzo with me for my concert? She likes music a lot. I think she's got talent. She already plays rather well. I think you should send her to music school."

That moment Giusi was sure she knew. Carmelina proved to be enthusiastic, as always when it came to suggestions coming from him. She looked at him fondly, pondering once again how much she owed him for his paternal attention towards her daughters.

Giusi went upstairs without saying a word. She found her stepfather revolting and her mother of a naiveté that bordered on idiocy. Peered out from the window, unseen, observing them while he got into the nice convertible car and held the door for little Rosaria who was wearing a short skirt and pink ballerina pumps. They left, looking happy. Now she was certain: the pianist had found another secret little bride.

That night, when her mother got back from work, tired and hungry, she sat next to her and confronted her.

"Mom, I have to tell you something."

"What's up, baby? You look so serious…"

"It's about your husband."

"What about him?"

"I wanted to tell you that he took me to bed."

"Bed? Whose bed?"

"Yours. His. Your bed."

"Don't talk nonsense, Giusi. You know he loves you like a father."

"How would you call a father who seduces the daughters of his beloved wife?"

"You are dreaming. He has always been affectionate with you. Maybe you've misunderstood. I know him well. He would never do anything like that. And he loves me, Giusi, he is my husband, we are always making love, what are you talking about?"

"And what if I tell you that right now he is taking Rosaria to bed too?"

"I don't want to listen to this rubbish anymore"

"He said I was his secret bride, Mom. He kept me quiet for two years with it. Now he has a new secret bride, and that is Rosaria. Mom, listen to me! Gigi is betraying both of us. And you're silly, in love and blind."

"I don't believe you, Giusi. You have a very strong imagination. You're always making up stories, I know you well, since you were a child, you're delusional…In fact, I think you're jealous of Rosaria and of the attention that Giorgio pays to her. Rosaria wants to be a pianist, you know, and he helps her learn."

And so, despite being a rational and honest woman, Carmelina did not want to believe her daughter. Perhaps, precisely because she was honest, she could not conceive of someone lying with such artful insolence. Was not her husband doting and kind with her? Were they not making love with the same passion as before? Did he not treat the "kids," as he used to call them, with paternal affection?

Giusi was desperate. What was she supposed to do? It hurt her that her little sister was going through all the pain, blackmailing, seduction and complicity that she herself had had to endure. And it finally became clear to her that the story of the secret bride was just an excuse to keep them quiet and do as he liked, behind their mother's back. It was not even true that their marriage was a farce, and that they did not make love. All horrible lies that he was spouting in order to deceive them.

One night, while she was listening to the great pianist practising on the keyboard in the living room with his usual sinuous grace, she had an idea. And she dashed out covering her ears. She no longer wanted to be seduced by that music, that voice, those sweet and lewd hands.

She went to an electronics shop and she bought a tiny recorder.

Then, at the first opportunity, one night that Carmelina was away on one of her business trips, she hid it behind the double bed and set it up so that it would start recording past midnight.

And so it went. That tiny recorder changed the life of the family. Carmelina listened, holding her breath, to the passionate words of her Gigi, his sighs, his gasps, and his repeating continuously: "You are my little bride, aren't you? You are my secret little bride, with your mother I've never made love, I swear, only with you, only with you, my love...But don't tell anyone, anyone. Otherwise, your mother will die. I will kill her like a rat. If you talk she dies, is that clear? You don't want your mother to die, do you?"

She heard Rosaria's sobs and then her silence.

"Next time we see each other I'll give you a golden ring" he went on, persuasively.

"It'll be our wedding ring. Do you understand my love? I love only you. You're the most beautiful, the sweetest, the most charming girl I've ever met. You're not a child, you're a woman, my woman, my one and only woman... But we have to keep our secret, remember that, even from your sister. It's a secret between you and me, remember, because a secret wedding is bigger and more beautiful."

Carmelina listened to all of this coming from the damned tape that Giusi put under her nose and sobbed in desperation.

"Now you believe me?" said Giusi wiping off her mother's tears.

Carmelina hugged her with such strength she thought she would crush her.

"I can't believe it but I have to."

That very morning mother and daughter went to the police station to report the husband and stepfather and took the little precious recording with them.

The handsome pianist ended up in prison, with the accusation of sexual assault on minors. To testify against him there were his wife, Carmelina, and one of her daughters, Giusi. The other one, Rosaria, did not want to press charges against him. She would some time later leave home and refuse to talk to her mother and sister again.

The pianist with butterfly-like hands on the other hand did not bat an eye when confronted with the major charge.

"I love women, I don't harm them" he said in his defence. "First I loved Carmelina, then Giusi and then Rosaria. I loved them with all my heart. It's not my fault if they've seduced me. They took my soul and tore it to pieces. I shouldn't have made Giusi jealous; this is the one mistake I've made. Women become dangerous when they are jealous. Think about Medea. She was capable of killing her sons to vindicate her betrayal. And Giusi acted just like Medea."

The judge listened to him attentively, with a seemingly consenting air. As soon as the pianist stopped talking, he told him wearily to return to his seat. Then, looking him in the eyes, he addressed him gently, yet peremptorily: "You certainly are a greatly talented artist, I've seen the articles that your lawyers have sent me." We know that you play in churches and that in your room you keep a photograph of a bishop with an inscription. Your lawyer didn't spare us any detail about your greatness and your connections. But you understand that all of this doesn't have anything to do with sexual violence, don't you...? Who told you that an artist has the right to behave as he likes, disrespecting the law? You took advantage of the two children your wife trustfully gave you custody of. The first one was ten years old when you raped her and blackmailed her calling her your secret wife and threatening her that you would kill her mother if she talked. Then, as soon as you got bored of the first one, you started to fool with the second one. Does this look like the behaviour of a father to you? Of a groom? Of an honest man?"

Two years later, when the great pianist was still in prison, Giusi died from an overdose. She had started to do heroin without her mother knowing. She had moved to a small flat with a young man who had taught her how to do drugs. Neither of them was working and they were living off Carmelina's money. In spite of this, they would still treat her with contempt and scorn.

Rosaria moved out too, to a commune, with some friends. She

seemed happy. She died her hair purple, wore trekking boots and tattered clothes. She had two dragons tattooed on her arms, a piano on her back and two flying birds on her neck.

Carmelina was left on her own. Her hair turned all white in just a few months. Now her hands shake when she drinks coffee. She is still working because she cannot do without it but she has become more and more listless and absent-minded, so much so that her boss does not take her with him on business trips anymore.

Sometimes she pays Rosaria a visit at the commune only to find her each time more ill-tempered and insufferable.

"What's the matter with you?"

"Nothing, mom, leave me alone."

"You're not doing drugs like Giusi, are you? I don't want you to end up like your sister."

"It's better if you shut up, mom. You made Giusi die. You sent Giorgio to prison. What do you want from me?"

"I only want you to be alright."

"You should have thought about that earlier."

Carmelina did not know what to do. She realised that her worries irritated her daughter, the only daughter she had left and whom she loved with pain and frustration.

One day she discussed it with a psychiatrist whom she eventually managed to send to the commune, under cover, to talk with Rosaria and try to talk some sense into her. Her daughter was looking so skinny, pale and unhappy lately!

The psychiatrist did go. She talked to Rosaria and reported that her daughter was not eating enough, was smoking like a chimney and was drinking, but not doing drugs. Just that, she added, she "makes an inconsiderate use of her body."

"What do you mean by inconsiderate?" Carmelina asked worried.

"It means that she doesn't care about her body and treats it like a dog, feeding it with leftovers, leaving it in the cold at night."

"What can I do for her?"

"She should get treated. But she wouldn't allow it. She is stubborn and happy with her unhappiness. Perhaps she will change with time. She should find a kind man, who truly loves her. The boys I saw in that house seemed to me even more lost and hopeless than she is."

"But how can I convince her to..."

"The psychiatrist looked at her with a sort of ironic compassion. "It's too late" it seemed like she wanted to say, "it's too late, Carmelina."

That night, on the way home, Carmelina looked at herself in the mirror and saw herself very old, with long and white hair falling over her shoulders. She thought of Giusi, the cheerful kid she used to be and what she had turned into: thin as a rake, with bruises on her arms. When she was dead she combed her hair for a long time and it seemed to her rough and prickly, like a wild bush. She thought of Rosaria and the cigarettes she left everywhere, half smoked. She thought of the psychiatrist's words: "She makes an inconsiderate use of her body." Two secret brides, two kids initiated into sex prematurely and who had become enemies of their own bodies. It was all her fault she thought, why had she not realised what was going on at home? Why had she not seen? Where did her maternal blindness come from? Could it be possible that love had made her so estranged from her own family? So detached from reality?

Her gloomy face seemed to command her from that mournful mirror that was moving like stagnant water. Yes, I'll do it, she said to herself. She took a razor; she shaved her head, like a Tibetan monk seeking expiation. She slipped her shoes off and went out, bold and barefoot, to face her new fate.

Some claim they have seen her by the river, begging. A delicate and still beautiful woman, her hair all white, her bare feet encrusted with mud, her hands worn out, her clothes ragged and torn.

---

26. See the interview with the author: "Dacia Maraini, l'impegno civile e la scrittura: 'Credo nel cambiamento'." *Tempo stretto*. Claudio Staiti. http://www.tempostretto.it/news/intervista-dacia-maraini-impegno-civile-scrittura-credo-cambiamento.html. Last accessed 5/01/2014. The translation is mine.
27. The term is Maraini's own coinage. It appeared for the first time in the introduction of *Storia di Piera* (1980), a published dialogue between the author and theatre actress Piera Degli Esposti. The allure of the world of the "padri" ("fathers") can be understood as the psychoanalytical (oedipal) metaphor of the little girl attracted to her father but also, in a broader frame, the seduction of patriarchy, whereby women, by yielding to it, become not only the victims but also the accomplices of a system which subjugates them. On the professed fascination of Maraini for her own father, Fosco, see *Bagheria* (Bagheria, 1993) and *La nave per Kobe. Diari giapponesi di mia madre* (*The Boat for Kobe. Japanese Diaries of my Mother*, 2001). As the title suggests, this latter book is based on the diaries of Maraini's mother, Topazia Alliata, written between 1938 and 1942. What emerges from these memories is the image of a strong-willed and affectionate woman, relentlessly recording details of Dacia and her two little sisters adjusting to their new life in Japan up until the family's interment in a concentration camp, due to the anti-fascist stances of Dacia's parents—which is when the narration stops. Most importantly, the book is an exploration of the author's relationship with her mother, and an attempt to rescue the maternal figure after it had been shadowed for so long, in her life as well as in her literary production, by the paternal presence. The translation is mine.

The Poet-Director and the Wonderful Soprano

Preface and translation by Adria Frizzi
The University of Texas at Austin*

Contrary to the classic film disclaimer, the characters and circumstances depicted in "The Poet-Director and the Wonderful Soprano" are not fictitious, but thinly disguised real persons and events. The four protagonists are Dacia Maraini herself, "the young writer;" Maria Callas, "the wonderful soprano;" Pierpaolo Pasolini, "the poet-director;" and Alberto Moravia, "the great fiction writer." All traveled to Africa together on two separate occasions in the late sixties. The story, however, is more than just a memoir, and quickly transports us beyond the limitations of time and place into the territory of narrative, transforming the record of experience into something larger, more universal and central to Maraini's themes through two portraits of women whose significance transcends their individual circumstances: the sophisticated, sensitive artist frustrated in her search for love in spite of world-wide acclaim; and the mother's ironclad determination and exclusive bond with her son.

The raw material of memory is decanted through the gaze of its witness and custodian, the aptly named "girl with pale blue eyes," who registers the splendors of a night at the opera in Paris, the landscapes and wild animals of Africa, the intensity of discoveries, moods, sensations, and difficulties. It's a steady but discreet gaze, one that doesn't gawk, as it records poignant details, images that abide in our memory: the Diva's white lace shirt against her perspiring skin, the poet-director's boots striking the red soil, the pink bow in his mother's hair, the prelate holding his skirts like a grand lady, elephants, termite nests, and crocodiles. An unflinching but compassionate gaze that momentarily dissolves in the presence of the primordial mystery of Africa and eventually brings the passage from experience to text full circle by returning the reader to words and literature through the voice of Antonio Machado.

---

* Original title of the short story: Dacia Maraini, "Il poeta-regista e la meravigliosa soprano," in *La ragazza di via Maqueda* (Milan: Rizzoli, 2009), 203-225.

The Poet-Director and the Wonderful Soprano

The vehicle speeds down the potholed road, its occupants bouncing in their seats. There are no windows or side panels. The air flows freely in and out of the open sides. The roof consists of a metal structure covered with a tarp. You have to hold on to the long iron rods that secure the seats to the floor to keep from falling out of the truck bed.

The landscape rolls past in a whirlwind of dust raised by the vehicle as it pushes ahead on the dirt road. Baobabs with their awkward bodies of porous wood, low acacia bushes with prickly thorns, piles of stones, wretched wind-twisted pines. A few wild goats. Blood-red paths merge and split apart in the middle of nowhere. Every now and then the road is interrupted by an ochre cupola rising more or less three feet out of the dry soil. They are termite nests. The driver brakes slightly, swerves onto the grass, crushing the pointy roots sticking out of the ground and giving the passengers a jolt.

And then he drives on. The grass is burnt and coated with dust. The driver, a young black man with a round smiling face, is wearing a short-sleeved flower shirt. At the end of his bare arms, his hands, encased in black felt gloves, glide indolently over the large steering wheel, hot from the scorching sun.

When the girl with pale blue eyes looks up and sees the white-clad creature desperately clutching the rods, she tells herself that she's traveling with the world's greatest singer and she doesn't even realize it. The matinée idol, "l'Admirable," as the French call her, is wearing hip hugging pants the color of snow and is perched stiffly on the uncomfortable dust-covered seat. The wide brim of a pure white cotton hat falls over her forehead, a pair of huge sunglasses hides half her face. The collar of her broderie anglaise shirt opens in two crisp winglets over her sweaty neck. The diva is right there, before her, her face tense as she strains not to inhale the dust whirling around inside the Land Rover, but there's nothing divine about her. She looks like a tired, frightened little girl. And yet she tries to put on a brave face. Every now and then she turns and casts an amorous glance at the poet-director. But her dark liquid eyes are laden with black clouds. Where the hell are we going in this most uncomfortable rattletrap? say those eyes accustomed to gazing at the soft seats of luxurious cars that glide over the pavement, barely touching it. But at the same time she doesn't want to seem difficult, and grits her teeth, putting up with the blinding dust and sun. She would like the director to notice her heroism and know she's doing it for him, for the tender feelings his young athlete's body stirs in her. I know it's not your fault, that crooked smile suggests, I know you love me, but don't you think these rides along potholed roads, in the middle of a muggy Africa full of leech-like mosquitoes are going too far?

They had all gone together to the Paris Opera to hear her sing: the poet-director, the great fiction writer and the girl with pale blue eyes. When they walked into the auditorium they felt out of place among the audience of ladies in evening gowns and gentlemen in tuxedos politely settling into the plush seats, while the orchestra rehearsed the final notes.

It was a gala night and the guests of honor were already seated in the royal box: the king and queen of Spain, together with the president of the French republic. At some point the orchestra stopped making discordant sounds and started to play the *Marseillaise*. Everyone stood up. And the king of Spain, turning to the audience, bowed slightly, an old-world bow. Flashing a modern smile, though, as if saying: we know we're playing a dead game, but here we are, alive and modern, and we don't mind performing. It's not a coincidence that we're paying homage to the *Marseillaise*, which in its time would have accompanied the chopping off of our sacred heads. But there you have it, kings are of little consequence these days. We are wandering symbols and as such I bow down, voilà, once more, as one of my ancestors would have done, with the utmost grace of a true sovereign.

Then the lights went out. Silence descended upon the packed auditorium. And the curtain, with its golden fringes, its embroidery in relief, opened with a rustle upon the interior of the church of Sant'Andrea della Valle in Rome. Great stone arches, a pale, twisted Christ hanging off to the side, a little Madonna with a beatific air wrapped in a stiff blue mantle, chubby angels perched on the columns, vases with seldom seen lilies. Puccini's music got in your nostrils, along with the scented smoke. But isn't the overture customarily played before the curtain rises? The originality of the direction consisted in this too: heightening an anticipation scented like lilies while the notes insisted on sculpting musical presentiments among the ghostly arches of a bare, empty church. Even though everyone knew what the story was about, it was as if it were told by a strolling minstrel to a clueless, innocent audience: once upon a time there was a Bonapartist rebel, escaped from the prison of Castel Sant'Angelo, whom a painter of madonnas, Cavaradossi, helped to hide from the pope's guards, themselves led by an intelligent and sadistic policeman named Scarpia.

When l'Admirable appeared on stage, in an ample lizard green gown, there was an open curtain applause. The girl with pale blue eyes sank into her seat, mentally isolating herself from the audience in order to listen undisturbed to that extraordinary voice. The poet-director sat next to her, quiet and concentrated as usual. The internationally-known writer drew close to whisper in her ear: "Did you see? She moves like a panther." And it was true. The soprano strode across the stage as if it were a jungle and she its queen and mistress. The powerful voice didn't seem to issue from that restless body, from that white throat, but from a deep volcano erupting incandescent lava among lapilli and fiery stones.

The girl with pale blue eyes breathlessly followed that body encased in green velvet as it ran from one side of the stage to the other, and it was both suffering and victorious, torn by fear and thirsty for revenge. A body that at times labored to keep up with the voice, which sought to escape, flying out of that female mouth into perverse and far-flung places, unknown to traditional musical experiences. It was the voice of a mighty dragon and at the same time of a goldfinch pleading for mercy.

The girl with pale blue eyes returned to the hotel drained by this all-consuming experience. She held in her memory Cavaradossi's screams while he was tortured in the prison of Castel Sant'Angelo. Scarpia's cruel voice trying to blackmail young Tosca and she, dripping honey, coming to terms with the torturer: I will lie with you if you don't execute my beloved painter. Scarpia agrees: I will pretend to execute him and set him free! he promises. All in exchange for the young female body he lusts after. The pact is sealed. Scarpia is sated. Tosca thinks she has saved her Cavaradossi. The time of the execution draws near. She reassures her love in secret: it will be just an act, you'll see, think about what comes after! But the execution is for real. And when Tosca discovers the deceit, she throws herself from the castle battlements.

After the performance they dined together at a *bistrot* near the theatre. She was there too, the panther, next to the poet-director who gazed at her fondly. "I have to go to Africa, will you come with me?" she heard him say in a sweet voice. "My friends are coming with us." The diva turned and looked at the girl with pale blue eyes. And it was as if she'd seen her for the first time. She gave her a courteous smile. But one of curiosity as well. Her voice, the voice of a woman in love, was thick, a little mannered. She told the director she was happy to go to Africa with them, she was happy to travel with her beau's friends. The poet-director placed a small nervous hand on l'Admirable's large white hand. Their eyes met and to the girl it seemed the gaze of a boundless promise of love.

The Land Rover has stopped in the middle of a field bristling with stubble and dead brush. Through the rising dust they glimpse large dark shapes. "Why, they're elephants!" l' Admirable says excitedly. Hers is the shrill, happy voice of a little girl discovering the universe. She raises her arm and points to a spot in the middle of the dust cloud, a gigantic shape slowly fanning its ears.

It was the first time the girl with pale blue eyes had seen an elephant outside a cage. Due to some strange nemesis, this time it was they, the humans, who were fenced in behind bars and nets. And there, before their eyes, a herd of wild elephants was peacefully grazing.

Strange, when seen up close. Ancient prehistoric animals with wrinkly, sagging skin, grey like the bark of an ancient, dying tree. Their eyes small and lively. The sensitive ears that open up like umbrellas and move to capture sounds and chase flies away. The short, pitiful tail hangs between the hind legs, which are so covered with folds and bags and wrinkles they look as if they were loose, worn pyjamas. The feet, firmly planted on the ground, move slowly and seem incapable of running. But they sure do! In fact, right at that moment the passengers see an elephant approaching the vehicle in long strides. The earth is shaking. The elephant seems to be heading straight toward them. L'Admirable shudders with fear. But when the animal gets close to the vehicle it stops, raises its long, steel-colored trunk, and trumpets like a cry of despair. Tired of these tourists taking pictures, laughing, gawking and circling around them like bothersome flies? No, it's actually looking for a calf that's wandered away.

In fact, here's a young elephant emerging from behind a pile of grey and silver stones, it approaches the mastodon-like female elephant with her curving tusks and grabs onto her tail with its trunk. The others, as if following an unspoken order, line up: the large females in front and the males behind. In the middle, the young animals clinging to the small tails of the ones in front of them. Like this, in a queue, they descend a slope to the wide red river flowing mightily and lazily downstream.

It's such a surprising and primordial vision that it leaves everyone speechless. No one dares speak a word. Even l'Admirable has forgotten the discomfort of the seat, the bouncing over potholes, the dust caked on her skin, the blinding sun, the mosquitoes sucking her blood, and is watching, captivated by these extraordinary African beasts who only ask to be left alone. Organized tourism hounds them, stares at them, hunts them down wherever they are and demands to witness their every movement with insufferable presumption.

Of course tourists don't kill as hunters used to do, but they are a nuisance, all right. The poor elephants watch them with a mixture of disinterest and impatience. They don't know that without these peeping toms of tourism even they would disappear. They don't know that tourism is the only guarantee for their survival.

The group of about thirty elephants, beautiful in their wild, archaic opaqueness, is now entering the water, sinking to their bellies and proceeding like this, in a line, the smallest protected by the largest, elegant, amiable, the memory of a fading world.

The girl with pale blue eyes would like to smile with joy at this vision of bygone days. But something keeps her from doing so. "Why are you crying?" L'Admirable asks her gently. "I'm not crying," the girl answers, not knowing that she's lying, as tears silently roll down her cheeks.

"Oh my god, a crocodile!" exclaims l'Admirable, who seems worried about the elephants now half-submerged in the waters of the river stretching majestically before them. The crocodile is lying in the sun with its mouth open. A little bird with long thin legs, feathers, and a long beak, balances itself like the captain of a ship on the crocodile's iron-colored scales and peers into the horizon inquisitively. From time to time it bends over to peck at something in those opaque muddy scales. If the crocodile shivers or stirs, the little white bird loses its footing for a moment, but it immediately recovers it by spreading its stout little wings half-way. And it glances around raising its small head with the impertinent tuft.

The elephants don't seem afraid of this large crocodile with its open jaws. "Why do they keep their mouth open?" asks l'Admirable.

"To cool off," replies the director lovingly.

"The better to eat you with, my dear," says the writer friend in a sing-song voice.

The elephants trudge past the nasty beast lying in wait in the sun without even looking at it. "Aren't they afraid?" "They could crush its head simply by stepping on it," insists the fiction writer and the Divine One laughs and claps her hands like a delighted child. Now the elephants are no longer in a line, they've scattered in the water: some plunge their trunks into the river and raise them to their mouths as if they were long greedy arms. Others suck up the muddy liquid and spray it over their hot heads. They know nothing about the world but they seem to comprehend everything: they know its deep wonder, they know about its eternal invitation to live, its mad rush toward a future of death. They even seem to guess that no one will touch them as long as the ruthless, greedy law of mass tourism is in force. And this is what makes them so fragile in spite of their might, their mass and their umbrella-like ears, able to pick up the most distant sounds.

One day, at the poet-director's home, in the outskirts of Rome, l'Admirable had met the mother of the man she loved. The elderly schoolteacher welcomed them with a gaudy pink bow in her neatly pulled back brown hair. She squeezed the singer's large soft hands between her small knotty hands. She smiled, revealing her immaculate teeth, the canines slightly stained with purple lipstick. She took them to the garden, walking in front of them in small timid steps. She had them sit on wicker chairs in the shade of a huge horse chestnut tree, went inside and came back out carrying a tray with ice tea and cumin cookies. They drank the tea and talked about this and that. Then the director asked his mother to stand next to the Divine One and he took their picture. Next to the great singer her son was in love with, the tiny, skinny schoolteacher looked like a dwarf. But she didn't seem to be embarrassed. Her eyes sparkled. Her smile was becoming increasingly liquid and sweet. Anything that brought joy to her surviving son—the other one had been killed in the war—gave her joy as well. Just as Don Ottavio wonderfully sings when speaking about Donna Anna, the only one to rebel against Don Giovanni's abuse, "Quel che a lei piace, vita mi rende/quel che a lei spiace, morte mi dà.—What pleases her/gives me life,/what displeases her/gives me death."

The poet-director was happy, but ill at ease. That's why he had asked the girl with pale blue eyes to be present at the encounter. Maybe he was afraid his beloved mother wouldn't like the great soprano. Or that she'd be jealous. Wasn't he constantly telling her that she was the only woman in his life? And now, where did this foreign woman with large hands, a stork's neck and a frog's mouth pop out of?

But the indomitable little schoolteacher from Friuli was too smart to show any jealousy, assuming she was capable of harboring such a devastating feeling in that tiny, frail breast of hers. She wanted the great soprano to feel at ease in their home, she wanted her son to be happy about this encounter, she wanted everything around them to smile. Besides, this had been her lifelong resolve: a resolve that had turned into docile submission to her increasingly unhappy and violent husband. A resolve that had led her to invest everything into her increasingly intimate and symbiotic relationship with her son. A resolve that made her speak like a timorous little girl: never raising her voice, marveling at everything, taking umbrage at any harsh word. Only playful angels flew about in her heavens, ready to shower fragrant petals upon mortals' bodies. Only smiles of joy and welcome were allowed in her house. Her love of sobriety and courtesy made her peep like a little bird, barely breathing for fear of being a nuisance, hardly eating in order not to give room to life's passions, which she viewed as extreme and inimical.

"Can it be true that there are men who love other men?" she said one day to the girl with pale blue eyes in a thin, scandalized voice. The girl looked at her in astonishment, without knowing what to answer. The great poet-director spoke openly about his homosexuality, he didn't keep it a secret from his friends. But with his mother he did. Probably because it would have been like taking her away from her world of flowers, angels and delicate sentiments. That's why he refused to talk about it, especially with the press. He didn't want the little schoolteacher to read, perhaps by accident, about his night escapades in search of boys. And she avoided magazines, gossip, even though she'd never tolerated prohibitions.

That day the great poet-director had brought home a woman, a diva, famous all over the world, whom he wanted his mother to meet. Many doubted the director's love for l'Admirable.

"What is he drawn to in her? Success, glory?" But they didn't know him. The girl with pale blue eyes had seen them together. She knew he was in love, just like any man can be with a woman. But what about his bizarre sexuality? His habit of boy-hunting at night? An inexplicable contradiction, his friends said. But love is more complicated and mysterious than one might think. There are passions born of enthusiasm, admiration, the desire to learn and revere. As Stendhal says: "A monarchist falls in love with princesses, a revolutionary with rebels." The brilliant poet-director, a lover of music and theatre, had fallen in love with an extraordinary performer. Even though his body still preferred boys? Yes, even so.

It was a sweet new love, almost adolescent-like, made of furtive kisses, small promises, hugs with closed eyes, chasing after each other, long phone chats. And above all a great deal of admiration: hers for his poetic art, his for her wonderful, amazing voice.

With time the famous poet-director had learned to divide himself with feline grace. By day, the woman of an intoxicating and impossible dream, at night the furious, exciting battles with elusive adolescent bodies that never really belonged to him.

The vehicle skids, sputters, and stops with a jerk. The great singer's hat flies away as she stretches out an arm with a theatrical gesture. The driver with the wide smiling face turns the ignition key. The engine fires up again, but the wheels only spin. He tries again. Now the wheels are spraying mud and the engine stalls with a scream that turns into wheezing and then an unsettling silence.

"*Il faut descendre*," the driver says, "You have to get out, too much weight, *il faut descendre*." His long black hands move with fabulous elegance. They can't be assertive, those fingers: he looks as if he were shooing flies away from the face of a loved one. "*Il faut descendre!*" he repeats, and he jumps out of his seat. He opens the door on the director's side, who plants his boots on the red earth with a hop.

"What about the crocodiles we just saw?" L'Admirable says hesitantly. She's taken off her sunglasses, which she is now holding in her gloved hand. Around her eyes, where the dust hasn't settled, two pale circles appear.

The director holds out his hand to help her out. She hesitatingly puts one foot on the metal running board and looks around. The view has been the same for hours: burnt earth, a few baobabs, thorny bushes, an ochre dirt path unrolling before the car for miles. There's no sign of life, houses, people. They've left the park behind, heading for a desert-like, inhospitable North.

The director and the girl with pale blue eyes get busy along with the fiction writer, attempting to push the front wheels out of the rut. The driver, in his cab, is showing signs of impatience. But clearly the three don't have the strength to move a Land Rover. Gesticulating angrily, the young man gets out of the driver's seat, takes a wicker mat from the trunk and sticks it under the front wheels. "*Prenez des pierres!*" he says. But there are no rocks. Only parched dirt, some shrubs covered with spines, the small red pyramids, termite nests, and nothing else.

The driver climbs back into the Land Rover and urges them to push. The girl, the poet-director and the fiction writer place their hands on the back and try to push while the wheels again spin in place. The mat flies away in shreds. The driver climbs out again, dejected, to take a close look at the wheels, which are digging deeper and deeper into the dirt. He clutches his head in his hands in despair.

"And now what?" says the writer, who's always having dramatic presentiments. "We'll be stuck here all night, we'll be eaten by animals. Remember the story about the island in Lake Victoria? The explorers were left alone on the cliffs, with tents and rifles, but when someone went back to get them, a month later, all they found were some gnawed bones. "

The director regards l'Admirable. But she doesn't seem scared. Suddenly the grotesque side of the situation becomes apparent and all four burst out laughing. "We need to find some rocks," the poet-director finally says. But no one dares to venture far from the Land Rover, knowing that the river nearby is infested with crocodiles that blend in with the ground and run like fiends if they see an appetizing prey. The driver gets all kinds of tools out of the trunk, but none are the right ones.

"We should have one of those iron ladders I've seen attached to the back of the buses that cross the desert."

"But he doesn't have one."

That's how they discover that the young driver recommended by the hotel hasn't anticipated anything: he's driving around without a shovel, without a ladder, maybe not even a spare tire. And who knows if he even has a driver's license.

They try again to get some traction under the wheels with broken branches and rolled up cardboard. But it's pointless. The rut gets deeper and deeper, and the car isn't budging. Indeed, at one point the engine stops altogether and silence descends upon the five as night begins to fall. It's getting dark. The few trees take on a bluish hue, the bushes turn into ungainly black shapes standing out against the horizon and the little dirt road slowly becomes indistinguishable from the sky. What to do?

"*Il faut monter. C'est dangereux.*" Says the driver, who climbs back into the cab, slamming the door. Then they see him drink from a small flat bottle filled with a yellow liquid. The director, who never loses his cool, opens the door, takes the bottle from him, and tells him that they need to keep trying. They can't stay there all night. The driver languidly complies. They start pushing again, the driver with them, while the girl with pale blue eyes sits behind the wheel. But the car is definitely stuck. And the engine seems dead.

L'Admirable is displaying unexpected courage. She's as hungry as everyone else, but she doesn't complain. She sits again on the plastic lined seat and looks around patiently. "Can crocodiles climb up a Land Rover?" The driver laughs. Then he explains that he's not afraid of crocodiles, but of *"les bandits"*, as he says widening his eyes. Apparently people armed with guns prowl around at night, assaulting anyone they find on their path, and they take everything— cameras, money, papers.

Night has fallen now. There's a great silence around them. Broken from time to time by the guttural cries of a bird of prey. In the silence you can also hear the crickets, chirping in that senseless way of theirs, and the mosquitoes, which are becoming insistent and intrusive. "Cover up, the most serious danger here is malaria, not bandits," says the fiction writer. But they have nothing except their light cotton windbreakers. The singer has even lost her hat, it blew away and they couldn't find it. The mosquitoes are getting hungrier by the minute. Their hissing is louder than the crickets'. From time to time the frogs' croaking reminds them that the river isn't far. They can also hear elephants trumpeting. But they sound far away, and in any case there's nothing to fear from elephants, says the driver, who insists on talking about bandits. Even the two flashlights they had in their pockets are about to die. They're getting dimmer and dimmer. Tired and hungry, they have given up pushing. All five of them are sitting in the vehicle trying to shoo away the mosquitoes with their hats. All they can do is wait for dawn. Or a passing car. Which seems improbable, since they've been here for three hours and not one car has gone by.

They've almost fallen asleep, the singer with her head leaning against the poet-director's shoulder, when they hear the distant sound of an engine approaching.

"Someone's coming!" cries l'Admirable.

The driver has fallen asleep and doesn't look like he wants to move. The director jumps out and stands in the middle of the small dirt road to make himself visible. He points the flashlight at the car approaching in a big cloud of dust. The headlights are a foot and a half off the ground. It can't be a truck. It looks like a car. Which is rapidly advancing. Its driver turns on the high beams. The car is getting closer and closer, but without slowing down. When it reaches them, it suddenly speeds up and flies past them with a loud honk that makes the director jump to the side. And then it drives off while they wave their arms, crying *"au secours!"*

"They were afraid!" says the fiction writer looking at them dejectedly.

But just as they begin to resign themselves to a night in the Land Rover, they hear the sound of an engine again and see the car coming towards them in reverse. It's a large champagne-colored Mercedes, low and sleek, but with four-wheel-drive. A black chauffeur gets out and starts speaking animatedly with their driver. Finally he bows and says *"Venez! Monsigneur vous attend."*

The girl approaches the luxurious Mercedes first. And to her surprise she finds, sitting composedly, a small and very elegant black prelate in a long purple habit, with a crimson hat and a huge solid gold ring on his finger.

"Je vous avais pris pour des bandits," he says, smiling. And immediately holds out his hand to be kissed. His clothes give off a faint scent of bergamot. *"Montez, montez,"* he urges them. He orders his chauffeur to load their luggage in the large trunk, then he makes room next to himself by removing some rolls of paper. He doesn't even get out to greet l'Admirable, and she plops down next to him, happily speaking French.

The director introduces them: "This is an Italian writer, read and admired all over the world, this is l'Admirable, a great soprano, queen of the New York and Paris stages, and then there's her, the young writer, and me, I'm a director scouting shooting locations for my next film. The monsignor greets them, smiling benevolently. He holds out his hand for each of them to kiss. But he doesn't appear to recognize any of their names. The Mercedes softly rolls off again and quickly heads south along small red dirt roads. The trip takes roughly half an hour. Then the Mercedes abruptly turns right, the dirt road miraculously turns into a paved road and suddenly they find themselves in front of a gate bristling with iron spikes. *"Nous sommes arrivés,"* says the monsignor, and finally gets out of the car holding his skirts up the way a grand lady would.

Immediately barefoot maids come running and bow to kiss the small knotty hand of their lord, with the gold ring on which a miniature Christ on the cross sticks out. Before the five, the doors of a newly built mission open, with baby pink walls, large freshly painted windows, a bell tower of sun-baked bricks, a spacious, bare church. The country house, made of bricks and surrounded by circular huts made of dried mud, here called adobe, has a thatched roof.

The bishop asks them if they've had supper. Upon their negative reply, he instructs the cook to prepare a meal for everyone. In the meantime he asks how many rooms they need. Four, the director replies. But there aren't four rooms available. Just two. "Two's fine," the director responds. "One for the men and one for the women," he adds quickly, ignoring the singer's offended look, who had already placed her suitcase next to his with a conspiratorial air.

And this is how the girl with pale blue eyes finds herself sharing a tiny room with a concrete floor, two iron cots and a chipped sink with the great diva of the white dusty clothes. "I'm sorry," she murmurs, understanding her disappointment. But the diva graciously replies: "We're in a house of priests, he didn't want to shock them." And now they take turns washing their faces and hands in the tiny sink sticking out of the freshly made wall.

Shortly afterward the bell rings. *"Le dîner est servi,"* a melodious voice calls out. And the five are led into a spacious dining room where, at a long table, already sit four elderly friars and a young secretary with a flushed face and languid eyes. The supper consists of plantain mash with meat sauce, small river fish fried in palm oil, and a papaya and ginger cake. The monsignor entertains them in excellent French. His manners are polished. He talks about Paris, Rome, the pope.

But his passion is soccer, he confesses after they drink a delicious coffee served in Limoges demitasses. And he rattles off the names of all the Roma players as if he knew them personally. The director looks at him astonished. The soprano asks him politely if he's ever been to the opera. "Foo!" he says, indolently raising his hand in a gesture of contempt and indifference. And he begins again to talk about a wingback particularly dear to him and all the games he's played in, against Juventus and against Milan, and how he is wont to score nonchalantly, dribbling past the players from the opposing team with quick, skillful moves. *"Il est africain,"* he says proudly, and he gets up to personally take out of a locked wooden cabinet a bottle of Pernod he pours in his guests' glasses along with the water that, he guarantees, was boiled for an hour and the ice, also made with sterilized water. "To Roma!" he toasts, raising his crystal glass.

After dinner the friars hurry back to their cells, barely taking leave of the guests. But the monsignor invites them to stay. And so they spend hours on an incense-scented terrace, drinking Pernod on ice, eating peanuts and fried banana balls. The bishop wants to know everything about the pope, the piazzas and the fountains of the eternal city, which he hasn't seen for a long time. But above all his questions revolve around the "magical Roma" and its strikers, its amazing goalie, its midfielders. The only one who responds is the poet-director, who's been playing soccer since he was a boy, but doesn't know much about Roma's latest exploits. His writer friend, who knows nothing about soccer, tries to ask him something about the famous "bandits with guns prowling around at night." But all he gets from him are generic reassurances: "No guns here," says the monsignor bringing the opalescent glass to his lips. *"Ici, la paix,"* he repeats, drinking and laughing. Only to start extolling the virtues of yet another striker's quick moves.

But the time has come to turn in. A barefoot maid shows them to their rooms, where their dusty bags sit. The girl notices that l'Admirable is scratching her arms, which are covered with red welts. She hands her a tube of cream for mosquito bites. And the other timidly thanks her. She doesn't seem happy to be sharing with her the small room with cement floor and enameled iron cots. She would have preferred to sleep with her love, but *"il faut avoir patience,"* she murmurs.

The girl with pale blue eyes goes to the bathroom and when she returns she finds her undressing with acrobatic gestures.

"I can go back out if you're embarrassed," she says.

"No, no, I'm almost done," l'Admirable replies. But she's really funny: it's hard to take off your bra with your shirt on and pull out your underpants with your legs wrapped in a long brick red sarong. She seems to be terrified of being seen naked. Even though the girl is politely sitting on her cot with her back turned.

Finally they're under the covers, beneath the mosquito net that opened over the bed as soon as they removed the bedspread. "An ingenious system," l'Admirable comments while she pulls up her long dark hair with both hands and ties it with a rubber band.

"I wonder if there are fleas, what do you think?"

"I don't think so, everything seems very clean."

"Well, good night."

"Good night."

But an hour later she hears her sighing loudly and turning incessantly.

"You can't sleep?"

"No. What time is it?"

"Three, I think."

"These mosquito bites...I hope I don't get malaria."

"They say this is not a malaria-prone area."

"Let's hope so."

More silence. But neither of them can sleep.

"Have you known him long?" L'Admirable asks, and the girl with pale blue eyes stares into the darkness before answering. She doesn't remember how long she's known him, the poet-director with the austere face, the sad innocent eyes: maybe five years, maybe six.

"Do you think he's capable of love?"

"I think so."

"I've never had any luck with men. I hope I didn't make another mistake. "

The girl with pale blue eyes is afraid to speak. If l'Admirable doesn't bring up his homosexuality, she won't say a word, she vows to herself.

"Are you asleep?"

"No."

"Why do you think a woman who's lucky in everything would be so unlucky in love?"

"I don't know. Maybe you're not looking for the right person."

"Maybe."

Silence.

And then: "Are you trying to tell me that I was wrong again?"

"I don't know. He's a generous man, capable of love. Maybe he's too attached to his mother."

"Too in love with her to fall in love with another woman?"

"Maybe."

"I thought about that too. But he's always talking to me about love."

Silence. What can she say?

"When a man talks so much about love it means he doesn't want to take you into his arms," muses the diva.

The girl with pale blue eyes would like to tell her that it's her impression as well. But she keeps quiet out of discretion. A little later she hears her breathing regularly, like someone who's slipped into sleep without realizing it.

The next morning, at the dining room table, while they gulp down black coffee with hot milk, they tell each other about their dreams. L'Admirable says she didn't get much sleep. But during the brief sleep intervals she walked among elephants. And she even saw a big beast that held out its foot to her like a dog would with its paw.

"I took the foot in my hand and shook it as if in greeting. Then I realized it was a man's hand, jet black, but very soft and giving off a slight smell of sun-baked grass. When I let it go it became an elephant foot again."

The director says he dreamed he was playing soccer with a group of black kids. Among them there was one with bright blue eyes, "He said he was Christ," he comments, smiling. "But he didn't want the others to know. So he hid his eyes behind a pair of dark glasses."

"What about you?" the director asks his writer friend.

"I dreamed I was in Africa with you all, that I had gotten stuck in the middle of a red dirt road, and that a monsignor came to our rescue in a champagne-colored Mercedes. And that he knew the names of all the Roma players by heart."

"What kind of dream is that?"

"You think that if you go to Mars or Jupiter you'll discover who knows what. But in my opinion you're going to find the same things that exist on Earth. Merely repeated. Even after you die, what do you expect will happen to you? You start all over again and that's that."

The girl with pale blue eyes is about to tell them about her disjointed, fragmented dream, when they are interrupted by a barefoot African woman with wide white skirts who bows and hands them a handwritten slip of paper.

"Use of two twin bed rooms for one night: $400.00. Dinner: $100.00. Transportation to the mission and back to the car accompanied by two assistants: $300.00. Thank you and have a good trip!"

L'Admirable bursts out laughing. And the poet-director and the writer friend follow. Worse than if they had stayed in a five star hotel! The director goes over the figures again, wide-eyed. And he reads them out loud. The writer says that explains the beautiful Mercedes. The girl with pale blue eyes takes out all the money she has left, and it's not much. Luckily there are the common funds. There are the travelers' checks they had put aside for the rest of the trip.

But where is monsignor?

"He's praying and is not to be disturbed."

One morning, a call comes from Paris while the girl with pale blue eyes is sitting at her work desk.

"Did you hear? L'Admirable died last night."

She hadn't heard from her in years. After the film she'd shot with the poet-director, which hadn't been very successful, they had lost touch. The poet-director often went to Paris to visit her, but she had already begun to pine after another lover. Who would turn out to be not much better than the others.

Then, suddenly and inexplicably, the poet-director had died. A man who was still young: his small strong body, accustomed to running, playing soccer, night chases, had been found by the sea shore, with his heart burst by the weight of a car wheel and his face, legs, and arms covered with wounds and blood. The young man who'd been with the poet-director that night immediately declared that he had killed him. But how come he didn't even have one drop of blood on his new suit? "Someone else was with you, admit it!" the investigators insisted. But he claimed that he was alone, that he had acted alone. And the police believed him. After all, when someone pleads guilty what else are you looking for? The case is closed, that's it.

The girl with pale blue eyes was so wounded by that unjust, premature death that she still hadn't gotten over it. Every night she dreamed he was coming back. After all, even his mother acted as if he were still alive: "He's in the garden writing," she'd say when she saw her, "do you want me to tell him you're here?" And she leaned out of the French windows to let him know. But then she'd draw back, tucking her little head in her shell like an old turtle. "He's too busy now. Wait a bit, tell me about your theatre. He'll be back soon."

So the girl with pale blue eyes would sit next to the old schoolteacher with her wrinkly face, her blank eyes, and tell her about the theatre with which she was involved in a neighborhood in the city's outskirts.

One night she dreamed he was calling to her. He told her: "Look, I came back: aren't you happy? And she hugged him, ecstatic. But while she held him she felt the cold of his bones pressing against her chest.

The radio is screaming the news of l'Admirable's death. The entire world is mourning her. They are constantly broadcasting her sublime voice soaring toward the heavens like a banner of grief.

The girl with pale blue eyes thinks back on their trip to Africa, the diva's childish joy before the elephants, the night spent together in the little room at the mission. Too bad she didn't go see her in Paris after the death of the poet-director. She would have listened to her talk about love and jewels. The clumsier she felt about the passions she aroused and she herself felt, the more she wrapped herself in precious jewels. But they had nothing to do with that stupid, vulgar thing that is money. For her a diamond ring was a magical object with which to open secret doors. A necklace was a chain with which to imprison time. A bracelet was a token of devotion. A pair of earrings, the dangling memory of passing hours that bring glory and oblivion.

Suddenly she remembers that on one occasion, when the poet-director was still alive, l'Admirable had sent her a little book. It was a poetry collection. Inside she had found her signature in her large, determined hand: "To the girl with pale blue eyes, from a far-away friend."

Now her hands are searching for the little poetry book on the shelves. She doesn't even remember who wrote those short poems. She remembers they were printed like small flowers on precious Japanese paper.

Here it is. Fortunately it has remained intact on the poetry shelf, a little dusty, but still whole and fresh.

She opens it and reads:

All love is fantasy;
Inventing the year, the day,
the hour and its melody.
It invents the lover, and even
the beloved. This proves nothing
against love, since the beloved
never existed anyway.[28]

In small print, the name of a famous Spanish poet, Antonio Machado.

---

28. Antonio Machado, *Border of a Dream: Selected Poems*, trans. Willis Barnstone (Port Townsend, WA: Copper Canyon Press, 2004).

A Woman, a Man, a Donkey

Translated by Michelangelo La Luna and ReenMary Varkey
University of Rhode Island*

The man and the girl had walked all night. Her swollen feet pushed against the bandages around her ankles. The man, who was older was leaning on a staff. They moved slowly toward the small city where they were heading, that by now was only a few miles away. Suddenly they heard the noise of a cart pulled by two horses lifting a cloud of reddish dust. They pulled back on the grassy edge of the road and waited for the cart to pass. The horses had foam on their mouths, a standing man whipped them pitilessly. The girl covered her mouth with both hands. The dust whirled and penetrated under their tunics' worn, shredded hems. "Are you tired," the man asked? She responded yes. Her swollen belly under her long tunic seemed to shake. The man placed a hand on her belly and smiled, content, "The baby is moving with energy. It will definitely be a boy!" The young woman nodded. "We have to get off the road," he added with a worried voice. "We are eating dust and have nothing to drink."

From far away they saw a donkey trotting along the dusty road, and an old man with long, thin legs on top. A swarm of flies covered the head of the poor donkey, which seemed even thinner and older than his owner. "Do you have a bit of water for my wife who is pregnant and has a mouth full of dust?" asked the man when the old man reached them. The farmer stopped the animal with a click of his tongue. The donkey was more than content for this unexpected break. He began to shake his head and his long, gray tail to shoo away the flies.

The Birth

The old man looked at the young woman with the swollen belly breathing badly; he saw the blue, dusty veil that covered her sweaty hair; he observed the man leaning on the long, knotty staff. She is a little girl, he thought, she is barely sixteen. He felt pity. He climbed off the donkey and offered her his place. She shook her head. It did not seem fair to her to

---

* Original title of the short story: Dacia Maraini. "'Lo chiameremo Gesù.' E da allora il mondo cambiò," in *Il Messaggero*, December 24, 2015: 1 and 21.

take the place of that old man who looked as though he could hardly stand. And then, how would she mount the donkey without falling? Besides, she was embarrassed to show the calloused, muddy heels under her tunic. She thanked him, she got closer to the donkey and started to pet its mouth. The flies swarmed gluttonously on her hand. But she did not show that she was annoyed by them. With her open hands she tried to catch the insects that were whirling around the animal's stocky mouth. But the old man insisted. And finally, with the help of her husband, the woman mounted the donkey and the three of them thus proceeded toward the small city of pink rocks that was waiting for them beyond the hills.

But while riding under the hot sun, surrounded by a swarm of flies growing more and more dense, the woman became pale and began to shake, doubling over. "What is it?" asked the man with concern. "The baby..." she murmured, bowing her head. The pangs in her womb had become increasingly strong and she felt a warm liquid trickle down her legs. The old man stopped the donkey and helped her down. He looked around, searching for a shelter.

"There is a cave over there," he said, pointing toward the small, dry valley, beneath gray, rocky cliffs. "Let's go, I'll help you, too, we cannot let her give birth in the middle of the road." The old man showed a surprising energy. With one hand he grabbed the donkey's rope, and with the other hand he hooked the girl's arm and began to pull both toward the cave, crossing a burnt clearing, sprinkled with thorny bushes. The man hurried to support his wife, grabbing her other arm. When they reached the cave, they saw that inside there was straw and in a corner the embers of a fire that someone had started and then abandoned. They sat on the straw and waited. The woman moaned in a low voice, with shyness and discretion, holding her big worker's hands open on her moving belly. Her husband supported her back. The old man said, "I'm going to look for a bit of water," and left the cave.

When he returned with a clay jug from a local farmer, he saw that the baby was already born, and his father was cleaning him with the veil of the young mother. The woman was lying on the straw—moaning with the voice of a little bird. The baby had such a clear skin that seemed to illuminate the cave with its splendor. He did not cry and did not shout like all newborn babies do, but he was already sitting on the ground, crossing his small legs, and looking around curiously. "He has eyes like two stars," said the old man, surprised by that creature just born and yet so ready to take on the world. He noted also that, while he was away to look for water, a white ox had entered the cave, with small, twisted horns, calmly eating the hay on which the newborn lay. Nearby, his emaciated, old, and exhausted donkey seemed content that in the shadows the flies had disappeared leaving his mouth free. He wasn't eating the hay, but stood silent and enchanted staring at the baby who, although toothless and bald, burst out laughing when the soft, warm snout of the ox tickled one of his cheeks.

The old man handed the pitcher to the young mother who drank with avidity, in large gulps, as if she had not touched water in months. She did not leave even a single drop for her husband who also suffered from thirst. When she realized she had drunk all the water, she was ashamed of her avidity and started to get up to go get more, but her legs wouldn't hold her and she went back to sit on the straw next to her child.

The Ox and the Donkey

The baby flailed in silence. The mother stooped down by him murmuring: "Come, so that I can give you milk." She pulled the newborn toward her and he let her caress him and pick him up. To make herself modest, the girl pulled out, from the opening of her dirty and wrinkled tunic, a small adolescent breast and gave it to her son who started to suck sweetly, closing his eyes in contentment. The father watched, worried that in that cave, naked as he was, he would be cold. For this, he took off his long tunic, tore a strip from the hem, and wrapped it around the little body of his son. It was the only moment when the baby, away from the delight of mother's milk, made a dull noise of opposition. He opened his eyes that were brown, liquid filled, and thoughtful and looked around, furrowing his eyebrows.

The young mother laughed at the worry, and his elderly father grabbed the baby's little white leg, brought it to his mouth and kissed him tenderly. The owner of the donkey, meanwhile, was patrolling the cave, to chase away snakes and mice. He started reinvigorating the fire with fresh wood and the cave was filled with a pungent smoke that made the young mother cough. The old man leaned over blowing with all his might, stopping only when he saw that the logs were starting to burn and the smoke had become thin and slipped out through the mouth of the cave. "I am leaving to work," he said falling to his knees for a moment to stare at the beautiful baby who shone like a lamp. "I have to take the donkey. But towards evening I will come back, so that we can reach the city with the woman seated and the newborn in her arms. Is there something you need?" The father responded with no and thanked him for the help he had given them. The other responded that at his age, it was a joy to see a new creature born.

"What will you name him?" He asked distractedly.

"Jesus," responded the man, "We are heading to Bethlehem."

Pier Paolo Pasolini and Maria Callas in Sabaudia, Italy (1970). Photo by Dacia Maraini.

Dacia Maraini in the United States of America.

IV

Poems

Translations by Genni Gunn
Novelist, poet, and translator

At Night*

At night mountains sleep
at night thoughts sleep
at night mouths sleep
at night hair sleeps
at night trees sleep
at night someone does not sleep...
at night those whose bones ache do not sleep
at night those who are lost do not sleep
at night those who write novels do not sleep
at night those who are lovesick do not sleep.
Who sleeps in a night without night of a
winter night?

* Original title of the poem: "La notte" (unpublished typescript).

Rome*

Roam roam roam
my pilgrim
you've tattered seven pairs of shoes
you've wept seven flasks of tears
roam roam roam
you've arrived in the city of woe
in this city of stone arches
in this city of glorious columns
roam roam roam
my pilgrim
what will you find at the end of your journey,
will you find a cross of climbing vines
will you find a sword corroded by rust
will you find a serpent of love
will you find a stone in the shape of bread
or bread in the shape of a stone?
Roam roam roam
my pilgrim
in the end in the end in the end
you'll find churches that spy
clocks that cry
bells that peal
and maybe maybe maybe a little compassion.

* Original title of the poem: "Roma" (unpublished typescript).

Like Sea Bass Underwater*

Sometimes at night
they come to visit
bring cloth shoes
they don't know how to walk
but oddly, very oddly:
they know how to sing,
their voices like sea bass
underwater,
like one who knows
the sound of stones
and of the new moon rising.
Sometimes at night
they come to visit
my sister with her butterfly neck
my father with his elephant smile
they don't ask me to respond
they don't ask me to go;
they sit on a stone
like in days of our great picnics
along the river Karisawa
and they sing without opening their mouths
like sea bass underwater.

* Original title of the poem: "Come spigole sott'acqua" (unpublished typescript).

If By Loving Too Much*

If by loving too much
we end up not loving at all
I say that
love is a bitter ruse
those eyes, half-mast
sail and sail
on waves of milk
my god, what hides
behind those blue eyelids
a thought of flight
a scheme of defiance
a decision to possess?
the ship with black sails
now turns westward
glides on waves of foam
among swirls of wind
and famished gulls
I know that on that bridge
I'll leave a shoe, a tooth
and a good part of me.

---

* Original title of the poem: "Se amando troppo," published in Dacia Maraini, *Viaggiando con passo di volpe: poesie 1983-1991* (Milan: Rizzoli, 1991), 37. Then published in Dacia Maraini, *Se amando troppo: poesie 1966-1998*, (Milan: Rizzoli, 1998), 13.

A Grass Theatre*

The bat flies low
perches breathless
on a dry well
the sycamore whips
its sick leaves
shrouds itself in resin drops
we pull the ropes
of a grass theatre
in this frail summer
of frayed edges
A summer theatre
in the belly of Villa Borghese
among rotting paper and other urban wonders
a tenacious Roman dream
a theatre of vegetables
with its brown and blue curtains
its earthen floor
trailed by yellow roots
like hardened elbows
our thoughts fly
toward the light of a confused logic
ready to become flesh and word
under the radiant play of spotlights,

* Title of the poem: "Un teatro di erbe." Revised version of "Il pipistrello vola basso," published in *Viaggiando con passo di volpe: poesie 1983-1991*, pp. 67-68; then in *Se amando troppo: poesie 1966-1998*, pp.102-103.

Villa Borghese is languid
toward seven in the evening
in a milk of dormant leaves
we hear the roar of a lion
behind the wall of the zoo
in the giant aviary
an imprisoned eagle flies furiously
we pull on the curtain
with its bordered edges
to enfold the scene
of our excessive artifices
a ladybird perches on a finger
light, enamelled, red and black
she resembles the back
of a teaspoon from Sèvre,
I swear she'll bring us luck!

In the Theatre*

The stage flies
and we cling to her sails
our ears filled with the mute music
of mermaids
we tell ourselves yes, when it's no,
we dance like trained fleas
on those planks that sway in the wind,
while eating salami sandwiches
and we kiss furiously,
it's all make-believe, right?
Never before this journey from yesterday to tomorrow
have we been filled with such turmoil and wounds,
our mouths full of mushrooms,
sprung between the chairs of the audience.
This desire to risk, my God, what is it?
The face of the bureaucrat smiles eternally
and I who wanted to sing the fury
of Antigone who buries her brothers
under the planks of the stage,
between January and March,
in a year of misdeeds and heavy losses
we are still there to part a crimson curtain
the scent of strawberries and mould
the bloody curtain of a bloodless theatre.
Everyone looks up and thinks it's daylight
but it's only the orange gel of a spotlight
that creates wispy shadows on the wooden floor.

---

* Title of the poem: "In teatro." Revised version of "Il palcoscenico vola," published in *Viaggiando con passo di volpe: poesie 1983-1991*, pp. 39-40; then in *Se amando troppo: poesie 1966-1998*, pp. 99-100.

But we chase away the dead
who turn madly
between the undulating curtains
dressed in blue jeans and vest
asking to be buried
cheerfully, while from above
a stagehand spits sunflower seeds.
Your electric sun doesn't burn
but strokes you with paper wings
it's always you beyond the scrim
beyond the light
beyond sensible words
and you laugh a full-throated joy
that renders your eyes bright and happy.

My Nights*

My nights
of bitter orange
were inhabited
by clumsy white whales
and flying serpents,
I recognized the swing
of milk-white curtains,
I planted a medlar tree
in the hollow of a dead dog
out sprung a sapling
twisted and angry
that I will call extinction
my nights
of sweet jasmine
how strong the wings
and liquid the memories
in that distant untamed island
where every morning
I awakened taller
and happier
my nights
of valerian
have become dark and shameless
and however much I lay
my head on feathered pillows
in upturned cities
inside strange rooms
I no longer dream of whales
my nights
of diazepam
tighten my shoulders
how will I summon the swallow
that carries my life in its beak?

---

* Original title of the poem: "Le mie notti," published in *Viaggiando con passo di volpe: poesie 1983-1991*, pp. 35-36; then in *Se amando troppo: poesie 1966-1998*, pp. 47-48.

War in a Plate*

War in a plate
but only for curious eyes:
a woman pulls a dead girl
by the arm
a house breaks to pieces
biscuit walls crumble
how often have we spoken of war
seated, peacefully
at either side of the table?
In the air, a car tumbles
above the salad bowl
a man screams staring at the void
in his bloody pant leg
a war overseas
surges on the gigantic screen
explodes, unravels, lacerates
our tainted thoughts,
what will we call
the ghosts of others' suffering, my god
if not offshoots, secretions
of an elated heart?
A war beyond the bread
consumed during dinner
fields burn
a school burns
a forest burns
the terraces of a luxury hotel burn
while we filet the fish
a boy laughs triumphantly
he has lost all his teeth,
a war overseas
and we who pry, wary
beyond a pearly glass

---

* Original title of the poem: "Guerra dentro un piatto," published in *Viaggiando con passo di volpe: poesie 1983-1991*, pp. 29-30; then in *Se amando troppo: poesie 1966-1998*, pp. 73-74.

drink beer
inside a violet evening
and listen, surprised
to the sound of a motor,
is the war outside or inside?
Will the plane explode
or slide through clouds?
A girl runs, barefoot
a child cries soundless
we are not the ones watching the war
it is spying on us
beyond the scratched split screen
another grenade
a helmet flies
the body of a soldier
soft and inert folds into itself
a war overseas
falls sweetly into our plate
and we eat it with the potatoes
or does it eat us
like many scattered children
ruining forever
the carnal experience of sorrow?

Sweet Deluge*

I have in mind a sweet deluge
a light sliding of stones
perhaps the chatty bird
that yesterday morning paused on a branch
under my window
will approach me whistling.
With nun's shoes
I will climb windy paths
among so many hanging dresses
so many floppy collars,
seated under a lamp, a man reads
his hands in his lap
the tobacco sign
casts a square light,
the cautious step of a cat
leaves wet triangles on asphalt
I await the return of a man
I loved a million years ago.

---

* Title of the poem: "Diluvio dolce." Revised version of "Ho in mente un diluvio dolce," published in *Viaggiando con passo di volpe: poesie 1983-1991*, p. 52; then in *Se amando troppo: poesie 1966-1998*, p. 95.

You Loved to See Her Run[*]

You loved to see her run and jump
I'm speaking of Bionda our dog
with bat ears
short paws, flat tummy
her tail wagging.
Bring her to the hospital
you said, your eyes bright
in a flash of cunning
a small deception against the rules
of nurses, of doctors,
hide her under your coat
and bring her here
I'd like to pet her
just once,
but you knew I couldn't
you knew the danger
for you without defense
the white dog
with the wagging tail
greeted you
from the street, her nose high
sniffing the dirty air
of a muddy Roman evening.

---

[*] Title of the poem: "Ti piaceva vederla correre e saltare," published in Dacia Maraini, *Notte di capod'anno in ospedale* (Rome: Ed. Lepisma, 2009) no. 12, 39-40. In the collection, which contains a "Prefazione" by Dante Maffia (pp. 9-14), each poem is indicated with a number and not with a title. For this reason, we will use the first line as a title of each poem, and indicate the number of it, followed by the page numbers.

Now that the window
is forever shut
the dog searches for you
and when she sees a blue car
she leans her paws
against the window
to see if inside
you're still seated there
with short breath
and the joyous smile of a child
awaiting her
and you whisper: Bionda, get in, let's go!

Hours of snow[*]

Hours of snow, the sky white
the house sealed
the fire devours oxygen
with blue and orange tongues
you left by that door
on a holiday,
little king without a crown
walker without shoes
musician without instrument,
you left by that window
leaving in our dresser
a blue-checked shirt
stretched with the imprints of your elbows
a pair of ski boots
size forty-three
a red and white shirt
whose threadbare collar holds your scent
one heavy woollen blue glove
and two short-sleeved T-shirts,
but where is your body now?
Where are your agile feet
of a walker, your long neck
your two beautiful hands nails bitten to the quick?
Where is your clever face
your mouth with thin lips?
Where are your brown eyes?
It snows behind the double glass
and the woods of the Marsica fill
with a magnificent flurry of wonder
wolves are ready to ambush
a loitering lamb
bears sleep within hidden caves
with your voice the mountain sings
a distant song of love.

---

[*] Title of the poem: "Nevica da ore," in *Notte di capod'anno in ospedale*, no. 2, pp. 19-20.

In January*

In January, a year ago,
you determined to leave us,
choosing a tomb
over a house,
but you didn't want to die
I know, you told me
in the dark, in a soft voice
while I squeezed your hand
to keep you here, with us
in the stupid world of the living,
your sleep tasted of anise
while serpents usurped your life
you were a hairless cherub
wanting to drink when it was prohibited
wanting to sing when it was banned
wanting to laugh when it was forbidden
and you wanted to leap from your bed
but already had marble feet
weak calves without wings
your head so heavy on the pillow
the dream of butterflies useless
your threadbare shoes
already gone
while you asked for a little water
and one more hour to live.

* Title of the poem: "A gennaio, un anno fa," in *Notte di capod'anno in ospedale*, no. 3, pp. 21-22.

At Night I Wake*

At night, I wake with your hand
on my shoulder, your breath at my neck
I rise, frightened
are you still here? I ask
but you do not respond
you have the small smile
of a child and you hide
behind my shoulder
behind the pillow
behind the curtains
you are mischievous as a cricket
and would like to bite my ear
like a puppy would
I have to remind you that you are dead
that you left without goodbyes
how cruel are the thoughts
of the living while the dead play
with their careless shadows
and snow falls gracefully
and water boils
and mandarins scent the room
I so want you to be here
but when I extend my hand
to grasp you, you escape
and recede into the pale stars
of a moonless night.

---

* Title of the poem: "Di notte mi sveglio con la tua mano," in *Notte di capod'anno in ospedale*, no. 4, pp. 23-24.

All Night a Dog*

All night a dog howled
but was it a dog?
or was it the voice of grief
along the thorns of thought?
while you shed your gloves
encrusted with ice
while you removed your shoes
covered in snow
while you shook off your hood
and your eyelids defied
night with feathered lashes
while you smiled
and gazed at friendly stars
you were alone and sighed
but you wanted to laugh, I know
that laughter like a light
shower of water
pushed you towards
the sleeping forest
of a Marsican winter.

* Title of the poem: "Tutta la notte ha pianto un cane," in *Notte di capod'anno in ospedale*, no. 5, pp. 25-26.

V

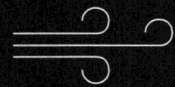

Bibliography

1. Writings by Dacia Maraini Featured in This Volume (1984-2013)*

Maraini, Dacia. *Woman at War*, translated by Mara Benetti and Elspeth Spottiswood. London: Lighthouse Books, in association with Writers and Readers Publishing Cooperative Society Ltd, 1984. [Pages selected: 151-163].

------. *Viaggiando con passo di volpe: poesie 1983-1991*. Milan: Rizzoli, 1991. [Selected poems: "Guerra dentro un piatto," 29-30; "Le mie notti," 35-36; "Se amando troppo," 37; "Il palcoscenico vola," 39-40; "Ho in mente un diluvio dolce," 52; "Il pipistrello vola basso," 67-68]

------. *L'età del malessere*. Turin: Einaudi, 1996. [Pages selected: 5-6, 9-24].

------. *Se amando troppo: poesie 1966-1998*. Milan: Rizzoli, 1998. [Selected poems: "Se amando troppo," 13; "Le mie notti," 47-48; "Guerra dentro un piatto," 73-74; "Ho in mente un diluvio dolce," 95; "Il palcoscenico vola," 99-100; "Il pipistrello vola basso," 102-103].

------. *Colomba*. Milan: Rizzoli, 2004. [Pages selected: 9-16].

------. *Notte di capod'anno in ospedale*. Rome: Lepisma, 2009. [Selected poems: 2. "Nevica da ore," 19-20; 3. "A gennaio, un anno fa," 21-22; 4. "Di notte mi sveglio con la tua mano," 23-24; 5. "Tutta la notte ha pianto un cane," 25-26; 12. "Ti piaceva vederla correre e saltare," 39-40].

------. *La ragazza di via Maqueda*. Milan: Rizzoli, 2009. [Selected short stories: "Tanto vale vivere," 83-87; "La sposa Serena," 136-138; "Una suora siciliana," 158-170; "Splendor," 173-179;; "La bambina e il terremoto," 246-254].

------. *Buio*. Rizzoli, 2012. BUR Scrittori contemporanei 8. [Selected short stories: "Viollca la bambina Albanese," 23-39; "Un numero sul braccio," 137-145].

------. *L'amore rubato*. Milan: Rizzoli, 2012. [Selected short stories: "Marina è caduta per le scale," 8-24; "La sposa segreta," 115-147].

------. *La grande festa*. Milan: Rizzoli, 2012. [Pages selected: 95-102, 115-120, 128-130, 148-209].

---

* This chronological list is an important tool to identify the specific editions of the books by Dacia Maraini used for this volume.

------. *La nave per Kobe. Diari giapponesi di mia madre*. Milan: Rizzoli, 2012. [Pages selected: 165-176].

------. "Splendor," translated by Adria Frizzi. *ELQ Magazine/Exile: The Literary Quarterly* 36.2 (October 2012): 108-112.

------. *Chiara di Assisi: Elogio della disobbedienza*. Milan: Rizzoli, 2013. [Pages selected: 9-16, 61-62, 126-131, 131-132, 136-141, 185-189, 249-250].

3. Books by Dacia Maraini (1962-2015)*

Maraini, Dacia. *La vacanza*. Milan: Lerici, 1962; Milan: Bompiani, 1976; Turin, Einaudi, 1998; Einaudi, 2005.

------. *L'età del malessere*. Turin: Einaudi, 1963; Einaudi, 1996.

------. *Crudeltà all'aria aperta*. Milan: Feltrinelli, 1966. Poesia 9.

------. *A memoria*. Milan: Bompiani, 1967.

------. *Mio marito: racconti*. Milan: Bompiani, 1968; Milan: Rizzoli, 1999.

------. , and Salvatore Samperi. *Cuore di mamma*. Milan: Forum, 1969.

------. *Il ricatto a teatro e altre commedie*. Turin: Einaudi, 1970. [Includes: *Recitare, La famiglia normale, Manifesto dal carcere*].

------. *Memorie di una ladra*. Milan: Rizzoli, 1972.

------. *Viva l'Italia*. Turin: Einaudi, 1973. [Includes: *La rosa serpentina indovina, Farsa popolare, Peppa e Carlino, Arruolamento, Farsa contadina, Crocifissa e Garibaldi*].

------. *E tu chi eri? Interviste sull'infanzia*. Milan: Bompiani, 1973; Milan: Rizzoli, 1998.

------. *Donne mie*. Turin: Einaudi, 1974.

---

* This chronological list includes the most important books written by Dacia Maraini from 1962 to 2015. For a more detailed bibliography, please see: Dacia Maraini. *Bibliografia delle opere e della critica (1953-2014). Una prima ricognizione*. Federica Depaolis and Walter Scancarello eds. (Pontedera, Pisa: Bibliografia e Informazione, 2015).

──────. *Fare teatro: materiali, testi, interviste.* Milan: Bompiani, 1974; Milan: Rizzoli, 2000.

──────. *Donna in guerra.* Turin: Einaudi, 1975.

──────. *La donna perfetta; seguito da Il cuore di una vergine.* Turin: Einaudi, 1975.

──────. *Don Juan.* Turin: Einaudi, 1976.

──────. *Mangiami pure.* Turin: Einaudi, 1978.

──────. , and Anne Denner. *Arte, il rituale dell'inquietudine: creativita artistica e disagio esistenziale: dipingere e amare di nuovo.* Melegnano: Ussl 57, 1991.

──────. *Dialogo di una prostituta con un suo cliente e altre commedie: con un dibattito sulla decisione di fare il testo e la preparazione dello spettacolo.* Padua: Mastrogiacomo-Images 70, 1978; Milan: Rizzoli, 2001. [The most recent edition includes: *Mela, Donna Lionora Giacobina, Stravaganza, Un treno, una notte*].

──────. , and Giustina Laurenzi. *Sor Juana.* Rome: Teatro La Maddalena, [1979?].

──────. , and Piera Degli Esposti. *Storia di Piera.* Milan: CDE, 1980; Milan: Rizzoli, 1997.

──────. , *Suor Juana.* In *Risposta a suor Filotea. Suor Juana Ines de la Cruz*, edited by Angelo Morino. Turin: La Rosa, 1980.

──────. *I sogni di Clitennestra e altre commedie.* Milan: Gruppo Editoriale Fabbri-Bompiani-ETAS, 1981. [Includes: *Due donne di provincia, Zena, Una casa di donne, Donna Lionora Giacubina, Maria Stuarda*].

──────. *Lettere a Marina.* Milan: Bompiani, 1981.

──────. *Dimenticato di dimenticare.* Turin: Einaudi, 1982.

──────. *Lezioni d'amore, e altre commedie.* Milan: Bompiani, 1982. [Includes: *Bianca Garofani, Fede o Della perversione matrimoniale, Felice Sciosciammocca, Mela, Reparto speciale antiterrorismo*].

──────. *Isolina: la donna tagliata a pezzi.* Milan: Mondadori, 1985.

──────. *Il bambino Alberto: interviste.* Milan: Bompiani, 1986.

──────. *Stravaganza.* Rome: Serarcangeli, 1987.

──────. *La bionda, la bruna e l'asino: con gli occhi di oggi sugli anni settanta e ottanta*. Milan: Rizzoli, 1987.

------. *Delitto*. Lungro (Cosenza): C. Marco, 1990.

------. *La lunga vita di Marianna Ucrìa*. Milan: Rizzoli, 1990.

------. *L'uomo tatuato*. Naples: A. Guida, 1990 [Included work: Menichella, Giada: *Pomeriggio*].

------. *Nuovi racconti campani*. Naples: Guida, 1990.

------. *Erzbeth Báthory; Il Geco; Norma '44*. Rome: Editori & Associati, 1991.

------. *Viaggiando con passo di volpe. Poesie 1983-1991*. Milan: Rizzoli, 1991.

------. *Occhi di Medusa: poesie*. Calcata: Edizione del Giano, 1992.

------. *Veronica meretrice e scrittora*. Milan: Bompiani, 1992; Milan: Rizzoli, 2001. BUR. [Includes: *La terza moglie di Mayer, Camille*].

------. *Bagheria*. Milan: Rizzoli, 1993, La Scala; Milan: CDE, 1993; Rizzoli, 1994, La Scala; Rizzoli, 1995, La Scala; Rizzoli, 1996, Superbur; Milan: RL Libri, 1997, SuperPocket; Rizzoli, 1999, BUR; Rizzoli, 2004, BUR Scrittori Contemporanei; Rizzoli, 2005, BUR Scrittori Contemporanei; Rizzoli, 2012, BUR Contemporanea; Rizzoli, 2014, BUR Contemporanea.

------. *Un clandestino a bordo: le donne, la maternità negata, il corpo sognato*. Rome: Gabriele e Mariateresa Benincasa, 1993. Milan: Rizzoli, 1996.

------. *Cercando Emma*. Milan: Rizzoli, 1993; Rizzoli, 1996. BUR.

------. *Mulino, Orlov e il gatto che si crede pantera*. Viterbo: Piccola Biblioteca Millelire, 1994.

------. *Voci*. Milan: Rizzoli, 1994.

------. *La ragazza con la treccia*. Rome: Viviani Editore, 1994; Zovencedo: Il Narratore Audiolibri, 2009 [Audio production with readings by Alessandra Bedino, Eleonora Calamita, Maria Grazia Mandtruzzato...*et al.*].

------. *La casa tra due palme*. Salerno: Edizioni Sottotraccia, 1995.

------. *Mulino, Orlov e Il gatto che si crede una pantera*. Rome: Stampa alternativa, 1995.

------. *Conversazione con Dacia Maraini: Il piacere di scrivere*. Omicron, 1995.

------. *Silvia*. Ravenna: Edizioni Del Girasole, 1995.

------. *Dolce per sé*. Milan: Rizzoli, 1997.

------. *Se amando troppo*. Milan: Rizzoli, 1998.

------. *Buio*. Milan: Rizzoli, 1999; Rizzoli, 2000. BUR.

------. *Amata scrittura. Laboratorio di analisi, letture, proposte, conversazioni*. Milan: Rizzoli, 2000.

------. *Maria Stuarda e altre commedie*. Milan: Rizzoli, 2001.

------. *Memorie di una cameriera e altre commedie*. Milan: Rizzoli, 2001.

------. *Storie di cani per una bambina*. Milan: Bompiani, 1996, 1998; Milan: Fabbri, 1999; Milan: Rizzoli, 2001.

------. *Sicilia ricordata*. Milan: Rizzoli, 2001.

------. *No alle leggi forza ladri*. Rome: Gruppo Editoriale L'Espresso, 2001.

------. *La pecora Dolly e altre storie per bambini*. Milan: Fabbri, 2001; Milan: Rizzoli, 2009.

------. *Berah di Kibawa: Un racconto con dodici finali*. Rome: Gremese, 2003.

------. , Anna Salvo, Finzi Silvia Vegetti, and Maddalena Tulanti. *Madri e figlie: Ieri e oggi*. Rome: GLF Editori Laterza, 2003.

------. *La nave per Kobe. Diari giapponesi di mia madre*. Milan: Rizzoli, 2003.

------. *Colomba*. Milan: Rizzoli, 2004.

------. , and Piera Degli Esposti. *Piera e gli assassini*. Milan: Rizzoli, 2004.

------. , and Gioconda Marinelli. *Dentro le parole: aforismi e pensieri*. Cava De' Tirreni (Salerno): Marlin, 2005.

------. *In volo*. Mantova: Corraini, 2005.

------. , and Paolo Di Paolo. *Ho sognato una stazione. Gli affetti, i valori, le passioni. Conversazione*. GLF Editori Laterza, 2005.

------. *Un sonno senza sogni. Gita in bicicletta a mongerbino*. Bagheria (Palermo): Drago, 2006.

------. , and Gioconda Marinelli. *Dacia Maraini in cucina: Sapori tra le righe*. Cava De' Tirreni (SA): Marlin, 2007.

------. *I giorni di Antigone*. Milan: Rizzoli, 2007.

------. *Passi affrettati*. Pescara: Ianieri, 2007; Rome: Giulio Perrone, 2015.

------. *Ragazze di Palermo*. Milan: Corriere Della Sera, 2007.

------. *Notte di capod'anno in ospedale*. Rome: Edizioni Lepisma, 2009.

------. *La ragazza di via Maqueda*. Milan: Rizzoli, 2009.

------. *Sulla mafia: piccole riflessioni personali*. Rome: Giulio Perrone Editore, 2009.

------. *Il treno dell'ultima notte*. Milan: Rizzoli, 2009.

------. *La seduzione dell'altrove*. Milan: Rizzoli, 2010.

------. *La grande festa*. Milan: Rizzoli, 2011.

------. , and Gabriele Marchesini. *In viaggio da Itaca*. Cesena (Forlì): Il Ponte Vecchio, 2011.

------. *Per Giulia*. Rome: Giulio Perrone, 2011.

------. *La notte dei giocattoli*. Latina: Casalini Libri, 2012.

------. *L'amore rubato*. Milan: Rizzoli, 2012.

------. *Il treno per Helsinki*. Milan: Rizzoli, 2012. BUR.

------. *Chiara di Assisi: Elogio della disobbedienza*. Milan: Rizzoli, 2013.

------. *Per proteggerti meglio, figlia mia*. Rome: Giulio Perrone, 2013.

------. *Gita a Viareggio*. Rome: Edizioni Fahrenheit 451, 2013.

------. , and Eugenio Murrali. *Il sogno del teatro: cronaca di una passione*. Milan: Rizzoli, 2013.

------. *Teresa la ladra*. Rome: Giulio Perrone, 2013.

------. , and Joseph Farrell. *La mia vita, le mie battaglie*. Pisa-Cagliari: Della Porta Editori, 2015.

------. *La bambina e il sognatore*. Milan: Rizzoli, 2015.

------. , *Bibliografia delle opere e della critica (1953-2014). Una prima ricognizione*, edited by Federica Depaolis and Walter Scancarello. Pontedera (Pisa): Bibliografia e Informazione, 2015.

Others (1968-2014)

Maraini, Dacia, and Michiko Nojiri, eds. *La protesta poetica del Giappone. Antologia di cent'anni di poesia giapponese*. Rome: Officina, 1968.

Maraini, Dacia. *Il sommacco: piccolo inventario dei teatri palermitani trovati e persi*. Palermo: Flaccovio, 1993.

Joseph Conrad: *Il compagno segreto*, translation and introduction by Dacia Maraini. Milan: Rizzoli, 1996.

Maraini Dacia, and Fosco Maraini. *Il gioco dell'universo*. Milan: Mondadori, 2007.

Maraini Fosco, and Topazia Alliata. *Love Holidays. Introduzione di Dacia Maraini; nota storica di Toni Maraini; acquisizione dei materiali a cura di Yoi Maraini*. Milan: Rizzoli, 2014.

4. Dacia Maraini's Books Translated into English (1963-2015)

Maraini, Dacia. *The Age of discontent*, translated by Frances Frenaye. London: Weidenfeld & Nicolson, [1963].

——. *The Age of Malaise*, translated by Frances Frenaye. New York: Grove, 1963.

——. *The Holiday*, translated by Stuart Hood. London: Weidenfeld and Nicholson, 1966; London: Panther Books, 1968.

——. *Memoirs of a Female Thief*, translated by Nina Rootes. London: Abelard-Schuman, 1973.

——. *Woman at War*, translated by Mara Benetti and Elspeth Spottiswood. London: Lighthouse Books, in association with Writers and Readers Publishing Cooperative Society Ltd, 1984; New York: Italica Press, 1988.

——. *Devour Me Too*, translated by Genni Gunn. Montreal: Guernica Editions, 1987.

——. *Letters to Marina*, translated by Dick Kitto and Elspeth Spottiswood. London: Camden Press, 1987.

——. *Traveling in the Gait of a Fox*. Poetry 1983-1991, translated by Genni

Gunn. Kingston, ON: Quarry, 1992.

------. *Isolina,* translated by Siân Williams. London: Peter Owen, 1993; London: Women's Press, 1995.

------. *Only Prostitutes Marry In May,* translated by Nicolette Kay and Tony Mitchell. Toronto: Guernica Editions, 1994. [Includes: *Dreams of Clytemnestra* and *Mary Stuart*]

------. *Bagheria,* translated by Dick Kitto and Elspeth Spottiswood. London: Peter Owen, 1994.

------. *Voices,* translated by Dick Kitto and Elspeth Spottiswood. London: Serpent's Tail, 1997.

------. *Searching for Emma: Gustave Flaubert and Madame Bovary,* translated by Vincent J. Bertolini. Chicago: University of Chicago Press, 1998.

------. *The Silent Duchess,* translated by Dick Kitto and Elspeth Spottiswood. New York: The Feminist Press at CUNY, 1998.

------. *The Train,* translated by Dick Kitto and Elspeth Spottiswood. London: Camden Press, 1989.

------. *Stowaway on Board,* translated by Giovanna Bellesia and Victoria Offredi Polletto. West Lafayette, IN: Bordighera Press, 2000.

------. *The Violin,* translated by Dick Kitto and Elspeth Spottiswood. London: Arcadia, 2001.

------. *Darkness,* translated by Martha King. South Royalton, Vt.: Steerforth Press, 2002.

------. *Love Letters,* translated by Thomas Simpson. Toronto: Guernica Editions, 2004.

------. *My Husband,* translated by Vera F. Golini. Waterloo, Ont.: Wilfrid Laurier University Press, 2004.

------. *Train to Budapest,* translated by Silvester Mazzarella. London: Arcadia Books, 2011.

------. *Extravagance and Three Other Plays,* translated by James R. Schwarten. Lanham, Maryland: John Cabot University Press/Co-Published with the Rowman & Littlefield Publishing Group, Inc., 2015. [Includes: *Stravaganza/Extravagance, Camille, Storia di Isabella di Morra raccontata da Benedetto Croce/The Story of Isabella di Morra as Told by Benedetto Croce, I digiuni di Catarina da Siena/The Fasting of Catherine of Siena*].

Others (1984-2012)

Maraini, Dacia. "My Hands" [short story] translated by By Martha King. *Literary Review* 27.3 (1984): 315-335.

------. "Reflections on the Logical and Illogical Bodies of My Sexual Compatriots." Introduction to *La bionda, la bruna, e l'asino*, translated by By Rodica Diaconescu-Blumenfeld, 21-38. In *The Pleasure of Writing: Critical Essays on Dacia Maraini*, 2000.

Cutrufelli, Maria Rosa, ed., and Vincent J. Bertolini, trans. *In the Forbidden City: An Anthology of Erotic Fiction by Italian Women*. Chicago, London: University of Chicago Press, 2000, [Includes: Maraini's short story: "The Zipper," 111-114].

Sartini Blum, Cinzia, and Lara Trubowitz, eds. *Contemporary Italian Women Poets: A Bilingual Anthology*. New York: Italica Press, 2001. [Includes: Maraini's poems: "Ho sognato un porco; L'uomo dalle gambe lunghe; Amore se questo è amore; Storie famigliari; Io sono due; Ho passato la notte; La tua faccia non ha nome; Limone, acqua calda e un grumo di sangue; Una piccola donna dagli occhi di medusa." 156-166].

Barr, Alan P., ed. *Modern Women Playwrights of Europe*. New York: Oxford University Press, 2001. [Includes: Maraini's play: "*Dialogue Between a Prostitute and Her Client*. (Italy 1978)," translated by Tony Mitchell, 289-303].

Maraini, Dacia. "Splendor," translated by Adria Frizzi. *ELQ Magazine/Exile: The Literary Quarterly* 36.2 (October 2012): 108-112.

------. "Two Stories. The Bride, Serena. Roman Dream," translated by Adria Frizzi. *ELQ Magazine/Exile: The Literary Quarterly* 39.2 (June 2015): 57-59.
Achilli, Tina. *Mariti e Regine: Il gioco violento delle coppie nel teatro di Luigi Pirandello e Dacia Maraini*. Bari: Progedit, 2007.

5. Books about Dacia Maraini and Her Writings

Antonucci, Giorgio. *Diario dal manicomio: ricordi e pensieri dall'agosto 1973 al settembre 1996*. Milan: Spirali, 2006.

Cruciata, Maria Antonietta. *Dacia Maraini*. Fiesole (Firenze): Cadmo, 2003.

De Miguel Y Canuto, Juan Carlos. *Scrittura civile: studi sull'opera di Dacia Maraini*. Rome: G. Perrone, 2010.

Diaconescu-Blumenfeld, Rodica, and Ada Testaferri. *The Pleasure of Writing: Critical Essays on Dacia Maraini*. West Lafayette, IN: Purdue University Press, 2000.

Gabriele, Tommasina. *Dacia Maraini's Narratives of Survival: (Re)Constructed*. Lanham, Maryland: Fairleigh Dickinson University Press, 2016.

Gaglianone, Paola. *Conversazione con Dacia Maraini. Il piacere di scrivere*. Rome: Nuova Omicron, 1995.

Marinelli, Gioconda, and Angela Matassa. *Dacia Maraini in scena*. Pescara: Ianieri, 2008.

Merry, Bruce. *Dacia Maraini and the Written Dream of Women in Modern Italian Literature*. Townsville, Australia: Dept. of Modern Languages, James Cook University of North Queensland, 1997.

------. *Dacia Maraini and Her Place in Contemporary Italian Literature*. Oxford: Berg, 1994.

Montini, Ileana. *Parlare con Dacia Maraini*. Verona: Bertani, 1977.

Panizza, Letizia, and Sharon Wood. *A History of Women's Writing*. Cambridge: Cambridge University Press, 2000.

Passione, Lina. *Sulle orme di Marianna Ucrìa*. Catania: CUECM, 1997.

Picchietti, Virginia. *Relational Spaces: Daughterhood, Motherhood, and Sisterhood in Dacia Maraini's Writings and Films*. Madison [NJ]: Fairleigh Dickinson University Press; London: Associated University Presses, 2002.

Sumeli Weinberg, Grazia. *Invito alla lettura di Dacia Maraini*. Pretoria: University South Africa, 1993.

Others

Frabotta, Biancamaria ed., and Corrado Federici, trans. *Italian Women Poets*. Toronto: Guernica, 2002. [Includes a "'Critical Note' by Dacia Maraini," 170-177].

Fraire, Manuela, Rosalba Spagnoletta, and Marina Virdis. *L'almanocco: luoghi, nomi, incontri, fatti, lavori in corso del movimento femminista italiano Dal 1972*. Rome: Edizioni Delle Donne, 1978.

Libreria delle donne di Milano, eds. *Non credere di avere dei diritti: la generazione della libertà femminile nell'idea e nelle vicende di un gruppo di donne.* Turin: Rosenberg & Sellier, 1987. [English translation: *Sexual Difference: A Theory of Social-Symbolic Practice*, translated by Patricia Cicogna and Teresa de Lauretis. Bloomington: Indiana University Press, 1990].

Meizei, Kathy, ed. *Ambiguous Discourse: Feminist Narratology and British Women Writers.* Chapel Hill: University of North Carolina Press, 1996.

Muraro, Luisa. *L'ordine simbolico della madre*. Rome: Riuniti, 1991.

Sedgwick, Eve Kosofsky. *Epistemology of the Closet.* Berkeley: University of California Press, 1990.

Silvi, Maria Grazia. *Il teatro delle donne*. Milan: La Salamandra, 1980.

Violi, Patrizia. *L'infinito singolare: considerazioni sulle differenze sessuali nel linguaggio.* Verona: Essedue, 1987.

Wood, Sharon. *Italian Women Writing.* Manchester, Eng., and New York: Manchester University Press, 1993.

6. Articles about Dacia Maraini and Her Writings

Anderlini, Serena, Tracy Barrett, and Dacia Maraini. "Interview: Dacia Maraini: Prolegomena for a Feminist Dramaturgy of the Feminine." *Diacritics* 21.2/3 (1991): 148-160.

Andersen, Marguerite, and Ada Testaferri. "Interview with Italian Feminist Writer, Dacia Maraini." *Resources for Feminist Research; RFR=Documentation sur la recherche féministe* 16.2 (1987): 60-63.

Bertone, Manuela. "Pandora's Box: A Conversation with Dacia Maraini." *Harvard Review* 1 (Spring 1992): 76-79.

Calamai, Silvia. "Dalla parola al palcoscenico: Le lingue di Chitti, Malpeli, Maraini, Russo, Scimone, Tarantino, in *Varietà dell'italiano nel teatro contemporaneo.*" *Atti della giornata di studio, a cura di Stefania Stefanelli, scuola normale superiore,* Pisa 2009: 195-238.

Cannon, Joann. "Rewriting the Female Destiny: Dacia Maraini's *La lunga vita di Marianna Ucrìa.*" *Symposium* 49.2 (1995): 136-146.

Carini, Lucia. "Dacia Maraini: une force tranquille di féminisme." *La parole Métèque* 5 (1988): 9-11.

Cavallaro, Daniela, "*I sogni di Clitennestra: The Oresteia* According to Dacia Maraini." *Italica* 72.3 (Fall 1995): 340-355.

De Miguel Y Canuto, Juan Carlos. "*Los pasos apresurados* de Dacia Maraini." *Signa: Revista de la Asociación Española de Semiótica* 21. (2012): 349-367.

De Paco Serrano, Diana M. "Cassandra e le donne tragiche." *Myrtia* 26. (2011): 123-139.

Gabriele, Tommasina. "From Prostitution to Transsexuality: Gender Identity and Subversive Sexuality in Dacia Maraini." *MLN* 117.1 (2002): 241-256.
------. "Suor Attanasia and the Metaphor of Arrested Maternity in Dacia Maraini" *Italica* 81.1 (Spring, 2004): 65-80.

Guida, Patrizia. "La ricostruzione dell'io nell'itinerario poetico di Dacia Maraini." *Italica* 78.1 (2001): 74-89.

Hanafin, Patrick. "An Ethics for Dead Voices: Law and the Politics of Sexual Difference in Dacia Maraini's *Isolina.*" *Law & Humanities* 4.2 (2010): 195-209.

Hostert, Anna Camaiti. "Intervista con Dacia Maraini." *Forum Italicum: A Journal of Italian Studies* 28. (1994): 111-115.

King, Martha. "*La nave per Kobe* (Book)." *World Literature Today* 76.3/4 (2002): 140.

La Luna, Michelangelo. "'Viollca, la bambina albanese' di Dacia Maraini: dal racconto al testo teatrale." *Italica* 92.3 (Fall 2015): 702-712.

Messina, Claudia. "Per un teatro necessario. La prima drammaturgia di Dacia Maraini." *Scaffale aperto* 3 (2012): 142-147.

Mitchell, Tony. "'Scrittura femminile': Writing the Female in the Plays of Dacia Maraini." *Theatre Journal* 42.3 (1990): 332-349.

Murrali, Eugenio. "*I sogni di Clitennestra* di Dacia Maraini: eredità di Eschilo, suggestioni moderne e autobiografiche." *Quaderni del '900* 8 (2008): 63–88.

Pallotta, Augustus. "Dacia Maraini: From Alienation to Feminism." *World Literature Today* 58.3 (1984): 359–362.

Ramsey-Portolano, Catherine. "The Evolution of the Theme of Sexual Difference as Revealed Through the Experience of Rape in Sibilla Aleramo's *Una donna* and Dacia Maraini's *La lunga vita di Marianna Ucrìa*." *Cahiers d'études italiennes* 7 (2008): 231–240.

Rita Dos Santos, Elsa, and Pietro Tavoracci. "Gioco di narratori in *Donna Lionora Giacubina*. Atto unico di Dacia Maraini." *Studi Novecenteschi* 72.2 (2006): 191–214.

Rosenberg, Marion Lignana. "Silence and Violence." *The Women's Review Of Books* 16.6 (1999): 7–8.

Santagostino, Giuseppina. "*La lunga vita di Marianna Ucrìa*: tessere la memoria sotto lo sguardo delle chimere." *Italica* 73.3 (1996): 410–428.

Schifino, Elena. "Della crudeltà: *Erzbeth* di Dacia Maraini." *Misure Critiche* 2008–2009: 198–209.

Scott, Joan M. "The Evidence of Experience." *Critical Inquiry* 17.4 (1991): 773–97.

Seger, Monica. "A Conversation with Dacia Maraini." *World Literature Today* 85.4 (2011): 27–32.

Showalter, Elaine. "Feminist Criticism in the Wilderness." *Critical Inquiry* 8.2 (1981): 179–206.

Siggers Manson, Christina. "In Love with Cecchino: Opening the Door to Violence in Dacia Maraini's *Colomba* and *Voci*." *Journal of Romance Studies* 5.2 (2005): 91–102.

Standen, Alex. "Politicizing the *Puttana*: Changing Representations of the Prostitute in Works of Dacia Maraini." *Italianist* 32.3 (2012): 437–452.

Sumeli Weinberg, Grazia. "All'ombra del padre: la poesia di Dacia Maraini in *Crudeltà all'aria aperta*." *Italica* 67.4 (1990): 453–465.

Taffon, Giorgio. "Figure regali femminili nella letteratura teatrale italiana di fine Novecento (D. Fo, G. Testori, D. Maraini)." In *Presenze femminili nel Novecento italiano. Letteratura, teatro, cinema,* edited by Graziella Pagliano Ungari, 137–166. Naples: Liguori, 2003.

Tamburri, Anthony J. "Narrative Plenitude in Limited Space: Dacia Maraini's 'Il calciatore di Bilbao'." *Italica* 92.3 (Fall 2015): 747-748 [Followed by the short story: Maraini, Dacia: "Il calciatore di Bilbao:" 749-753].

------. "Dacia Maraini's *Donna in guerra*: Victory or Defeat?" *Contemporary Women Writers in Italy: A Modern Renaissance*, edited by Santo L. Aricò, 139-151. Amherst: University of Massachussetts Press, 1990.

Wood, Sharon. "Invito alla lettura di Dacia Maraini." *Modern Language Review* 91.2 (1996): 500-501.

------. "The Language of the Body and Dacia Maraini's *Marianna Ucria*." *Journal of Gender Studies* 2.2 (Nov 1993): 223-237.

Wright, Simona. "Intervista a Dacia Maraini: Pascasseroli, 13 luglio 1996." *Italian Quarterly* 34.133-34 (1997): 71-91.

------. "Dacia Maraini: Charting the Female Experience in the Quest-Plot: *Marianna Ucrìa*." *Italian Quarterly* 34.2 (1997): 59-70.

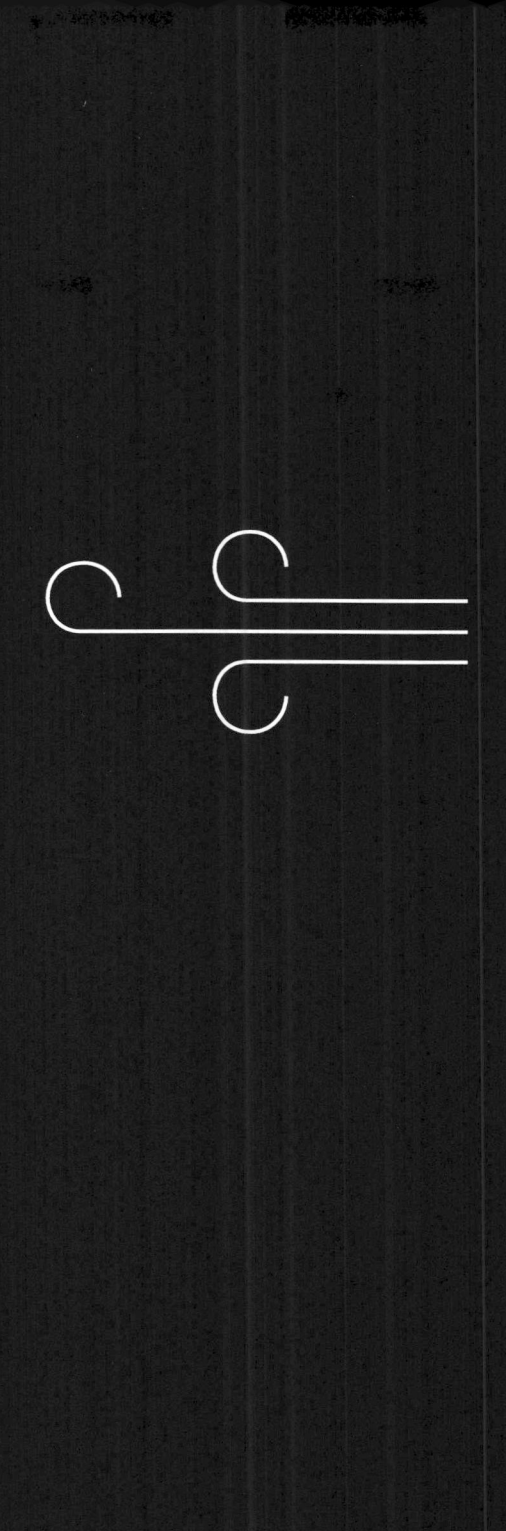

Index of Names*

Abraham, 108.
Ada, 183.
Adam, 28.
Addolorata, 173, 177, 178 [also Addoloratina and Ratina], 179-180.
Addoloratina (see Addolorata).
Admirable (see Callas, Maria).
Afola, Gianmaria, 39.
Agave, 57.
Agnes of Bohemia, 102.
Agostina (see Laminti, Agostina).
Alberto?, 32.
Alessandra?, 32.
Alfio, 104.
Alighieri, Dante, 102.
Alliata, Topazia, 13, 22, 205n.
Amalia, 165.
Amodio, Barbara, 37-39, 42, 47.
Andreuccio da Perugia, 105.
Angiolieri, Cecco, 52.
Anjeza, 131.
Anna (Donna), 212.
Antigone, 236.
Anton, 131.
Antonella (see Maraini, Antonella).
Antonello?, 32.
Antonia (Abbess), 166.
Antonio, 82-83.
Antonio (see Maraini, Antonio).
Apollo, 59.
Ariosto, Ludovico, 102.
Aristaeus, 54.
Aurora (see Gaudenzi, Aurora).
Austen, Jane, 17.
Barbara (see Amodio, Barbara).
Barthes, Roland, 64, 64n.
Bastianin, Renzo, 90 [Renzo].
Baudelaire, Charles Pierre, 32.
Benetti, Mara, 76, 78n.
Bennu, 53, 55.
Beppe (see Lancianesi, Beppe).
Bergman, Ingrid, 179-180.
Bettelheim, Bruno, 24.
Beyle, Marie-Henri, 213 [Stendhal].
Bigoncia, Zaira, 96-98 [Zà and Zaira], 99 [also Zaira], 100-101 [Zaira].
Bionda, 39, 45, 47, 242-243.
Boccaccio, Giovanni, 105.
Boccuccia (see Pinocchio).
Bonaventura of Bagnoregio (Saint; born Giovanni Fidanza), 115.
Bovary, Emma (Madame), 177.
Brecht, Bertolt, 182.
Cadmus, 57.
Calderón de la Barca, Pedro, 98.
Callas, Maria, 206, 207-210 [Admirable], 211 [Admirable and Divine One], 212 [Divine One], 213-216 [Admirable], 218-221 [Admirable], 227.
Candida?, 32.
Carbone, 36.
Carlo, 70-75.
Carlo (see Gaudenzi, Carlo).
Carmelina (see Croci, Carmelina).
Carrà, Raffaella, 133, 168 [also Raffaella].
Cate, 132-135, 138-140.
Caterina, 178-179.
Caterina (see Moretti, Caterina).
Catherine of Siena (Saint; born Caterina Benincasa), 55, 116.
Cavalchini?, 15.
Cavalli, Patrizia, 53.
Cavaradossi, Mario, 208-209.
Cerberus, 54-55.
Cesare, 65-69, 72-73.
Cetti (see Concettina).
Chantal?, 32.
Charon, 54.
Chevalier, Jean, 17.
Chiara di Assisi (Saint; born Chiara Offreduccio), 102-103 [also Clare of Assisi], 103n, 104 [Clare], 105 [Saint Clare], 106 [Clare, Clare of Assisi, and Saint Clare], 107-108 [Clare and Clare of Assisi], 109 [Clare], 110 [Clare and Clare of Assisi], 111 [Clare], 112 [Clare, Clare of Assisi, and Madonna Clare], 113 [Clare and Saint Clare], 114-116 [Clare], 116n, 158.
Chou, T'un-I, 17.
Christ (see Jesus).
Ciancimiglio, Giuseppe, 87.

* The index of names includes Maraini's fiction characters that, most of the time, appear with only their first names. For the rest, we tried to identify the people mentioned in the writings by giving their full names. When this is not possible, we add a question mark after the name. Other relevant names (such as of dogs, cats, teddy bears) are indicated in italics. In parenthesis are indicated the titles of important people, like King, Saint, Pope, etc. In brackets are indicated variations (pseudonyms, nick names, other names, names in translation, etc.) used in the volume for the name of each person.

Cinderella, 123.
Clare (see Chiara di Assisi).
Clare of Assisi (see Chiara di Assisi).
Collodi, Carlo, 25.
Concettina, 170 [Cetti], 175.
Cremaschi, Chiara Giovanna, 111-112.
Croci, Carmelina, 192 [Carmelina], 193 [also Carmelina], 195 [Carmelina], 198-204 [Carmelina].
D. M. (see Maraini, Dacia).
D'Annunzio, Gabriele, 52.
Da' (see Maraini, Dacia).
Dacia-ciàn (see Maraini, Dacia).
Dacina (see Maraini, Dacia).
Daciuzza (see Maraini, Dacia).
Damiani (*Sancti*; see Damiano San).
Damiano (San), 109, 111 [*Sancti Damiani*], 112-113.
Daniel (see McDonald, Daniel).
Daniela (see Moretti, Daniela).
Dante (see Alighieri, Dante).
David, 142.
Davoli, Ninetto, 27.
Deanna (see Frosini, Deanna).
Degas, Edgar, 195.
Degli Esposti, Piera, 191-191n [Piera], 205n [also Piera].
Demir, Nilufer, 128.
Di Fabio, Elvira, 23, 96.
Dionysus, 56-57.
Divine One (see Callas, Maria).
Domenica, 175.
Donatella?, 32.
Dürer, Albrecht, 28.
Eakin, Paul John, 149, 151.
Elisa, 71.
Elizabeth (see O'Connor, Elizabeth).
Emanuele, 141.
Emilio, 153.
Emma, 80, 95.
Enrica, 63-64, 69, 71, 73.
Erdogan, Recep Tayyip, 129.
Euripides, 57-58.
Eurydice, 53-56, 58.
Eve, 28.
Faele, 90.
Fain, Agathon Jean François, 16 [Baron Fain].
Fido, Franco, 29.
Foà, Robin, 44.
Fosco (see Maraini, Fosco).
Foscolo, Ugo, 52.
Francesca (see Gaudenzi, Francesca).
Francesco?, 32.
Francis (see Francis of Assisi).
Francis I (Pope), 102, 112.
Francis of Assisi (Saint; born Giovanni di Pietro di Bernardone), 103 [Francis], 107-108 [Francis], 110 [Francis and Saint Francis], 113 [Francis], 114 [Francis and Saint Francis], 115 [Francis].
Frizzi, Adria, 167, 206.
Fromm, Erich, 44.
Frosini, Deanna, 36.
Frugoni, Chiara, 107.
Furies, 54-55.
G. F., 169, 171.
Gabriele Fosco (see McDonald, Gabriele Fosco).
Gabriella (character in "Viollca the Albanian Girl"), 135-140.
Gabriella (character in *The Age of Malaise*), 71-72.
Garnett, David, 24.
Gassen?, 31.
Gaudenzi, Aurora, 30 [Aurora], 40 [Aurora], 45 [Aurora].
Gaudenzi, Carlo, 30 [Carlo].
Gaudenzi, Francesca, 30 [Francesca], 40 [Francesca], 45 [Francesca].
Gauguin, Paul Eugène Henri, 183-184.
Genoveffa (Saint), 104.
Georgia, 158-166.
Geppetto, 24, 26.
Gerardo, 175.
Gesù (see Jesus).
Gheerbrant, Alain, 17.
Gheo, 138.
Giacinto, 81, 91-92.
Gianluca?, 32.
Gianmaria (see Afola, Gianmaria).
Giannina, 86.
Gigi (see Politi, Giorgio).
Ginni, 36.
Ginzburg, Natalia, 52.
Giordani, 69-73.
Giordano, 126-128.
Giossi, 70.
Giottina, 91.
Giotto di Bondone, 115.
Giovanna, 76 [Vannina], 83 [Vanna], 87-90, 91-93 [Vannina], 94.
Giovanni, 175-178.
Giovanni (Don; see Tenorio, Giovanni).
Giuseppe (see Moretti, Giuseppe).
Giuseppina, 104.
Giusi, 191-192, 195-205.
Grado, Mara, 142-148, 148n.
Gregory IX (Pope), 111-112 [also Ugolino di Segni].
Guazzini, Monica, 36 [Monica].
Gunn, Genni, 15, 229.
G'vannitt', 99.

Hades, 53-54.
Hans (see Kurtmann, Hans).
Hasan, 87, 93.
Hayworth, Rita, 122.
Hermes, 54.
Herodotus, 53.
Heron, 53.
Hitar (see Hitler, Adolf).
Hitchcock, Alfred, 33.
Hitler, Adolf, 15 [also Hitar].
Honorious III (Pope), 111.
Hostiensi (Bishop), 111.
Iacurti, Luisa, 37-38, 42, 47 [Luisa]
Ingrid, 173, 179-180.
Innocent III (Pope), 111.
Innocent IV (Pope), 111.
Iorio, Maria Paola, 39, 44 [Maria Paola].
Isolina, 149.
Ixion (King), 55.
Jesus, 43 [Christ], 53, 108-109 [Christ], 111, 121 [Christ], 137 [Christ], 164 [Christ], 208 [Christ], 216 [Christ], 219 [Christ], 223n [Gesù], 225.
Josepha, 25, 29, 41-44, 52-54, 56, 58.
Karenina, Anna, 177.
Keiko, Kano, 20.
Kiku (see Maraini, Antonella).
Kitto, Dick, 76, 77 [Dick].
Kukuri, 17.
Kurdi (family), 128.
Kurdi, Abdullah, 129.
Kurdi, Aylan, 126, 126n, 127-129.
Kurdi, Tima Shenu, 127.
Kurtmann, Hans, 142 [also Georgy Ricciotto], 144, 145-147 [also Georgy Ricciotto], 148 [Hans], 148n.
La Luna, Michelangelo, 120, 126, 223.
Laminti, Agostina, 164 [also Agostina].
Lancianesi, Beppe, 36.
LaPenta, Kathleen, 65.
Laura?, 36.
Lavers, Annette, 64n.
Legret?, 31.
Lenti, Giovanni, 181-188.
Leopardi, Giacomo, 52.
Li, Shou-hsin, 43 [Shou-hsin].
Lillina, 91.
Ludovica, 198.
Luisa (see Iacurti, Luisa).
Luisa (see Maraini, Luisa).
Mà, 134-135, 139.
Machado, Antonio, 206, 222, 222n.
Madonna (see Mary).
Madonna of the Angel (see Mary).
Maenads, 56-58.
Mafalda, 82, 89-91.

Maffia, Dante, 242n.
Magistro, Elise, 157.
Magrelli, Valerio, 52.
Maira, Salvatore, 38-39.
Maldriks, 78.
Malek, 130, 134, 136-140.
Mandalà, Chiara, 102 [also Chiara], 103-104 [Chiara], 105 [also Chiara], 106 [Chiara], 107 [also Chiara], 108-109, 116n [also Chiara].
Mandelli, Franco, 44.
Mara (see Grado, Mara).
Maraini-Melehi, Mujah, 17 [Mujah], 45-46 [Mujah].
Maraini, Antonella, 16 [also Antonella, Kiku and Toni], 17-18 [Kiku and Toni], 19 [Toni], 45 [Toni].
Maraini, Antonio, 17.
Maraini, Dacia, 12, 13, 15n, 20 [Dacia-ciàn], 22, 23n, 27 [Da,' Dacina, and Daciuzza], 51 [Dacia], 59n, 60-61, 63, 63n, 65n, 76-77 [Dacia], 78n, 96n, 102-103, 103n, 105 [D. M.], 116n, 119, 120 [also Dacia], 120n, 126 [also Dacia], 126n, 130n, 141, 143n, 148n, 149-151, 152n, 155n, 157-158, 158n, 166n, 167, 168n, 173, 174n, 181-182, 183n, 191-192, 192n, 205n [also Dacia], 206, 206n, 223n, 227-228, 233n, 242n.
Maraini, Fosco, 13, 16-17 [Fosco], 20, 21 [Fosco], 22, 23 [Fosco], 205n [Fosco].
Maraini, Luisa, 16 [Yuki], 17 [Luisa and Yuki], 20 [Yuki].
Marina (see Savina, Marina).
Mario, 175.
Mariotti, Elisabetta, 130.
Marisa?, 32.
Marlene, 146.
Mary, 158 [Madonna of the Angel], 163 [Blessed Virgin], 166 [Madonna], 208 [Madonna].
Massimo, 32.
Mattei, Enrico, 52.
'Mbina (see Mitta, Colomba).
McDonald, Daniel, 18, 46 [Daniel].
McDonald, Gabriele Fosco, 18, 45-46 [Fosco].
McDonald, Ondina, 45-46 [Ondina].
Medea, 203.
Melehi, Nour-Shems, 17 [Nour].
Merini, Alda, 52.
Mina, 170.
Mitta, Colomba, 96 [Colomba and 'Mbina], 96n [Colomba], 97-98 [Colomba and 'Mbina], 99 [also Colomba], 101 [Colomba and 'Mbina], 149 [Colomba],
Mochizuki, Noriko, 120.
Monica (Saint), 164.
Monica (see Guazzini, Monica).
Montale, Eugenio, 52.
Morante, Elsa, 52.

Moravia, Alberto, 60-61, 206.
Morelli, Maria, 191.
Moretti, Caterina, 30, 38, 40, 46, 48-50, 52.
Moretti, Daniela, 30, 40, 46, 49 [Daniela].
Moretti, Giuseppe, 30-35, 36 [also Giuseppe] 37-41 [Giuseppe], 44-50 [Giuseppe], 52.
Moriokasan, Masako, 19, 24 [also Oka-chan], 27-28 [Oka-chan].
Mrozek (see Viollca).
Mujah (see Maraini-Melehi, Mujah).
Muses, 58.
Mussolini, Benito, 21n.
Nestore, 177-179.
Ninì, 73.
Nour (see Melehi, Nour-Shems).
Nuland, Sherwin B., 26, 59n.
O'Connor, Elizabeth, 79.
Oka-chan (see Moriokasan).
Oliver, 78, 80-81, 88.
Ondina (see McDonald, Ondina).
Orio, 84, 86, 92.
Orpheus, 53-54, 56-59.
Ortolana, 108.
Ottavio (Don), 212.
Parker, Dorothy, 150, 154.
Pascoli, Giovanni, 52.
Pasolini, Pier Paolo, 50-52, 59, 105, 149, 206, 227.
Pelosi, Giuseppe, 51.
Pentheus (King), 57.
Perrault, Charles, 24.
Philippa (Sister), 111.
Philomena (Sister), 157-160, 162-166.
Phoenix, 53, 55.
Picchietti, Virginia A., 141.
Piera (see Degli Esposti, Piera).
Pietro?, 33.
Pinocchio, 23-25, 26 [also Boccuccia].
Pinuccia Missirizzi (see Savina, Marina).
Pirandello, Luigi, 64.
Pizzocane, Santino, 81-83 [Santino], 86-87 [Santino], 89-92 [Santino].
Polipi, 126-127.
Politi, Giorgio, 192-193, 194 [also Gigi], 199 [Gigi], 200 [Giorgio], 201 [also Gigi], 202 [Gigi], 204 [Giorgio].
Preziosa, Vincenzo, 36 [Vincenzo].
Puccini, Giacomo, 208.
Raffaella (see Carrà, Raffaella).
Ramona, 150, 152, 154.
Rapettos, 68.
Ratina (see Addolorata).
Renata (see Zamengo, Renata).
Renzo (see Bastianin, Renzo).
Ricciotto, Georgy (see Kurtmann, Hans).
Rita da Cascia (Saint; born Margherita Lotti), 164.
Robert, 79-80.
Rosaria, 192, 195, 198-205.
Roswitha of Gandersheim, 108.
Russoniello, Marta, 63.
Salemme, Ernesto, 173.
Salvatore, 80.
Santino (see Pizzocane, Santino).
Savina, Marina, 181 [also Marina], 182 [Marina], 183, 183n [Marina], 184, 186-187 [also Marina], 188 [Marina and Pinuccia Missirizzi], 189-190 [Marina].
Scarpia (Baron), 208-209.
Segismund, 98.
Seneca, Lucius Annaeus, 54.
Serena, 149-150, 155, 155n, 156.
Sforza, Carlo, 15.
Slataper, Scipio, 169.
Smith, Colin, 64n.
Sòfia, Adele, 140.
Splendor, 167-168, 168n.
Spottiswood, Elspeth, 76, 77 [Elspeth], 78n.
Staiti, Claudio, 205n.
Standen, Alex, 149.
Stendhal (see Beyle, Marie-Henri).
Suna, 78-79, 81-84, 86-94.
Tenorio, Giovanni, 212 [Don Giovanni].
Teresa, 143.
Teuta, 131.
Tiresias, 57.
Toni (see Maraini, Antonella).
Toro, Angela, 182, 186-188.
Tortolani, Lisa, 173.
Tosca, Floria, 209.
Tylus, Jane, 102.
Ucrìa, Marianna, 106, 141.
Ugolino di Segni (Cardinal; see Gregory IX).
Ulysses, 25.
Vanna (see Giovanna)
Vannina (see Giovanna).
Varkey, ReenMary, 223.
Verlag, Rowohlt, 63.
Vienna?, 32.
Vincenzo (see Preziosa, Vincenzo).
Viollca, 130, 130n, 131 [also Mrozek], 132-140.
Virgil (Maro, Publius Vergilius), 54-55, 58.
Virgin (Blessed; see Mary).
Vittorio, 81-83, 87, 89-91, 95.
Welles, Orson, 120.
Wittemberg?, 18-19.
Wood, Sharon, 181.
Xhuvan, 130-131, 133.
Yuki (see Maraini, Luisa).
Zà (see Bigoncia, Zaira).
Zaira (see Bigoncia, Zaira).
Zamengo, Renata, 36 [Renata].

Index of Places*

Zeus, 59.
Abruzzo, Italy, 30, 96, 98, 101, 149, 157, 167, 177-179.
Addis?, Italy, 88, 91, 92.
Africa, 52, 206, 209, 219, 221.
America, 33, 40, 165, 173, 178.
Americas, 41.
Aniene (river), Italy, 40.
Antissa, Greece, 59.
Apostolic Seat (see Holy See).
Apulia (see Puglia).
Arezzo, Italy, 200.
Argentina, 112, 142, 143.
Assisi, Italy, 102-103 (refers to Chiara di Assisi and Clare of Assisi), 104-105, 106 (refers to Clare of Assisi), 107 (also refers to Clare of Assisi), 108 (also refers to Clare of Assisi), 109, 110 (refers to Clare of Assisi), 112 (also refers to Clare of Assisi), 116n (refers to Chiara di Assisi), 158 (refers to Chiara di Assisi)
   - San Damiano (Convent), 109, 112-113.
Auschwitz, Poland, 141-142, 146, 148n.
Bagheria, Italy, 28, 120, 192, 205n.
Bagnoregio (refers to Bonaventura da Bagnoregio), Italy, 115.
Benben (mound), Egypt, 53.
Berlin, Germany, 31.
Bethlehem, Palestine, 225.
Bevagna, Italy, 115.
Bodrum, Turkey, 127.
Boston, MA, United States of America, 56, 178-180.
Brescia, Italy, 192.
Brindisi, Italy, 131.
Budapest, Hungary, 141.
Buenos Aires, Argentina, 142-143
   - De Gama Street, 143.
C.?, Italy, 158, 161-163.
Caltanisetta, Italy, 88.
Canada, 127-128.
Casablanca, Morocco, 18.
Castelli Romani, Italy, 37.
Ciampino, Italy, 37.
Cithaeron (mount), Greece, 57.

Cocytus (river in the underworld), 55.
Dublin, Ireland, 79.
Durres, Albania, 131.
Dutch West Indies, 15.
Ebro (river), Greece, 56.
Erebus, 55.
Ermellina (woods), Abruzzo, 98.
Etna (Mt.), Italy, 103, 107.
Figline Valdarno, Italy, 32.
Florence, Italy, 31-32, 121, 123.
Florida, United States of America, 18.
France, 177.
Friuli, Italy, 212.
Galway, Ireland, 79.
Genoa, Italy, 67, 195.
Germany, 21, 63.
Gioia dei Marsi, Italy, 52, 173-174, 178, 180.
Guadalcanal, Solomon Islands, 18.
Gubbio, Italy, 114.
Hawaii, United States of America, 182.
Heaven, 28, 41.
Heliopolis, Egypt, 53.
Hiroshima, Japan, 19.
Holland, 66.
Holy Land, 108.
Holy See, Vatican, 111 [Apostolic Seat], 112.
Ireland, 79.
Italy, 17, 25, 33, 35, 43, 52, 111-112, 120, 123, 130-131, 133, 150, 173-174, 178-179, 181, 227.
Ithaca, United States of America, 151n.
Japan, 13, 15, 17-19, 22, 29, 60-61, 119-120, 165, 205n.
Karisawa (river), Japan, 232.
Kobanî, Syria, 127.
Kobe, Japan, 15, 15n, 120, 191, 205n.
Kos, Greece, 127.
Leningrad, Russia (see Saint Petersburg).
London, England, 77, 78n, 79.
Lyon, France, 31.
Marsala, Italy, 88.
Marsica, Abruzzo, Italy, 96, 99, 244.
Middle East, 82.
Milan, Italy, 15n, 23n, 96n, 103n, 130n, 143n, 151, 152n, 155n, 158n, 166n, 168n, 174n, 183n,

---

* The index of places includes Maraini's fiction locations that are invented (Santo Pellegrino) and abbreviated (C. and T.). Those locations are followed by a question mark. Given the importance they have for Maraini's works translated in this volume, mythological and religious places (Erebus, Tartarus, Paradise, etc.) are also included in the index. We identified the rest of the places mentioned in the writings, by giving their full name and state. Other relevant information (such as rivers, mountains, etc.) are indicated in parenthesis. In brackets are indicated variations (abbreviations, names in translation, etc.) used in the volume for some places.

191-192, 192n, 206n, 217, 233n.
Modena, Italy, 33.
Morocco, 18, 108.
Nagoya, Japan, 18, 19, 20, 21, 120.
Naples, Italy, 78, 80, 88, 112.
New England, 173.
New York, NY, United States of America, 12, 17-18, 33-34, 46, 59n, 64n, 216.
North America, 178.
Ostia, Italy, 51.
Padua, Italy, 38.
Palermo, Italy, 106
- Via:
    Emiri (degli), 153
    Generale Cadorna, 154
    Maqueda, 149, 152n, 155n, 157, 158n, 166n, 167, 168n, 173, 174n, 206n
- Villa Igea, 155
- Zisa, 152.
Paradise, 28.
Paris, France, 32, 206, 208, 216-217, 220, 221.
Perugia (refers to Andreuccio da Perugia), Italy, 105.
Pescasseroli, Italy, 24, 30.
Podgora (mount), Croatia, 169.
Pozzuoli, Italy, 90.
Puglia, Italy, [Apulia], 175.
Rignano, Italy, 36.
Roma, Italy, 17 [Rome], 27 [Rome], 31 [Rome], 33 [Rome], 35-36 [Rome], 44 [Rome] 50 [Rome] 81 [Rome], 88 [Rome], 131 [Rome], 135 [Rome], 149 [Rome], 157 [Rome], 167 [Rome], 180 [Rome], 208 [Rome], 211 [Rome], 217 [also Rome], 219, 231 [also Rome], 231n, 242n [Rome]
- Castel Sant'Angelo, 208-209
- Corso Vittorio, 168
- Eur, 50
- Monte Mario, 91
- Piazza Cancelleria (della), 168
- Sant'Andrea della Valle (church), 208
- Trastevere, 30
- Via/Street:
    - Barchetta (della), 170
    - Benevento, 44-45
    - Cappellari (dei), 168
    - Marsala, 69
    - Montoro (di), 168-170, 172
    - Moroni, 75
    - Pellegrino (del), 168
    - Serbatoio, 81
    - Slataper, 169
- Vicolo Sant'Eligio, 169
- Villa Borghese, 234-235.
Romania, 104.
Rome (see Roma).

Sabaudia, Italy, 227.
Saint Petersburg, Russia, 15 [Leningrad].
Salò, Italy, 15, 21, 21n.
San Severino, Italy, 15.
Sant'Oreste, Italy, 36
Santo Pellegrino?, Italy, 103, 107.
Scotland, 128.
Sèvre, France, 235.
Shijak, Albania, 132-133, 140.
Sicilia, Italy, 102-103 [Sicily], 107 [Sicily], 120 [Sicily], 123 [Sicily], 149 [also Sicily] 150 [Sicily], 157-158 [Sicily], 167 [Sicily].
Siena, Italy, 55.
Solomon Islands, 15, 18.
South (of Italy), 192.
South Seas, 155.
Spain, 208.
Styx, 54-55.
Switzerland, 80.
T.?, Italy, 162.
Tartarus, 55 [The House of Death].
The House of Death (see Tartarus).
Thrace, Greece, 58.
Tokyo, Japan, 15, 55, 120-123, 125.
Torino, Italy, 63n [Turin], 78n [Turin], 145, 151 [Turin].
Touta, Italy, 99.
Trevi, Italy, 30, 32.
Trieste, Italy, 169.
Tulagi, Solomon Islands, 18.
Turin (see Torino).
Turkey, 80, 94, 124.
United Kingdom, 76.
United States (see United States of America).
United States of America, 15 [USA], 178 [United States], 228.
University:
    - College London, 76, 77 [UCL], 149
    - Columbia, 35
    - Connecticut, 173
    - Fordham, 65
    - Harvard, 23, 29, 96
    - Leicester (of), 181, 191
    - Middlebury, 180
    - Montclair State, 63
    - New York, 102
    - Rhode Island (of), 120, 126, 223
    - Scranton (of), 141
    - Scripps College, 157
    - Texas (of) at Austin, 167, 206.
USA (see United States of America).
Vancouver, Canada, 127.
Vermont, United States of America, 149, 180.
Victoria (African lake), 214.
Yugoslavia, 90.

Index of Topics

Abuse, 130-141, 167-172, 181-205, 191-205
- Child abuse, 130-141, 167-172, 191-205
- Domestic violence, 181-205
- Child prostitution, 130-140, 167-172.

Death, 26-29
- Cremation, 29
- Death traditions in Japan 29
- Sense of death in America 26-29

Family of Dacia Maraini, 15-21, 23-24, 26, 45, 120-125
- Relationship with her father Fosco, 15-21, 23, 26, 120-125
- Relationship with her mother Topazia, 15-21, 24, 26, 120-125
- Relationship with her sisters Antonella and Luisa, 16-20, 45.

Human Rights, 76-95
- Disability rights, 76-95
- Feminism, 76-95.

Marriage, 155-156.

Politics and Society, 76-95, 126-129, 149-154, 173-180
- Italian emigration to the USA, 173-180
- Italian politics of the '70s, 76-95
- Precariousness in Italy, 149-154
- Syrian refugees, 126-129
- Unemployment in Italy, 149-154.

Religion, 17, 27-28, 53, 102-116, 157-166, 121, 216, 219, 223-225
- Buddhism and reincarnation, 17, 27
- Christianity, 28, 53, 108-109, 111, 121, 216, 219, 223-225
- Convent life, 102-116, 157-166
- Religion and politics in the Middle Ages, 102-116.

Sex and Sexuality, 52, 56-59, 63-95, 149, 181-190, 212-213
- Dominance, 58
- Female adolescence, 63-75, 149
- Female coming of age, 63-75
- Gender violence, 181-190
- Homosexuality, 56-57, 59, 212-213
- Lesbian and gay movement, 76-95
- Sex in religion, 52.

World War II, 15-16, 18-21n, 23, 82, 90, 120, 122, 124-125n, 141-148n, 205n
- Atomic bomb (Hiroshima), 19
- Concentration camp (Auschwitz), 141-142, 146, 148n
- Concentration camp (in Japan), 18-21, 23, 120, 122, 124, 125n, 205n
- Fascism, 15-16, 21, 21n, 82, 90, 205n
- Guadalcanal fight, 18
- Holocaust, 141-148
- Nazism, 21.

Published by
LISt Lab
info@listlab.eu
listlab.eu

Produzione
GreenTrenDesign Factory
Piazza Manifattura, 1
38068 Rovereto (TN) - Italy
T: +39 0464 443427
info@greentrendesign.it

Author
Dacia Maraini

Editor
Michelangelo La Luna

Editorial Director
Pino Scaglione

Editorial Assistant
Gioia Marana

**Art Director &
Graphic Design**
Blacklist Creative Studio, Barcelona
blacklist-creative.com

ISBN 9788898774814

**Printed and bound in the European Union,
September 2016**

Italian printed texts published by arrangement with RCS Rizzoli Libri S.p.A. and Giulio Einaudi Editore S.p.A.

**All rights reserved:
of the edition © 2016 by LISt Lab
of the original Italian texts © 1991-2015 by Dacia Maraini
of the original Italian printed texts © 1991, 1998, 2004, 2009, 2012, 2013 by RCS Rizzoli Libri S.P.A.
© 1975, 1996 by Einaudi © 2009 by Lepisma © 2015 by Il Messaggero
of the edited English texts © 2016 by Michelangelo La Luna
of the pictures © 2016 by Dacia Maraini, Fosco Maraini, Elvira Di Fabio**

Promotion and distribution in Italy
Messaggerie Libri, Spa, Milano,
Numero verde 800.804.900
assistenza.ordini@meli.it
amministrazione.vendite@meli.it

International promotion and distribution
ACC, London
Sandy Lane, Old Martlesham,
Woodbridge, Suffolk, IP12 4SD, UK
T +44 (0) 1394 389950
F +44 (0) 1394 389999
sales@antique-acc.com

Scientific Board of the List Edition
Eve Blau (Harvard GSD), Maurizio Carta (Università di Palermo), Alfredo Ramirez (Architectural Association London) Alberto Clementi (Università di Chieti), Alberto Cecchetto (Università di Venezia), Stefano De Martino (Università di Innsbruck), Corrado Diamantini (Università di Trento), Antonio De Rossi (Università di Torino), Franco Farinelli (Università di Bologna), Carlo Gasparrini (Università di Napoli), Manuel Gausa (Università di Genova), Giovanni Maciocco (Università di Sassari/Alghero), Antonio Paris (Università di Roma), Mosè Ricci (Università di Trento), Roger Riewe (Università di Graz), Pino Scaglione (Università di Trento).

LISt Lab is an editorial workshop, based in Europe, that works on the contemporary issues. LISt Lab not only publishes, but also researches, proposes, promotes, LISt Lab produces, creates networks.

LISt Lab is a green company committed to respect the environment. Paper, ink, glues and all processings come from short supply chains and aim at limiting pollution. The print run of books and magazines is based on consumption patterns, thus preventing waste of paper and surpluses. LISt Lab aims at the responsibility of the authors and markets, towards the knowledge of a new publishing culture based on an intelligent resource management.

GreenTrenDesign Factory, member of Progetto Manifattura, is a multiplatform structure, that provides advanced design services. In the balance between sustainability and quality, craftsmanship and digital experimentation, the company operates in partnership with LISt Lab.